**Adobe Dreamweaver**

# Classroom in a Book®

The official training workbook from Adobe

Jim Maivald

Writer: James J. Maivald
Executive Editor: Laura Norman
Development Editor: Robyn G. Thomas
Technical Reviewer: Candyce Mairs
Senior Production Editor: Tracey Croom
Copyeditor: Scout Festa
Composition: Kim Scott, Bumpy Design
Proofreader: Kim Wimpsett
Indexer: John Lewis, JJ Indexing
Cover Illustration: RETOKA
Interior Designer: Mimi Heft

ISBN-13: 978-0-13-687523-9

ISBN-10: 0-13-687523-8

# WHERE ARE THE LESSON FILES?

Purchase of this Classroom in a Book in any format gives you access to the lesson files you'll need to complete the exercises in the book.

1 Go to www.adobepress.com/DreamweaverCIB2021.

2 Sign in or create a new account.

3 Click Submit.

● **Note:** If you encounter problems registering your product or accessing the lesson files or web edition, go to www.adobepress.com/support for assistance.

4 Answer the questions as proof of purchase.

5 The lesson files can be accessed through the Registered Products tab on your Account page.

6 Click the Access Bonus Content link below the title of your product to proceed to the download page. Click the lesson file links to download them to your computer.

● **Note:** If you purchased a digital product directly from www.adobepress.com or www.peachpit.com, your product will already be registered. However, you still need to follow the registration steps and answer the proof of purchase question before the Access Bonus Content link will appear under the product on your Registered Products tab.

# CONTENTS

● **Note:** You will find this lesson on your Account page once you register your book, as described in "Accessing the lesson files and Web Edition."

# GETTING STARTED

Adobe® Dreamweaver is one of the leading web-authoring programs available. Whether you create websites for others for a living or plan to create one for your own business, Dreamweaver offers all the tools you need to get professional results.

## About Classroom in a Book

*Adobe Dreamweaver Classroom in a Book® (2021 release)* is part of the official training series for graphics and publishing software developed with the support of Adobe product experts.

The lessons are designed so that you can learn at your own pace. If you're new to Dreamweaver, you'll learn the fundamentals of putting the program to work. If you are an experienced user, you'll find that Classroom in a Book teaches many advanced features, including tips and techniques for using the latest version of Dreamweaver.

Although each lesson includes step-by-step instructions for creating a specific project or achieving a specific result, you'll have room for exploration and experimentation. You can follow the book from start to finish or complete only those lessons that correspond to your interests and needs. Each lesson concludes with a review section containing questions and answers on the subjects you've covered.

## TinyURLs

At several points in the book, I reference external information available on the internet. The uniform resource locators (URLs) for this information are often long and unwieldy, so we have provided custom TinyURLs in many places for your convenience. Unfortunately, the TinyURLs sometimes expire over time and no longer function. If you find that a TinyURL doesn't work, look up the actual URL provided in the appendix.

# Prerequisites

Before using *Adobe Dreamweaver Classroom in a Book (2021 release)*, you should have a working knowledge of your computer and its operating system. Be sure you know how to use the mouse, standard menus, and commands, as well as how to open, save, and close files. If you need to review these techniques, see the printed or online documentation included with your Windows or macOS operating system.

# Conventions used in this book

Working in Dreamweaver means you'll be working with code. We have used several conventions in the following lessons and exercises to make working with the code in this book easier to follow and understand.

## Bolded text

Certain names, words, and phrases will be bolded from time to time, usually when cited in an instruction. This styling will include text, other than HTML or CSS code, that needs to be entered into program dialogs or into the body of a webpage, like this:

Type **Insert main heading here**

Filenames, like **favorite-styles.css**, will also be bolded as needed to identify crucial resources or targets of a specific step or exercise. Be aware that these same names may not be bolded in introductory descriptions or general discussion. Be sure to identify all resources required in a specific exercise prior to commencing it.

## Code font

In many instructions, you will be required to enter HTML code, CSS rules and properties, and other code-based markup. To distinguish the markup from the instructional text, the entries will be styled with a code font, like this:

Examine the code `<h1>Heading goes here</h1>`.

In instances where you must enter the markup yourself, the entry will be formatted in color, like this:

Insert the following code: `<h1>Heading goes here</h1>`

Enter the code exactly as depicted, being careful to include all punctuation marks and special characters.

## Strikethrough

In several exercises, you will be instructed to delete markup that already exists within the webpage or style sheet. In those instances, the targeted references will be identified with strikethrough formatting, like this:

Delete the following values:

```
margin: 10px 20px 15px 25px;
background-image: url(images/fern.png), url(images/stripe.png);
```

Be careful to delete only the identified markup so that you achieve the following result:

```
margin: 10px 20px;
background-image: url(images/fern.png);
```

## Missing punctuation

HTML code, CSS markup, and JavaScript often require the use of various punctuation, such as periods (.), commas (,), and semicolons (;), and can be damaged by their incorrect usage or placement. Consequently, I have omitted periods and other punctuation expected in a sentence or paragraph from an instruction or hyperlink whenever it may cause confusion or a possible error, as in the following two instructions:

Enter the following code: `<h1>Heading goes here</h1>`

Type the link `http://adobe.com`

## Element references

Within the body of descriptions and exercise instructions, HTML elements may be referenced by name or by class or id attribute. When an element is identified by its tag name, it will appear as `<section>` or `section`. When referenced by its class attribute, the name will appear with a leading period (`.`) in a code-like font, like this: `.content` or `.sidebar1`. References to elements by their id attribute will appear with a leading hash (#) and in a code font, like this: `#top`. This practice matches the way these elements appear in Dreamweaver's tag selector interface.

# Windows vs. macOS instructions

In most cases, Dreamweaver performs identically in both Windows and macOS. Minor differences exist between the two versions, mostly because of platform-specific issues out of the control of the program. Most of these are simply differences in keyboard shortcuts, how dialogs are displayed, and how buttons are named. In most cases, screen shots were made in the macOS version of Dreamweaver and may appear different from your own screen.

Where specific commands differ, they are noted within the text. Windows commands are listed first, followed by the macOS equivalent, such as Ctrl+C/Cmd+C. Common abbreviations are used for all commands whenever possible, as follows:

| Windows | macOS |
| --- | --- |
| Control = Ctrl | Command = Cmd |
| Alternate = Alt | Option = Opt |

As lessons proceed, instructions may be truncated or shortened to save space, with the assumption that you picked up the essential concepts earlier in the lesson. For example, at the beginning of a lesson you may be instructed to "choose Edit > Copy" or "press Ctrl+C/Cmd+C." Later, you may be told to "copy" text or a code element. These should be considered identical instructions.

If you find you have difficulties in any particular task, review earlier steps or exercises in that lesson. In some cases, if an exercise is based on concepts covered earlier, you will be referred to the specific lesson.

# Installing the program

Before you perform any exercises in this book, verify that your computer system meets the hardware requirements for Dreamweaver, that it's correctly configured, and that all required software is installed.

If you do not have Dreamweaver, you will first have to install it from Creative Cloud. Adobe Dreamweaver must be purchased separately; it is not included with the lesson files that accompany this book. Go to **helpx.adobe.com/dreamweaver/system-requirements.html** to obtain the system requirements.

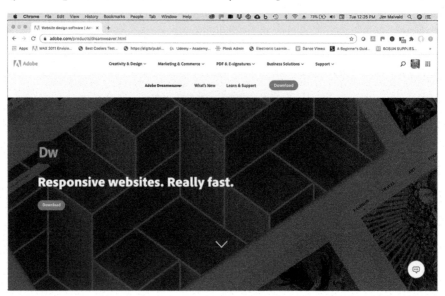

Go to www.adobe.com/creativecloud/plans.html to sign up for Adobe Creative Cloud. Dreamweaver may be purchased with the entire Creative Cloud family or as a standalone app. Adobe also allows you to try Creative Cloud and the individual applications for seven days for free.

Check out www.adobe.com/products/dreamweaver.html to learn more about the different options for obtaining Dreamweaver.

# Updating Dreamweaver to the latest version

Although Dreamweaver is downloaded and installed on your computer hard drive, periodic updates are provided via Creative Cloud. Some updates provide bug fixes and security patches, while others supply amazing new features and capabilities.

The lessons in this book are based on Dreamweaver (2021 release) and may not work properly in any earlier version of the program. To check which version is installed on your computer, choose Help > About Dreamweaver (in Windows) or Dreamweaver > About Dreamweaver (on macOS). A window will display the version number of the application and other pertinent information.

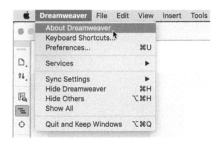

If you have an earlier version of the program installed, you will have to update Dreamweaver to the latest version. You can check the status of your installation by opening the Creative Cloud manager and logging in to your account.

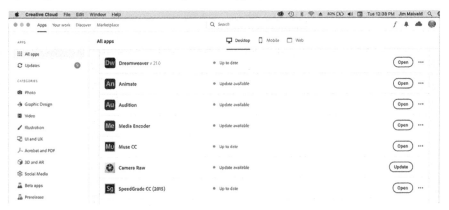

Check out helpx.adobe.com/creative-cloud/help/download-install-trial.html to learn how to download and install a limited-period trial of Creative Cloud to your computer or laptop.

# Online content

Your purchase of this Classroom in a Book includes online materials provided by way of your Account page on adobepress.com.

## Lesson files

To work through the projects in this book, you will need to download the lesson files by following the instructions in the "Accessing the lesson files and Web Edition" section.

## Web Edition

The Web Edition is an online interactive version of the book, providing an enhanced learning experience. Your Web Edition can be accessed from any device with a connection to the internet, and it contains:

* The complete text of the book
* Hours of instructional video keyed to the text
* Interactive quizzes

## Accessing the lesson files and Web Edition

You must register your purchase on adobepress.com to access the online content:

1  Go to www.adobepress.com/DreamweaverCIB2021.

2  Sign in or create a new account.

3  Click Submit.

4  Answer the question as proof of purchase.

5  The **lesson files** can be accessed from the Registered Products tab on your Account page. Click the Access Bonus Content link below the title of your product to proceed to the download page. Click the lesson file link(s) to download them to your computer.

   The **Web Edition** can be accessed from the Digital Purchases tab on your Account page. Click the **Launch** link to access the product.

   ● **Note:** If you purchased a digital product directly from www.adobepress.com or www.peachpit.com, your product will already be registered. However, you still need to follow the registration steps and answer the proof of purchase question before the Access Bonus Content link will appear under the product on your Registered Products tab.

The files are compressed into ZIP archives to speed up download time and to protect the contents from damage during transfer. You must decompress (or "unzip") the files to restore them to their original size and format before you use them with the book. Modern Mac and Windows systems are set up to open ZIP archives by simply double-clicking.

**Note:** Windows may treat ZIP archives like a file folder, allowing you to access the contents without decompressing them first. To use the files in Dreamweaver, you must decompress each archive first.

6   Do one of the following:

- If you downloaded **DWCC2021_lesson_files.zip**, unzipping the archive will produce a folder named **DWCC2021_Lesson_Files** containing all the lesson files used by the book.

**Note:** The files are updated from time to time, so the dates depicted in screen shots may be different from the ones you download.

| Name | Date Modified | Size | Kind |
|---|---|---|---|
| ▼ Lessons | Today at 12:46 PM | -- | Folder |
| ▶ lesson01 | Nov 7, 2019 at 5:06 PM | -- | Folder |
| ▶ lesson02 | Aug 18, 2019 at 4:37 PM | -- | Folder |
| ▶ lesson03 | Aug 11, 2020 at 9:47 AM | -- | Folder |
| ▶ lesson04 | Sep 14, 2020 at 7:56 PM | -- | Folder |
| ▶ lesson05 | Sep 24, 2019 at 10:10 AM | -- | Folder |
| ▶ lesson06 | Sep 14, 2020 at 8:03 PM | -- | Folder |
| ▶ lesson07 | Sep 18, 2020 at 8:42 AM | -- | Folder |
| ▶ lesson08 | Oct 21, 2019 at 11:22 AM | -- | Folder |
| ▶ lesson09 | Sep 30, 2020 at 2:03 AM | -- | Folder |
| ▶ lesson10 | Oct 2, 2020 at 11:07 AM | -- | Folder |
| ▶ lesson11 | Oct 5, 2020 at 9:11 PM | -- | Folder |
| ▶ lesson12 | Oct 8, 2020 at 11:17 AM | -- | Folder |

MacHD > webs > DW2021

- If you downloaded the lessons individually, create a new folder on your hard drive and name it **DW2021**. Unzip the individual lesson files to this folder. That way, all the lesson files will be stored in one location. Do not share or copy files between lessons.

# Recommended lesson order

The training in this book is designed to take you from A to Z in basic to intermediate website design, development, and production. Each new lesson builds on previous exercises, using supplied files and assets to create an entire website. We recommend you download all lesson files at once.

**Note:** Lesson 12 is included as a bonus lesson that you can access via your Account page as described in "Accessing the lesson files and Web Edition."

Start with Lesson 1 and proceed through the entire book to Lesson 12. We recommend that you do not skip any lessons, or even individual exercises. Although ideal, this method may not be a practicable scenario for every user. Each lesson folder contains all the files needed to complete every exercise within it using partially completed or staged assets, allowing you to complete individual lessons out of order, if desired.

However, don't assume that the staged files and customized templates in each lesson represent a complete set of assets. It may seem that these folders contain duplicative materials, but these "duplicate" files and assets cannot, in most cases, be used interchangeably in other lessons and exercises. Doing so will probably cause you to fail to achieve the goal of the exercise.

For that reason, you should treat each lesson folder as a standalone website. Copy the lesson folder to your hard drive, and create a new site for that lesson using the Site Setup dialog. Do not define sites using subfolders of existing sites. Keep your sites and assets in their original folders to avoid conflicts.

One suggestion is to organize the lesson folders in a single *web* or *sites* master folder near the root of your hard drive. But avoid using the Dreamweaver application folder. In most cases, you'll want to use a local web server as your testing server, which is described in Lesson 11, "Publishing to the Web."

## Bonus material

This book has so much great material that we couldn't fit it all in the printed pages, so we placed Lesson 12, "Working with Mobile Design," on the adobepress.com website.

You will find this lesson on your Account page once you register your book, as described in "Accessing the lesson files and Web Edition."

# On first launch

Right after installation or upon first launch, Dreamweaver will display several introduction screens. First, the Sync Settings dialog will appear. If you are a user of previous versions of Dreamweaver, select Import Sync Settings to download your existing program preferences. If this is the first time you've used Dreamweaver, select Upload Sync Settings to sync your preferences to your Creative Cloud account.

In the book, I use the lightest interface themes for the screen shots. This was done both to save ink in the printing and to place less stress on the environment. Feel free to pick the color themes you prefer.

# Choosing the program color theme

If you purchased the book after you installed and launched Dreamweaver, you may be using a different color theme than the one pictured in most screen shots in the book. All exercises will function properly using any color theme, but if you want to configure your interface to match the one shown, complete the following steps:

1   Choose Edit > Preferences (on Windows) or Dreamweaver > Preferences (in macOS).

    The Preferences dialog appears.

2   Select Interface from the Category list.

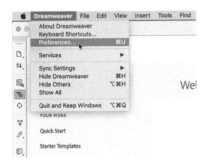 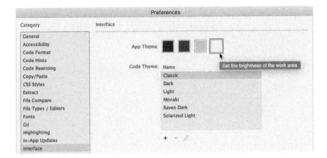

3   Select the lightest App Theme color.
    Select Classic from the Code Theme menu.

    The interface changes to the new theme. Depending on which app theme you select, the code theme may change automatically. The changes are not permanent yet. If you close the dialog, the theme will revert to the original colors.

4   Click the Apply button.

    The theme changes are now permanent.

5   Click the Close button.

Feel free to change the color theme at any time. Often, users select the theme that works best in their normal working environment. The lighter themes work best in well-lighted rooms, while the darker themes work best in the indirect or controlled lighting environments used in some design offices. All exercises will work properly in any theme color.

# Setting up the workspace

Dreamweaver (2021 release) includes two main workspaces to accommodate various computer configurations and individual workflows. For this book, the Standard workspace is recommended.

1  If the Standard workspace is not displayed by default, you can select it from the Workspace dropdown menu in the upper-right corner of the program interface.

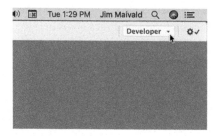
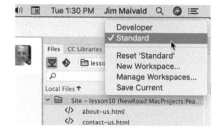

2  If the default Standard workspace has been modified—where certain toolbars and panels are not visible (as they appear in the figures in the book)—you can restore the factory setting by choosing Reset 'Standard' from the Workspace dropdown menu.

These same options can be accessed from the Window > Workspace Layout menu.

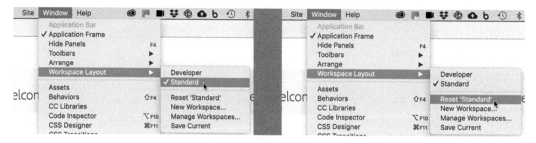

Most of the figures in this book show the Standard workspace. When you finish the lessons in this book, experiment with each workspace to find the one that you prefer, or build your own configuration and save the layout under a custom name.

For a more complete description of the Dreamweaver workspaces, see Lesson 1, "Customizing Your Workspace."

# Defining a Dreamweaver site

In the course of completing the following lessons, you will create webpages from scratch and use existing files and resources that are stored on your hard drive. The resulting webpages and assets make up what's called your *local* site. When you are ready to upload your site to the internet (see Lesson 11), you publish your completed files to a web-host server, which then becomes your *remote* site. The folder structures and files of the local and remote sites are usually mirror images of one another.

The first step is to define your local site.

1  Launch Adobe Dreamweaver (2021 release) or later.

2  Open the Site menu.

   The Site menu provides options for creating and managing standard Dreamweaver sites.

3  Choose New Site.

The Site Setup dialog appears.

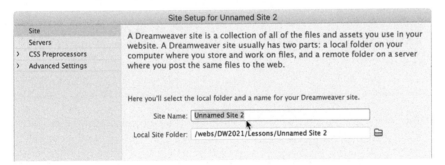

To create a standard website in Dreamweaver, you need only name it and select the local site folder. The site name should relate to a specific project or client and will appear in the Files panel Site dropdown menu. This name is intended for your own purposes only; it will not be seen by the public, so there are no limitations to the name you can create. Use a name that clearly describes the purpose of the website. For the purposes of this book, use the name of the lesson you intend to complete, such as lesson01, lesson02, lesson03, and so on.

◆ **Warning:** You must unzip the lesson files before you create your site definition.

4   Type **lesson01** or another name, as appropriate, in the Site Name field.

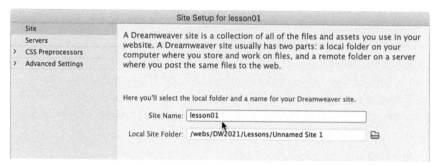

5   Next to the Local Site Folder field, click the Browse For Folder icon 📁.

6   Navigate to the appropriate folder containing the lesson files you downloaded
from www.adobepress.com/DreamweaverCIB2021 (as described earlier), and
click Select/Choose.

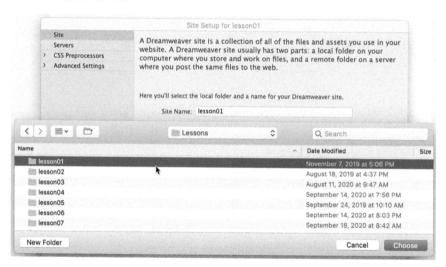

You could click Save at this time and begin working on your new website, but
you'll add one more piece of handy information.

7   Click the arrow to the left of the Advanced Settings category to reveal the
categories listed there.
Select Local Info.

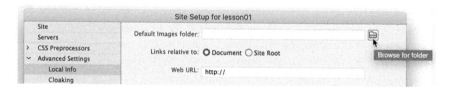

Although it's not required, a good policy for site management is to store different file types in separate folders. For example, many websites provide individual folders for images, PDFs, videos, and so on. Dreamweaver assists in this endeavor by including an option for a default images folder.

Later, as you insert images from other locations on your computer, Dreamweaver will use this setting to automatically move the images into the site structure.

8 Next to the Default Images Folder field, click the Browse For Folder icon 📁. When the dialog opens, navigate to the appropriate images folder for that lesson or site and click Select/Choose.

Note: The folder that contains the image assets will be referred to throughout the book as the site default images folder or the default images folder.

Note: Resource folders for images and other assets should always be contained within the main site root folder.

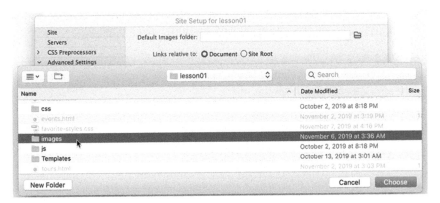

The path to the images folder appears in the Default Images Folder field. The next step is to enter your site domain name in the Web URL field.

9 Enter **http://favoritecitytour.com/** for the lessons in this book, or enter your own website URL, in the Web URL field.

Note: Many sites today use a secure socket layer (SSL) certificate to enable encrypted communication between a browser and a web server. If you have such a certificate installed, use https as your protocol in this field.

You've entered all the information required to begin your new site. In subsequent lessons, you'll add more information to enable you to upload files to your remote and testing servers.

10 In the Site Setup dialog, click Save.

The Site Setup dialog closes.

Note: The web URL is not needed for most static HTML sites, but it's required for working with sites using dynamic applications or to connect to databases and a testing server.

Whenever a site is selected or modified, Dreamweaver will build, or rebuild, a cache of every file in the folder. The cache identifies relationships between the webpages and the assets within sites and will assist you whenever a file is moved, renamed, or deleted to update links or other referenced information.

11 Click OK to build the cache, if necessary.

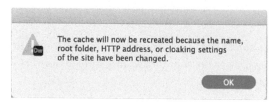

The cache is rebuilt, which should take only a few seconds at most.

In the Files panel, the new site name appears in the Site List dropdown menu. As you add more site definitions, you can switch between the sites by selecting the appropriate name from this menu.

Setting up a site is a crucial first step in beginning any project in Dreamweaver. Knowing where the site root folder is located helps Dreamweaver determine link pathways and enables many site-wide options, such as orphaned-file checking and Find and Replace.

# Checking for updates

Adobe periodically provides software updates. To check for updates in the program, choose Help > Updates. An update notice may also appear in the Creative Cloud update desktop manager.

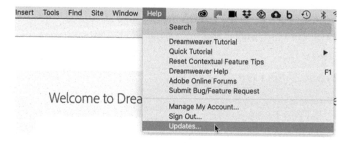

For book updates and bonus material, visit your Account page on peachpit.com and select the Lesson & Update Files tab.

# Additional resources

*Adobe Dreamweaver Classroom in a Book (2021 release)* is not meant to replace documentation that comes with the program or to be a comprehensive reference for every feature. Only the commands and options used in the lessons are explained in this book. For comprehensive information about program features and tutorials, refer to these resources:

**Adobe Dreamweaver Learn & Support:** helpx.adobe.com/dreamweaver/tutorials.html (accessible in Dreamweaver by choosing Help > Dreamweaver Tutorial) is where you can find and browse tutorials, help, and support on Adobe.com.

**Dreamweaver Help:** helpx.adobe.com/support/dreamweaver.html is a reference for application features, commands, and tools (press F1 or choose Help > Dreamweaver Help).

**Adobe Support Community:** forums.adobe.com lets you tap into peer-to-peer discussions and questions and answers on Adobe products.

**Resources for educators:** www.adobe.com/education.html offers a treasure trove of information for instructors who teach classes on Adobe software. You'll find solutions for education at all levels, including free curricula that use an integrated approach to teaching Adobe software and that can be used to prepare for the Adobe Certified Associate exams.

Also check out these useful links:

**Adobe Add-ons:** exchange.adobe.com/creativecloud.html is a central resource for finding tools, services, extensions, code samples, and more to supplement and extend your Adobe products.

**Adobe Dreamweaver product home page:** adobe.com/products/dreamweaver.html has more information about the product.

## Adobe Authorized Training Centers

Adobe Authorized Training Centers offer instructor-led courses and training on Adobe products. Go to https://learning.adobe.com/partner-finder.html to find a directory of AATCs.

# 1 CUSTOMIZING YOUR WORKSPACE

## Lesson overview

In this lesson, you'll familiarize yourself with the Dreamweaver CC (2021 release) program interface and learn how to do the following:

- Use the program Welcome screen.
- Switch document views.
- Work with panels.
- Select a workspace layout.
- Adjust toolbars.
- Personalize preferences.
- Create custom keyboard shortcuts.
- Use the Property inspector.
- Use the Extract workflow.

 This lesson will take about 60 minutes to complete. To get the lesson files used in this lesson, download them from the webpage for this book at www.adobepress.com/DreamweaverCIB2021. For more information, see "Accessing the lesson files and Web Edition" in the "Getting Started" section at the beginning of this book.

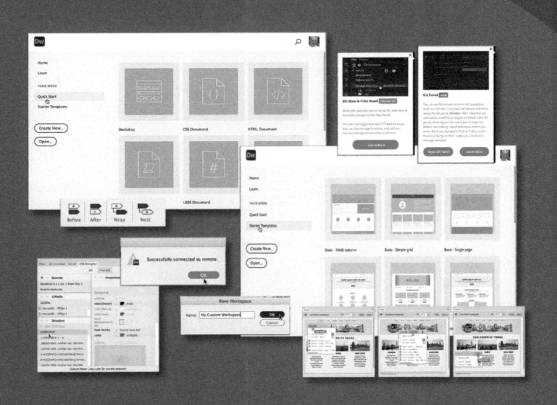

You'd probably need a dozen programs to perform
all the tasks that Dreamweaver can do—and none of
them would be as fun to use.

# Touring the workspace

**Note:** Before you begin this lesson, download the lesson files and create a new website for lesson01 as described in the "Getting Started" section at the beginning of the book.

Dreamweaver is the industry-leading Hypertext Markup Language (HTML) editor, with good reasons for its popularity. The program offers an incredible array of design and code-editing tools. Dreamweaver offers something for everyone.

Coders love the range of enhancements built into the Code view environment, and developers enjoy the program's support for a variety of programming languages and code hinting. Designers marvel at seeing their text and graphics appear in an accurate What You See Is What You Get (WYSIWYG) depiction as they work, saving hours of time previewing their designs in browsers. Novices certainly appreciate the program's simple-to-use and power-packed interface. No matter what type of user you are, if you use Dreamweaver, you don't have to compromise.

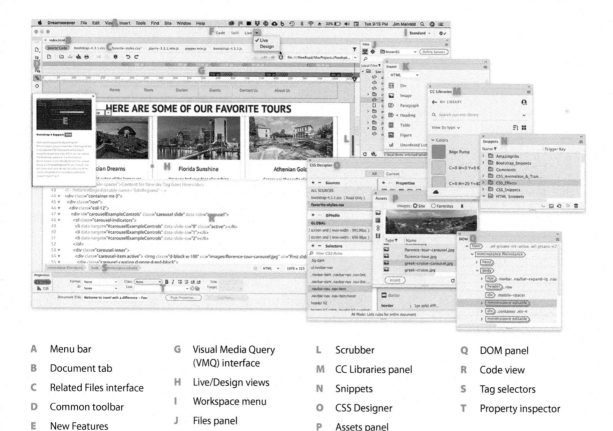

| | | | |
|---|---|---|---|
| **A** Menu bar | **G** Visual Media Query (VMQ) interface | **L** Scrubber | **Q** DOM panel |
| **B** Document tab | **H** Live/Design views | **M** CC Libraries panel | **R** Code view |
| **C** Related Files interface | **I** Workspace menu | **N** Snippets | **S** Tag selectors |
| **D** Common toolbar | **J** Files panel | **O** CSS Designer | **T** Property inspector |
| **E** New Features | **K** Insert panel | **P** Assets panel | |
| **F** Document toolbar | | | |

The Dreamweaver interface features a vast array of user-configurable panels and toolbars. Take a moment to familiarize yourself with the names of these components.

## Create New and Open

The Create New and Open buttons access the New Document dialog and the Open dialog, respectively. Previous users of Dreamweaver may be more comfortable using these options, which open familiar interfaces for creating new documents or opening existing ones.

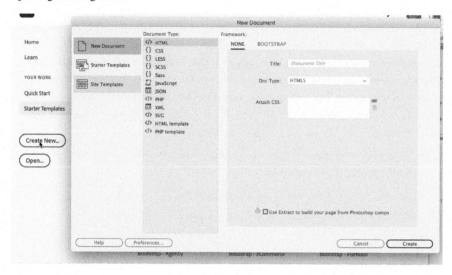

If you do not want to see the Start Screen anymore, you can disable it by accessing the option in the General settings in Dreamweaver Preferences and deselecting the checkbox.

# Exploring the New Feature guides

In Dreamweaver CC, the New Feature guides pop up from time to time as you access various tools, features, or interface options. The pop-ups call your attention to new features or workflows that have been added to the program and provide handy tips to help you get the most out of them.

When a tip appears, it may provide more extensive information or a tutorial you can access by following the prompts in the pop-up window. When you are finished, you can close the pop-up by clicking the Close icon in the upper-right corner of each tip. When you close the tip, it will not appear again. You can display the tips again by choosing Help > Reset Contextual Feature Tips.

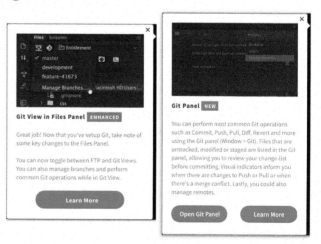

# Setting interface preferences

Dreamweaver provides users with extensive controls over the basic program interface. You can set up, arrange, and customize the various panels and menus to your own liking. One of the first places you should visit before you begin the lessons in this book is the Dreamweaver Preferences dialog.

As with other Adobe applications, the Preferences dialog provides specific settings and specifications that dictate how the program looks and functions. Preference settings are normally persistent, meaning that they remain in effect even after the program is shut down and relaunched. There are far too many options in this dialog to cover in one lesson, but let's make a couple of changes to give you a taste of what you can do. Some features of the program are not visible until you create or open a file for editing.

1  Define a new site based on the lesson01 folder as described in the "Getting Started" section at the beginning of the book.

2  Choose Window > Files or press F8 to display the Files panel.

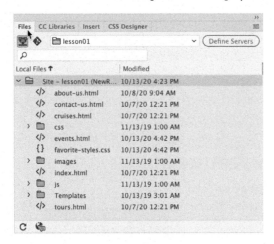

3  In the Files panel, select **lesson01** from the dropdown menu and reveal the site file list in the panel, if necessary.

4  Right-click the file **tours.html** from the lesson01 folder and choose Open from the context menu. You can also double-click a file in the list to open it.

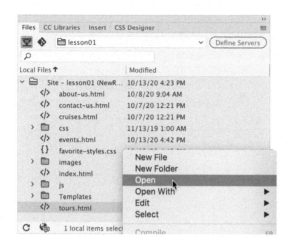

The file opens in the document window. If the program has not been used previously, the file may open in Live view. To get the full appreciation of the upcoming changes, let's also display the code-editing interface at the same time.

5 Select Split view at the top of the document window, if necessary.

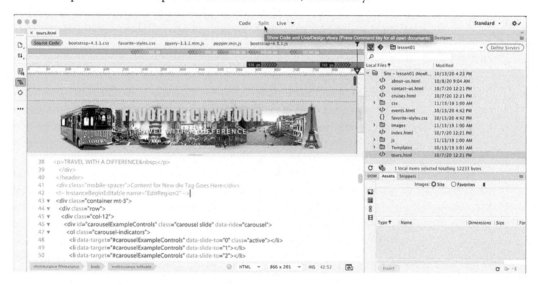

Dreamweaver may be sporting a different color scheme in Code view than you may see in the screen shots. The program enables you to control the interface coloring. You can change it completely or merely tweak it using Preferences. If you have already changed your interface theme, skip to the next exercise.

6 In Windows, choose Edit > Preferences.

In macOS, choose Dreamweaver > Preferences.

The Preferences dialog appears.

7  Select the Interface category.

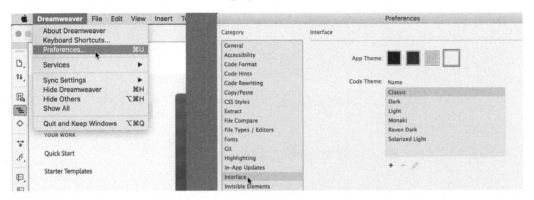

As you see in the dialog, Dreamweaver gives you control over the overall color theme as well as the code-editing window. You may change one or both.

Many designers work in controlled lighting environments and prefer the dark interface themes that are now the default in most Adobe applications. In this book, all screen shots from this point forward are taken in the lightest theme. This saves ink during printing, for less impact on the environment. You may continue to use the dark theme if you prefer, or switch now so that your screen will match the illustrations in the book.

8  In the App Theme window, select the lightest theme.

The theme of the entire interface changes to light gray. You will notice that the Code Theme setting changes to Light at the same time. If you prefer, you can switch the code theme back to Dark or choose another. The screen shots for code editing in the book use the Classic theme.

9  Select Classic in the Code Theme dropdown.

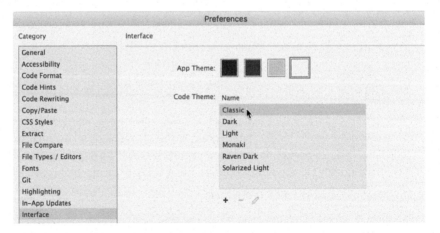

At the moment, the changes are not permanent. If you were to click the Close button in the dialog now, the theme would revert to dark.

10 Click Apply in the lower-right corner of the dialog.

The changes have now been applied permanently.

11 Click Close.

Saved preferences persist from session to session and through each workspace.

# Switching and splitting views

Dreamweaver offers dedicated environments for coders and designers.

## Code view

Code view focuses the Dreamweaver workspace exclusively on the HTML code and a variety of code-editing productivity tools. To access Code view, click the Code view button in the Document toolbar.

Code view

## Design view

Design view shares the document window with Live view and focuses the Dreamweaver workspace on its classic WYSIWYG editor. In the past, Design view provided a reasonable facsimile of the webpage as it would appear in a browser, but with the advancements in CSS and HTML, it is no longer as WYSIWYG as it once was. Although it can be difficult to use in some situations, you'll find that it does offer an interface that speeds up the creation and editing of your content. And at the moment, it's also the only way to access certain Dreamweaver tools or workflows, as you will see in the upcoming lessons.

To activate Design view, choose it from the Design/Live dropdown menu in the Document toolbar. Most HTML elements and basic cascading style sheets (CSS) formatting will be rendered properly within Design view, with the major exceptions being CSS3 properties; dynamic content; interactivity, such as link behaviors, video, audio, and jQuery widgets; and some form elements. In previous versions of Dreamweaver, you spent most of your time in Design view. That will no longer be the case.

Design view

## Live view

Live view is the default workspace of Dreamweaver. It speeds up the process of developing modern websites by allowing you to *visually* create and edit webpages and web content in a browser-like environment, and it supports and previews most dynamic effects and interactivity.

To use Live view, choose it from the Design/Live dropdown menu in the Document toolbar. When Live view is activated, most HTML content will function as it would in an actual browser, allowing you to preview and test most dynamic applications and behaviors.

Live view

In previous versions of Dreamweaver, the content in Live view was not editable. That has changed. You can edit text, add and delete elements, create classes and ids, and even style elements, all in the same window. It's like working on a live webpage right inside Dreamweaver.

Live view is integrally connected to the CSS Designer, allowing you to create and edit advanced CSS styling and build fully responsive webpages without having to switch views or waste time previewing the page in a browser.

## Split view

Split view provides a composite workspace that gives you access to both the design and the code simultaneously. Changes made in either window update in the other in real time.

● **Note:** Split view can pair Code view with either Design view or Live view.

To access Split view, click the Split button in the Document toolbar. Dreamweaver splits the workspace horizontally by default. When using Split view, you can display Code view with either Live view or Design view.

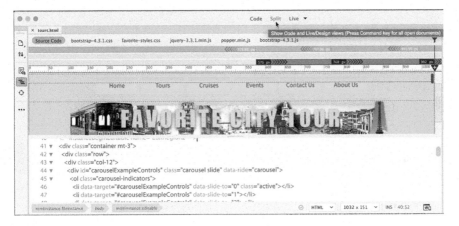

Split view (horizontal)

You can split the screen vertically by selecting the Split Vertically option on the View menu. When the window is split, Dreamweaver also gives you options for how the two windows display. You can put the code window on the top, bottom, left, or right. You can find all these options in the View menu. Most screen shots in the book that show Split view show Design or Live view at the top or on the left.

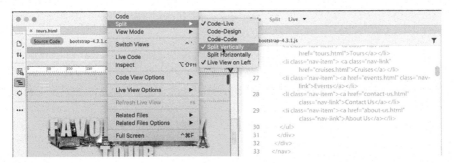

Split view (vertical)

## Live Code mode

● **Note:** The Live Code icon may not appear on the Common toolbar by default. You may need to activate it using the Customize Toolbar icon.

Live Code is an HTML code-troubleshooting display mode available whenever Live view is activated. To access Live Code, activate Live view and then click the Live Code icon in the toolbox at the left side of the document window. While active, Live Code displays the HTML code as it would appear in a live browser on the internet and gives you a peek at how the code changes when the visitor interacts with various parts of the page.

You can see this interaction firsthand by Ctrl-clicking/Cmd-clicking one of the three indicators in the image carousel in Live view. In Code view, the window will focus on the <ol> element that provides those controls. You will see that one of the controls shows the class active and that the class is then added to the code interactively each time you click a different indicator. Without Live Code mode, you would not be able to see this interaction and behavior, and it would make troubleshooting CSS errors more difficult.

Live Code mode

Be aware that while Live Code is active, you will not be able to edit the HTML code, although you can still modify external files, such as linked style sheets. To disable Live Code, click the Live Code icon again to toggle the mode off.

## Inspect mode

Inspect mode is a CSS troubleshooting display mode that is available whenever Live view is activated. It is integrated with the CSS Designer and allows you to rapidly identify CSS styles applied to content within the page by moving the mouse cursor over elements in the webpage. Clicking an element freezes the focus on that item.

The Live view window highlights the targeted element and displays the pertinent CSS rules applied or inherited by that element. You can access Inspect mode at any time by clicking the Live View icon whenever an HTML file is open and then clicking the Inspect icon in the Common toolbar.

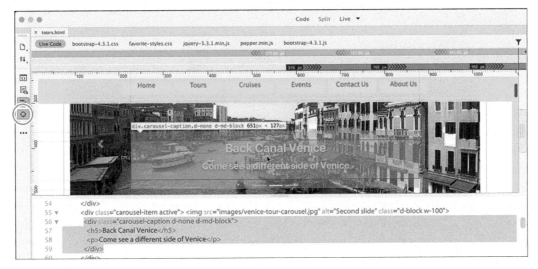

Inspect mode

# Selecting a workspace layout

A quick way to customize the program environment is to use one of the prebuilt workspaces in Dreamweaver. Experts have optimized these workspaces to put the tools you need at your fingertips.

Dreamweaver (2021 release) includes two prebuilt workspaces: *Standard* and *Developer*. To access these workspaces, choose them from the Workspace menu, located on the upper-right side of the program window.

## Standard workspace

The Standard workspace focuses the available screen real estate on the Design and Live view window. Standard is the default workspace for screen shots in this book.

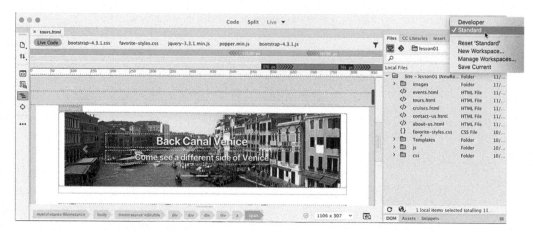

Standard workspace

## Developer workspace

The Developer workspace provides a code-centric layout of tools and panels ideal for coders and programmers. The workspace is focused on Code view.

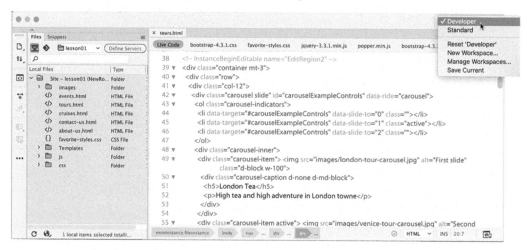

Developer workspace

# Working with panels

Although you can access most commands from the menus, Dreamweaver scatters much of its power in user-selectable panels and toolbars. You can display, hide, arrange, and dock panels at will around the screen. You can even move them to a second or third computer display if you desire.

Standard panel grouping

The Window menu lists all the panels available in the program. If you do not see a desired panel on the screen, choose it from the Window menu. A checkmark appears next to its name in the menu to indicate that the panel is open and visible. Occasionally, one panel may lie behind another on the screen and be difficult to locate. In such situations, simply choose the desired panel from the Window menu and the panel will rise to the top of the stack.

## Minimizing panels

To create room for other panels or to access obscured areas of the workspace, you can minimize or expand individual panels in place. To minimize a standalone panel, double-click the tab containing the panel name. To expand the panel, click the tab once.

Minimizing a panel by double-clicking its tab

Minimizing one panel in
a stack using its tab

To recover more screen real estate, you can minimize panel groups or stacks down to icons by double-clicking the bar appearing at the top of the panel. You can also minimize the panels to icons by clicking the double-arrow icon (>>) in the panel title bar. When panels are minimized to icons, you access an individual panel by clicking its icon. The selected panel will appear on the left or right of the icon, wherever room permits.

Collapsing a panel
to icons

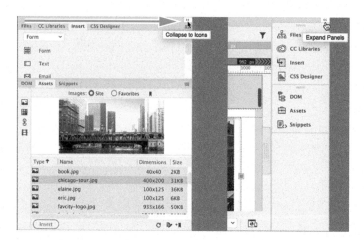

## Closing panels and panel groups

Each panel or panel group may be closed at any time. You can close a panel or panel group in several ways; the method often depends on whether the panel is floating, docked, or grouped with another panel.

To close an individual panel that is docked, right-click in the panel tab and choose Close from the context menu. To close an entire group of panels, right-click any tab in the group and choose Close Tab Group.

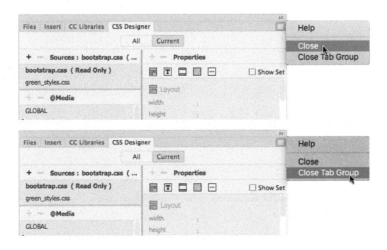

To close a floating panel or panel group, click the Close ✖ icon that appears in the upper-right corner of the panel in Windows or in the left corner of the title bar of the panel or panel group in macOS. To reopen a panel, choose the panel name from the Window menu. Reopened panels will sometimes appear floating in the interface. You may use them this way or attach, or dock, them to the sides, top, or bottom of the interface. You will learn how to dock panels later.

## Dragging

You can reorder a panel tab by dragging it to the desired position within the group.

Dragging a tab to change its position

## Floating

A panel that is grouped with other panels can be floated separately. To float a panel, drag it from the group by its tab.

Pulling a panel out by its tab

To reposition panels, groups, and stacks in the workspace, simply drag them by the title bar. To pull out a single panel group when it's docked, grab it by the tab bar.

Dragging a whole docked panel group to a new position

## Grouping, stacking, and docking

You can create custom groups by dragging one panel into another. When you've moved the panel to the correct position, Dreamweaver highlights the area, called the *drop zone*, in blue. Release the mouse button to create the new group.

Creating new groups

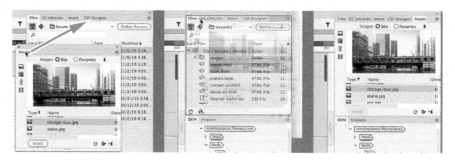

In some cases, you may want to keep both panels visible simultaneously. To stack panels, drag the desired tab to the top or bottom of another panel. When you see the blue drop zone appear, release the mouse button.

Creating panel stacks

Floating panels can be docked to the right, left, or bottom of the Dreamweaver workspace. To dock a panel, group, or stack, drag its title bar to the edge of the window on which you want to dock it. When you see the blue drop zone appear, release the mouse button.

Docking panels

# Personalizing Dreamweaver

As you continue to work with Dreamweaver, you'll devise your own optimal work-space of panels and toolbars for each activity. You can store these configurations in a custom workspace of your own naming.

## Saving a custom workspace

To save a custom workspace, create your desired configuration of panels, choose New Workspace from the Workspace menu, and then give it a custom name.

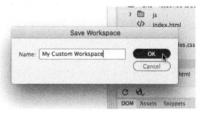

Saving a custom workspace

## Working with the Extract panel

Many web designers use Photoshop to create and edit web image assets. But did you know that Dreamweaver has a feature built right into the program that enables you to access Photoshop documents directly and create your assets from within Dreamweaver itself?

Dreamweaver can create web assets directly from your Photoshop file.

## Loading Photoshop documents into Extract

The first step is to load the Photoshop document into the Extract panel. Choose Window > Extract to open the panel.

Use the Extract panel to upload your Photoshop document.

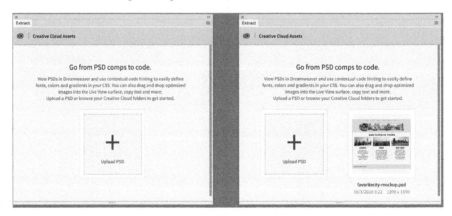

To select a document to upload, click the Upload PSD button in the panel. You must be logged in to your Creative Cloud account. The document will be added to your account assets. Once the file is uploaded, it will appear in the panel. Then, simply click it in the panel to start accessing the various layers and assets within the file.

Once a file is uploaded, the Extract panel can generate CSS, text, and image assets.

Extract can generate styling properties, text content, and even web-compatible image assets from the Photoshop file. You will use this feature extensively in Lesson 6, "Creating a Page Layout," to populate and style a webpage that you will use for your website's master design.

# Working with toolbars

Some program features are so handy you may want them to be available all the time in toolbar form. Two of the toolbars—Document and Standard—appear horizontally at the top of the document window. The Common toolbar, however, appears vertically on the left side of the screen. You can display the desired toolbar by choosing it from the Window menu.

## Document toolbar

The Document toolbar appears at the very top of the program interface and provides onscreen commands for switching between Live, Design, Code, and Split views. The toolbar is open by default. If it's not, you can enable this toolbar by choosing Window > Toolbars > Document when a document is open.

Document toolbar

## Standard toolbar

The Standard toolbar is an optional toolbar that appears between the Related Files interface and the document window and provides handy commands for various document and editing tasks, such as creating, saving, or opening documents; copying, cutting, and pasting content; and so on. The toolbar is not open by default. You can enable it by choosing Window > Toolbars > Standard when a document is open.

Standard toolbar

## Common toolbar

The Common toolbar appears on the left side of the program window and provides a variety of commands for working with code and HTML elements. The toolbar displays five tools by default in Live and Design view. However, the tools are context sensitive; insert the cursor in the code window, and you may see several more appear.

Common toolbar and dialog

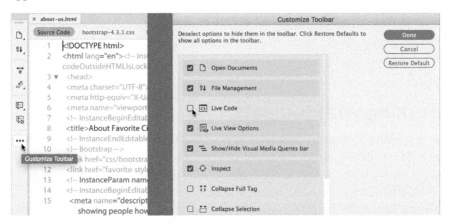

The Common toolbar was named the Coding toolbar in a previous version of Dreamweaver, and it is now user customizable. You can add and remove tools by clicking the Customize Toolbar icon. Be aware that some tools will be displayed and active only when using the Code view window.

# Creating custom keyboard shortcuts

Another powerful feature of Dreamweaver is the ability to create your own keyboard shortcuts as well as edit existing ones. Keyboard shortcuts are loaded and preserved independently of workspaces.

Is there a command you can't live without that doesn't have a keyboard shortcut or uses one that's inconvenient? Create one of your own.

● **Note:** The default keyboard shortcuts are locked and cannot be edited. But you can duplicate the set, save it under a new name, and modify any shortcut within that custom set.

1 Choose Edit > Keyboard Shortcuts (Windows) or Dreamweaver > Keyboard Shortcuts (macOS).

 You cannot modify the default shortcuts, so you have to create a list of your own.

2 Click the Duplicate Set icon to create a new set of shortcuts.

3 Enter a name in the Name Of Duplicate Set field. Click OK.

4 Choose Menu Commands from the Commands pop-up menu.

5 In the Commands window, choose File > Save All.

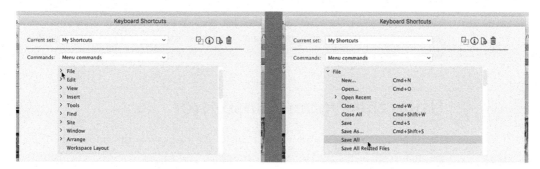

 Note that the Save All command does not have an existing shortcut, although you'll use this command frequently in Dreamweaver.

6 Insert the cursor in the Press Key field.
 Press Ctrl+Alt+S (Windows) or Cmd+Opt+S (macOS).

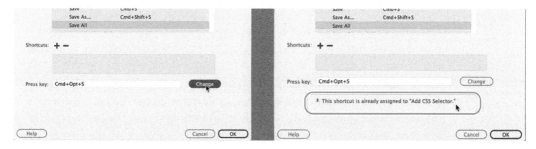

Note the error message indicating that the keyboard combination you chose is already assigned to a command. Although we could reassign the combination, let's choose a different one.

7   Press Ctrl+Shift+Alt+S (Windows) or Ctrl+Cmd+S (macOS).

This combination is not currently being used, so let's assign it to the Save All command.

8   Click the Change button.

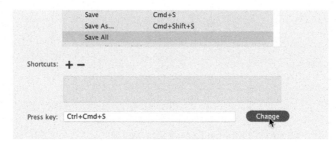

The new shortcut is now assigned to the Save All command.

9   Click OK to save the change.

You have created your own keyboard shortcut—one you can use in upcoming lessons. Whenever an instruction in one of the lessons says "save all files," use this keyboard shortcut.

# Using the Property inspector

One tool vital to your workflow and many of the exercises in this book is the Property inspector. In the predefined Dreamweaver workspaces, the Property inspector is no longer a default component. If it is not visible in your program interface, you can display it by choosing Window > Properties, and then dock it to the bottom of the document window, as described earlier. The Property inspector is context-driven and adapts to the type of element you select.

## Using the HTML tab

Insert the cursor into any text content on your page and the Property inspector provides a means to quickly assign basic HTML codes and formatting. When the HTML button is selected, you can apply heading or paragraph tags as well as bold, italics, bullets, numbers, and indenting, among other formatting and attributes. The Document Title metadata field is also available in the bottom half of the Property inspector. Enter your desired document title in this field, and Dreamweaver adds it automatically to the document <head> section. If you don't see the full Property inspector, click the triangle icon in the lower-right corner of the panel to expand its display.

HTML Property inspector

## Using the CSS tab

Click the CSS button to quickly access commands to assign or edit CSS formatting.

CSS Property inspector

## Accessing image properties

Select an image in a webpage to access the image-based attributes and formatting controls of the Property inspector.

Image Property inspector

## Accessing table properties

To access table properties, insert your cursor in a table and then click the table tag selector at the bottom of the document window. Once the Element Display appears on the table, click the Format Table icon ☰ and the Property inspector will display the table specifications.

● **Note:** Some users have reported difficulty accessing the Element Display on tables. If you have this experience, you can switch to Design view and use the table tag selector to access this feature.

Table Property inspector

# Using the Related Files interface

Webpages are often built with multiple external files that provide styling and programming assistance. Dreamweaver enables you to see all the files linked to, or referenced by, the current document by displaying the filenames in the Related Files interface at the top of the document window. This interface displays the name of any external file and will actually display the contents of each file—if the contents are available—when you simply select the filename in the display. The Related files interface displays by default when any web-type file is open. If you do not see it, you can enable it by choosing View > Related Files Options > Display External Files.

The Related Files interface lists all external files linked to a document.

To view the contents of the referenced file, click the name. Dreamweaver splits the document window and shows the contents of the selected file in the Code view window. If the file is stored locally, you'll even be able to edit the contents of the file when it's selected.

Use the Related Files interface to edit locally stored files linked to the webpage.

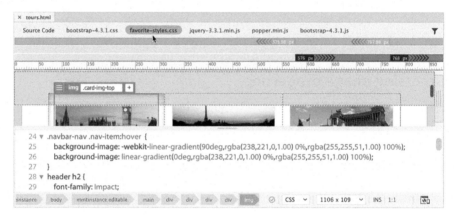

To view the HTML code contained within the main document, click the Source Code option in the interface.

Choose the Source Code option to see the contents of the main document.

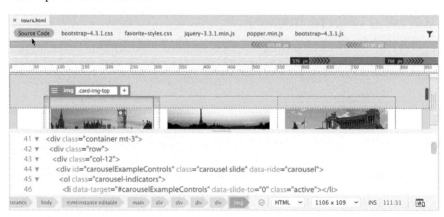

# Using tag selectors

One of the most important features of Dreamweaver is the tag selector interface that appears at the bottom of the document window. This interface displays the tags and element structure in any HTML file pertinent to the insertion point of, or that is selected by, the cursor. The display of tags is hierarchical, starting at the document root at the left of the display and listing each tag or element in order based on the structure of the page and the selected element.

The display in the tag selector interface mimics the structure of the HTML code based on your selection.

The tag selectors also enable you to select any of the displayed elements by simply clicking a tag. When a tag is selected, all the content and child elements contained within that tag are also selected.

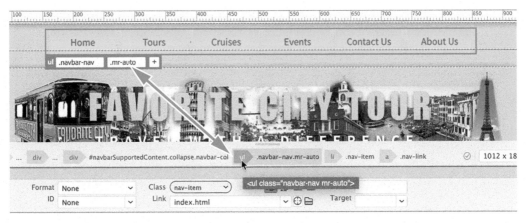

Use the tag selectors to select elements.

The tag selector interface is closely integrated with the CSS Designer panel. You may use the tag selectors to help you style content or to cut, copy, paste, and delete elements.

The tag selector is closely integrated with the styling and editing of elements.

# Using the CSS Designer

The CSS Designer is a powerful tool for visually inspecting, creating, editing, and troubleshooting CSS styling. The panel adapts to the size of the available workspace and displays in either a one-column or two-column layout.

The CSS Designer can be displayed in one or two columns. Simply drag the edge of the document window to the left or right until the panel displays the desired number of columns.

CSS Designer also allows you to copy and paste CSS styles from one rule to another. You can also decrease or increase the specificity of new selector names by pressing the up arrow or down arrow key, respectively.

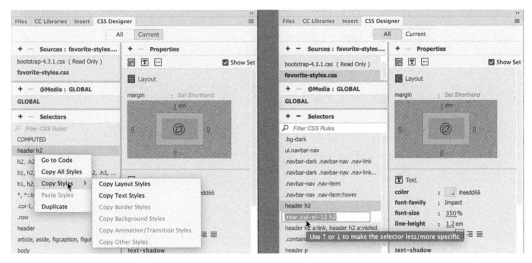

Copy and paste styles from one rule to another (left). Make selectors more or less specific by using the arrow keys (right).

The CSS Designer panel consists of four windows: Sources, @Media, Selectors, and Properties.

## Sources

The Sources window allows you to create, attach, define, and remove internal embedded and external linked style sheets.

## @Media

The @Media window is used to define media queries to support various types of media and devices.

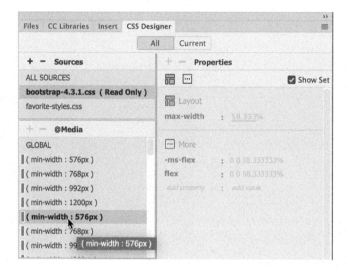

## Selectors

The Selectors window is used to create and edit the CSS rules that format the components and content of your page. Once a selector, or rule, is created, you define the formatting you want to apply in the Properties window.

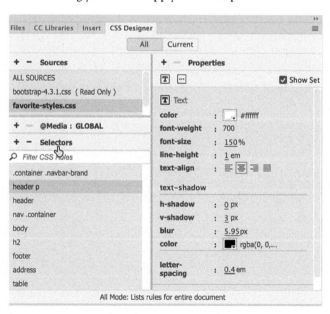

In addition to allowing you to create and edit CSS styling, the CSS Designer can also be used to identify styles already defined and applied, and to troubleshoot issues or conflicts with these styles.

## Properties

The Properties window features two basic modes. By default, the Properties window displays all available CSS properties in a list, organized in five categories: Layout, Text, Borders, Background, and More. You can scroll down the list and apply styling as desired or click the icon to jump to that category of the Properties panel.

● **Note:** Deselect the Show Set option to see all the CSS Designer categories and properties.

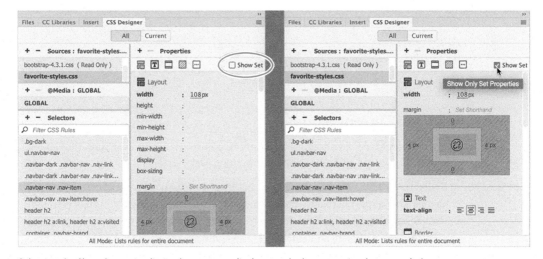

Selecting the Show Set option limits the property display to only the properties that are styled.

The second mode can be accessed by selecting Show Set at the upper-right edge of the window. In this mode, the Properties panel will filter the list down to only the properties actually applied to the rule chosen in the Selectors window. In either mode, you can add, edit, or remove style sheets, media queries, rules, and properties.

The Properties panel also features a COMPUTED option that displays the aggregated list of styles applied to the selected element when the Current button in CSS Designer is selected. The COMPUTED option will then appear anytime you select an element or component on the page. When you're creating any type of styling, the code created by Dreamweaver complies with industry standards and best practices.

The COMPUTED option collects all styles applied to the selection in one display.

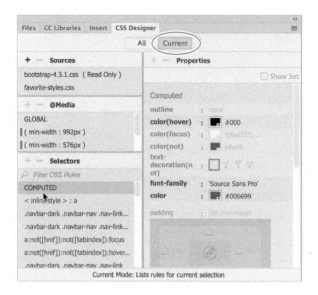

## All and Current modes

At the top of the CSS Designer panel are two buttons, All and Current, that enable specific functions and workflows within the panel.

When the All button is selected, the panel allows you to create and edit CSS style sheets, media queries, rules, and properties. When the Current button is selected, the CSS troubleshooting functions are enabled, allowing you to inspect individual elements in a webpage and assess existing styling properties applied to a selected element. In this mode, however, you will notice that some of the normal features in the CSS Designer are disabled. For example, when in Current mode you are able to edit existing properties and add new style sheets, media queries, and rules that apply to the selected element, but you cannot delete existing style sheets, media queries, or rules. This interaction works the same way in all document view modes.

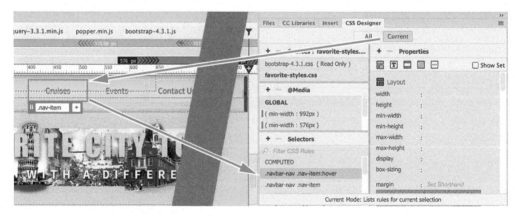

When the Current button is selected, the CSS Designer displays all the styling associated with a selected element.

In addition to using the CSS Designer, you may also create and edit CSS styling manually within Code view while taking advantage of many productivity enhancements, such as code hinting and auto-completion.

# Using the Visual Media Query (VMQ) interface

The Visual Media Query (VMQ) interface is a newer feature of Dreamweaver. Appearing above the document window, the VMQ interface allows you to visually inspect and interact with existing media queries, as well as create new ones on the fly using a simple point-and-click interface.

Open any webpage that is formatted by a style sheet with one or more media queries, like **tours.html**. If necessary, enable the VMQ interface by toggling the VMQ icon ⬚ in the Common toolbar.

# Using the DOM Viewer

The DOM Viewer allows you to view the Document Object Model (DOM) to quickly examine the structure of your webpage as well as interact with it to select, edit, and move existing elements and insert new ones. You'll find that it makes working in complex HTML structures simple.

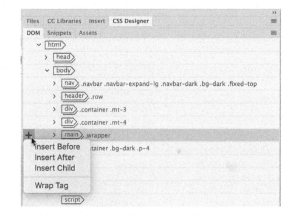

# Using element dialogs, displays, and inspectors

As Dreamweaver moves to make Live view the default workspace, it has driven the development of new methods for editing and managing HTML elements. You will find a handful of new dialogs, displays, and inspectors that provide instant access to important element properties and specifications. All of them, except the Text Display, allow you to add class or id attributes to the selected element and even insert references to those attributes into your CSS style sheets and media queries.

## Position Assist dialog

The Position Assist dialog appears whenever new elements are being inserted in Live view, using either the Insert menu or Insert panel. Typically, the Position Assist dialog will offer the options Before, After, Wrap, and Nest. Depending on what type of element is selected and what item is targeted by the cursor, one or more of the options may be grayed out.

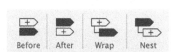

The Position Assist dialog allows you to control how elements and components are inserted in Live view.

## Element Display

The Element Display appears whenever you select an element in Live view. When an element is selected in Live view, you can change the selection focus by pressing the up arrow and down arrow keys; the Element Display will then highlight each element in the page, in turn, based on its position in the HTML structure.

The Element Display features a Quick Property Inspector icon where you can instantly access properties such as formats, links, and alignment. The Element Display also allows you to add a class or id to the selected element or to edit a class or id.

The Element Display enables you to quickly apply classes, ids, and links, as well as perform basic formatting.

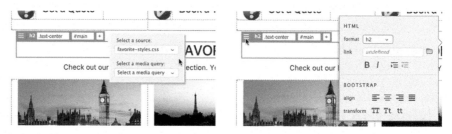

## Image Display

The Image Display provides a Quick Property inspector from which you can access the image source, alt text, and width and height attributes; it also contains a field from which you can add a hyperlink and several Bootstrap options.

The Image Display gives you quick access to the image source and allows you to add hyperlinks, as well as some Bootstrap options.

## Text Display

The Text Display appears whenever you select a portion of text in Live view. The Text Display allows you to apply bold <strong>, italic <em>, and hyperlink <a> markup to the selected text. Double-click the text to open the orange editing box. When you select some text, the Text Display will appear. When you are finished editing the text, click just outside the orange box to complete and accept the changes. Press Esc to cancel the changes and return the text to its previous state.

The Text Display lets you apply bold, italics, and hyperlink markup to selected text.

## Setting up version control in Dreamweaver

Dreamweaver CC (2021 release) supports Git, a popular open source version control system for managing the source code of your websites. Such systems are very valuable for preventing conflicts and loss of work when you have a number of people working together on a project.

Before you do the first step in Dreamweaver, you must create a Git account and set up a repository. Go to https://helpx.adobe.com/dreamweaver/using/git-support .html for full instructions on how to set up Git version control for your own project.

Once you have a repository set up, you must connect it to your site in Dreamweaver. First, select the option to associate the site with a Git repository within your site definition dialog.

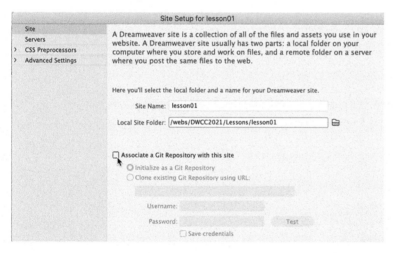

After that, click the Show Git View icon in the Files panel to toggle the Git panel.

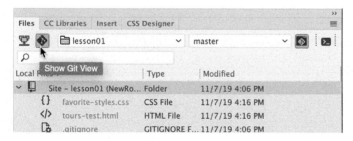

If you have not already configured a Git repository, Dreamweaver will prompt you to set up your Git credentials and the location of the repository.

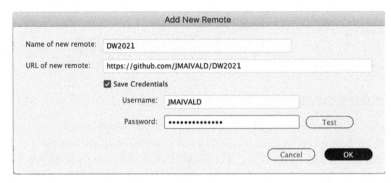

Test your credentials by clicking the Test button.

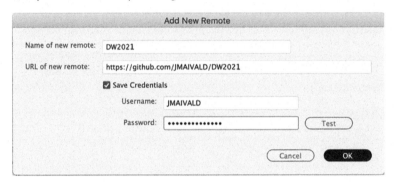

Once activated, the Git panel will display the contents of your site, and you can push and pull changes as needed.

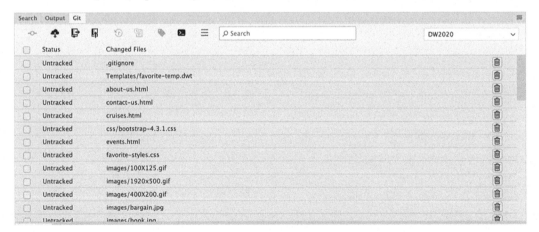

# Exploring, experimenting, and learning

The Dreamweaver interface has been carefully crafted over many years to make the job of webpage design and development fast and easy. It's a design in progress, and it's always changing and evolving. If you think you already know the program, you're wrong. Install the latest version and check it out. Feel free to explore and experiment with various menus, panels, and options to create the ideal workspace and keyboard shortcuts to produce the most productive environment for your own purposes. You'll find the program endlessly adaptable, with power to spare for any task. Enjoy.

## Review questions

1 Where can you access the command to display or hide any panel?

2 Where can you find the Code, Split, Design, and Live view buttons?

3 What can be saved in a workspace?

4 Do workspaces also load keyboard shortcuts?

5 What happens in the Property inspector when you insert the cursor into various elements on the webpage?

6 What features in the CSS Designer make it easy to build new rules from existing ones?

7 What can you do with the DOM Viewer?

8 Does the Element Display appear in Design or Code view?

9 What is Git?

## Review answers

1  All panels are listed in the Window menu.

2  The Code, Split, Design, and Live view buttons are components of the Document toolbar.

3  Workspaces can save the configuration of the document window, the open panels, and the panels' size and position on the screen.

4  No. Keyboard shortcuts are loaded and preserved independently of a workspace.

5  The Property inspector adapts to the selected element, displaying pertinent information and formatting commands.

6  The CSS Designer allows you to copy and paste styles from one rule to another.

7  The DOM Viewer allows you to visually examine the DOM and select and insert new elements and edit existing ones.

8  No. The Element Display is visible only in Live view.

9  Git is an open source version control system that enables you to manage your website source code.

# 2 HTML BASICS

## Lesson overview

In this lesson, you'll familiarize yourself with HTML and learn:

- What HTML is and where it came from
- Frequently used HTML tags
- How to insert special characters
- What semantic web design is and why it's important
- New features and capabilities in HTML

 This lesson will take about 30 minutes to complete. This lesson does not have support files.

```
<html>
    <head>
        <title>HTML Basics for Fun and Profit</title>
    </head>
    <body>
        <h1>Welcome to my first webpage</h1>
        <hr>
    </body>
</html>
```

HTML is the backbone of the web, the skeleton of
your webpage. It is the structure and substance of the
internet, although it is usually unseen except by the
web designer. Without it, the web would not exist.
Dreamweaver has many features that help you access,
create, and edit HTML code quickly and effectively.

# What is HTML?

"What other programs can open a Dreamweaver file?" asked a student in my Dreamweaver class. Although it might seem obvious to an experienced developer, it illustrates a basic problem in teaching and learning web design. Most people confuse the *program* with the *technology*. Some may assume that the extension .htm or .html belongs to Dreamweaver or Adobe. This isn't as unusual as it seems. Print designers are used to working with files ending with extensions, such as .ai, .psd, .indd, and so on; it's just a part of their jobs. They have learned over time that opening these file formats in a different program may be impossible, produce unacceptable results, or even damage the file.

On the other hand, the goal of the web designer is to create a webpage for display in a browser. The power or functionality of the originating program has little bearing on the resulting browser display, because the display is all contingent on the HTML code and how the browser interprets it. Although a program may write good or bad code, it's the browser that does all the hard work.

The web is based primarily on HyperText Markup Language (HTML). The language and the file format don't belong to any individual program or company. In fact, it is a *non*-proprietary, plain-text language that can be edited in any text editor, on any operating system, on any computer. Dreamweaver is, in part, an HTML editor, although it is also much more than this. But to maximize the potential of Dreamweaver, it's vital that you have a good understanding of what HTML is and what it can (and can't) do. This lesson is intended as a concise primer on HTML and its capabilities. It will be a helpful foundation for understanding Dreamweaver.

# Where did HTML begin?

HTML and the first browser were invented in 1989 by Tim Berners-Lee, a computer scientist working at the CERN (Conseil Européen pour la Recherche Nucléaire, which is French for European Council for Nuclear Research) particle physics laboratory in Geneva, Switzerland. He intended the technology as a means for sharing technical papers and information via the fledgling internet that existed at the time. He shared his HTML and browser inventions openly as an attempt to get the scientific community at large and others to adopt them and engage in the development themselves. The fact that he did not copyright or try to sell his work started a trend for openness and camaraderie on the web that continues to this day.

```
        CompuServe                    TOP

             1  Instructions/user Information
             2  Find a Topic
             3  Communications/Bulletin Bds.
             4  News/Weather/Sports
             5  Travel
             6  The Electronic MALL/Shopping
             7  Money Matters & Markets
             8  Entertainment/Games
             9  Home/Health/Family
            10  Reference/Education
            11  Computers and Technology
            12  Business/Other Interests


        >_
```

The internet before HTML looked more like MS DOS or the macOS Terminal application. There was no formatting, no graphics, and no user-definable color.

The language that Berners-Lee created more than 25 years ago was a much simpler construct of what we use now, but HTML is still surprisingly easy to learn and master. At the time of this writing, HTML is at version 5.2, officially adopted as of December 2017. The draft version of the next release (5.3) was published in October 2018 and is currently in development. Changes to the language are always in the works and often take several years to evolve before they are adopted officially.

HTML consists of over 120 *tags*, such as html, head, body, h1, p, and so on. The tag is inserted between less-than (<) and greater-than (>) angle brackets, as in <p>, <h1>, and <table>. These tags are used to identify, or *mark up*, text and graphics to signal the browser to display them in a particular way. HTML code is considered properly *balanced* when the markup features both an opening tag (<...>) and a closing tag (</...>), such as <h1>...</h1>.

When two matching tags appear this way, they are referred to as an *element*; an element encompasses any contents contained within the two tags, as well. Empty, or void, elements, like the horizontal rule, can be written in an abbreviated fashion using only one tag, such as <hr/>, essentially opening and closing the tag at the same time. In HTML5, empty elements can also be validly expressed without the closing slash, such as <hr>. Some older web applications require the closing slash, so it's a good idea to check before using one form over the other.

Some elements are used to create page structures, others to structure and format text, and yet others to enable interactivity and programmability. Even though Dreamweaver obviates the need for writing most of the code manually, the ability to read and interpret HTML code is still a recommended skill for any burgeoning web designer. Sometimes it's the only way to find an error in your webpage. The ability to read and understand code may also become an essential skill in other fields as more information and content is created and disseminated via mobile devices and internet-based resources.

Here you see the basic structure of a webpage:

You may be surprised to learn that the only text from all this code that displays in the web browser is "Welcome to my first webpage". The rest of the code creates the page structure and text formatting. Like an iceberg, most of the content of the actual webpage remains out of sight.

## Frequently used HTML elements

HTML code elements serve specific purposes. Tags can create distinct objects, apply formatting, identify content semantically, or generate interactivity. Tags that make their own space on the screen and stand alone are known as *block* elements; the ones that perform their duties within the flow of another tag are known as *inline* elements. Some elements can also be used to create *structural* relationships within a page, like stacking content in vertical columns or collecting several elements together in logical groupings. Structural elements can behave like block or inline elements or do their work entirely invisible to the user.

### HTML tags

**Table 2.1** shows some of the most frequently used HTML tags. To get the most out of Dreamweaver and your webpages, it helps to understand the nature of these elements and how they are used. Remember that some tags can serve multiple purposes.

**Table 2.1** Frequently used HTML tags

| TAG | DESCRIPTION |
| --- | --- |
| `<!--...-->` | Comment. Designates an HTML comment. Allows you to add notes within the HTML code (represented by … in the tag) that are not displayed within the browser. |
| `<a>` | Anchor. The basic building block for a hyperlink. |
| `<blockquote>` | Quotation. Creates a standalone, indented paragraph identifying content quoted from another source. |
| `<body>` | Body. Designates the document body. Contains the visible portions of the webpage content. |
| `<br>` | Break. Inserts a visual line break without creating a new paragraph. |
| `<div>` | Division. Used to divide webpage content into discernible sections. |
| `<em>` | Emphasis. Adds semantic emphasis. Displays as italics by default in most browsers and readers. |
| `<form>` | Form. Designates an HTML form. Used for collecting data from visitors. |
| `<h1>` to `<h6>` | Headings. Creates headings. Default formatting is bold. |
| `<head>` | Head. Designates the document head. Contains code that performs background functions, such as meta tags, scripts, styling, links, and other information not overtly visible to site visitors that may provide instructions on how to display the page or its contents. |
| `<hr>` | Horizontal rule. Empty element that generates a horizontal line visibly and is used to define a thematic change in content. |
| `<html>` | Root element of most webpages. Contains the entire webpage, except in certain instances where server-based code must load before the opening `<html>` tag. |
| `<iframe>` | Inline frame. A structural element that can contain another document or load content from another website. |
| `<img>` | Image. Provides the source reference to display an image. |
| `<input>` | Input. An input element for a form such as a text field. |
| `<li>` | List item. An element within an HTML list. |
| `<link>` | Link. Designates the relationship between a document and an external resource. |

| TAG | DESCRIPTION |
|---|---|
| `<meta>` | Metadata. Additional information provided for search engines or other applications. |
| `<ol>` | Ordered list. Defines a numbered list. List items display in an alpha, numeric, or roman numeral sequence. |
| `<p>` | Paragraph. Designates a standalone paragraph. |
| `<script>` | Script. Contains scripting elements or points to an internal or external script. |
| `<span>` | Span. Designates a section within an element. Provides a means to apply special formatting or emphasis to a portion of an element. |
| `<strong>` | Strong. Adds semantic emphasis. Displays as bold by default in most browsers and readers. |
| `<style>` | Style. Embedded or inline element or attribute containing CSS styling. |
| `<table>` | Table. Designates an HTML table. |
| `<td>` | Table data. Designates a table cell. |
| `<textarea>` | Text area. Designates a multiline text input element for a form. |
| `<th>` | Table header. Identifies a table cell containing a header. |
| `<title>` | Title. Contains the metadata title reference for the current page. |
| `<tr>` | Table row. Structural element that delineates one row of a table from another. |
| `<ul>` | Unordered list. Defines a bulleted list. List items display with bullets by default. |

## HTML character entities

Text content is normally entered via a computer keyboard. But many characters don't appear on a typical 101-key input device. If a symbol can't be entered directly from the keyboard, it can be inserted within the HTML code by typing the name or numeric value, referred to as an *entity*. Entities exist for every letter and character that can be displayed. Some popular entities are listed in **Table 2.2**.

● **Note:** Some entities can be created using either a name or a number, as in the copyright symbol, but named entities may not work in all browsers or applications. So either stick to numbered entities or test the specific named entities before you use them.

**Table 2.2** HTML character entities

| CHARACTER | DESCRIPTION | NAME | NUMBER |
|---|---|---|---|
| © | Copyright | &copy; | &#169; |
| ® | Registered trademark | &reg; | &#174; |
| ™ | Trademark | &trade; | &#153; |
| • | Bullet | &bull; | &#149; |
| – | En dash | &ndash; | &#8211; |
| — | Em dash | &mdash; | &#8212; |
| | Nonbreaking space |   |   |

Go to www.w3schools.com/html/html_entities.asp to see a complete list and description of entities.

# What's new in HTML5

Every new version of HTML has made changes to both the number and the purpose of the tags that make up the language. HTML 4.01 consisted of approximately 90 tags. HTML5 removed some HTML 4 tags from its specification altogether and adopted or proposed some new ones.

Changes to the list usually revolve around supporting new technologies or different types of content models, as well as removing features that were bad ideas or that were infrequently used. Some changes simply reflect customs or techniques that have been popularized within the developer community over time. Other changes have been made to simplify the way code is created, to make it easier to write and faster to disseminate.

## HTML5 tags

**Table 2.3** shows some of the important new tags in HTML5. The specification features nearly 50 new tags in total, while at least 30 old tags were deprecated. As we move through the exercises of this book, you will learn how to use many of these new HTML5 tags, as appropriate, to help you understand their intended role on the web. Take a few moments to familiarize yourself with these tags and their descriptions. Be aware that HTML support is not universal in all browsers. New tags may not be fully supported by every browser or even in the same way. Always test the use of new tags in various browsers and devices before basing your webpage on them.

Go to www.w3schools.com/tags/default.asp to see the complete list of HTML5 elements.

**Table 2.3** Important new HTML5 tags

| TAG | DESCRIPTION |
| --- | --- |
| `<article>` | Article. Designates independent, self-contained content that can be distributed independently from the rest of the page or site. |
| `<aside>` | Aside. Designates sidebar content that is related to the main content. |
| `<audio>` | Audio. Designates multimedia content, sounds, music, or other audio streams. |
| `<canvas>` | Canvas. Designates graphics content created using a script. |
| `<figcaption>` | Figure caption. Designates a caption for a `<figure>` element. |
| `<figure>` | Figure. Designates a section of standalone content containing an illustration, image, or video. |
| `<footer>` | Footer. Designates a footer of a document or section. |
| `<header>` | Header. Designates a section of the content that introduces a document or specific topic area. |
| `<hgroup>` | Heading group. Designates a set of <h1> to <h6> elements when a heading has multiple levels. |
| `<main>` | Main. Designates the unique content of a page. A page may have only one `main` element. |
| `<nav>` | Navigation. Designates a section containing a navigation menu or hyperlink group. |
| `<picture>` | Picture. Designates one or more resources for a webpage image to support the various resolutions available on smartphones and other mobile devices. This is a new tag that may not be supported in older browsers or devices. |
| `<section>` | Section. Designates a section within the content of a document. |
| `<source>` | Source. Designates media resources for video or audio elements. Multiple sources can be defined for browsers that do not support the default file type. |
| `<video>` | Video. Designates video content, such as a movie clip or other video streams. |

## Semantic web design

Many of the changes to HTML were made to support the concept of *semantic web design*. This movement has important ramifications for the future of HTML, its usability, and the interoperability of websites on the internet. At the moment, each webpage stands alone on the web. The content may link to other pages and sites, but there's really no way to combine or collect the information available on multiple pages or multiple sites in a coherent manner. Search engines do their best to index the content that appears on every site, but much of it is lost due to the nature and structure of old HTML code.

HTML was initially designed as a presentation language. In other words, it was intended to display technical documents in a browser in a readable and predictable manner. If you look carefully at the original specifications of HTML, it looks like a list of items you would put in a college term paper: headings, paragraphs, quotations, tables, numbered and bulleted lists, and so on.

The element list in the first version of HTML basically identified how the content would be *displayed*. These tags did not convey any intrinsic meaning or significance. For example, using a heading tag displayed a particular line of text in bold, but it didn't tell you what relationship or importance the heading had to the following text or to the story as a whole. Is it a title or merely a subheading?

HTML5 has added a significant number of new tags to help us add semantic meaning to our markup. Tags such as `<header>`, `<footer>`, `<article>`, and `<section>` allow you for the first time to identify specific content without having to resort to additional attributes. The result is simpler code and less of it. But most of all, the addition of semantic meaning to your code allows you and other developers to connect the content from one page to another in new and exciting ways—many of which haven't even been invented yet. It's truly a work in progress.

## New techniques and technology

HTML5 has also revisited the basic nature of the language to take back some of the functions that over the years have been increasingly handled by third-party plug-in applications and programming.

If you are new to web design, this transition will be painless because you have nothing to relearn, no bad habits to break. If you already have experience building webpages and applications, this book will guide you safely through some of these waters and introduce the new technologies and techniques in a logical and straightforward method. But either way, you don't have to trash all your old sites and rebuild everything from scratch.

Valid HTML 4 code will remain valid for the foreseeable future. HTML5 was intended to make web design easier by allowing you to do more with less work. So let's get started!

See www.w3.org/TR/2017/REC-html52-20171214 to learn more about HTML 5.2.

See www.w3.org to learn more about W3C.

## Review questions

1 What programs can open HTML files?

2 What does a markup language do?

3 HTML is composed of how many code elements?

4 What is the difference between block and inline elements?

5 What is the current version of HTML?

# Review answers

1  HTML is a plain-text language that can be opened and edited in any text editor and viewed in any web browser.

2  A markup language places tags contained within brackets, < >, around plain-text content to pass information concerning meaning, structure, and formatting from one application to another.

3  HTML5 contains more than 100 tags.

4  A block element creates a standalone element. An inline element can exist within another element.

5  HTML 5.2 was formally adopted at the end of 2017. A new draft version, 5.3, was published at the end of 2018. Full support of any new recommendations may take several years. And, as with HTML 4, some browsers and devices may support the specification in differing ways.

# 3

## CSS BASICS

## Lesson overview

In this lesson, you'll familiarize yourself with CSS and learn:

- CSS (cascading style sheets) terminology
- The difference between HTML and CSS formatting
- Different methods for writing CSS rules and markup
- How the cascade, inheritance, descendant, and specificity theories affect the way browsers apply CSS formatting
- The new features and capabilities of CSS3

 This lesson will take about 1 hour and 15 minutes to complete. To get the lesson files used in this lesson, download them from the webpage for this book at www.adobepress.com/DreamweaverCIB2021. For more information, see "Accessing the lesson files and Web Edition" in the "Getting Started" section at the beginning of this book.

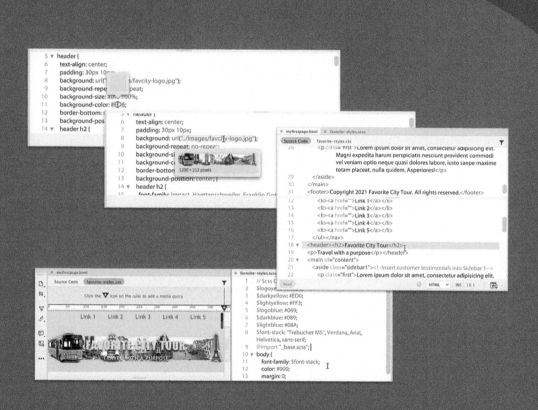

Cascading style sheets control the look and feel of a webpage. The language and syntax of CSS are complex, powerful, and endlessly adaptable. CSS takes time and dedication to learn and years to master, but a modern web designer can't live without it.

# What is CSS?

HTML was never intended to be a design medium. Other than allowing for bold and italic, version 1 lacked a standardized way to load fonts or even format text. Formatting commands were added along the way—up to version 3 of HTML—to address these limitations, but these changes still weren't enough. Designers resorted to various tricks to produce the desired results. For example, they used HTML tables to simulate multicolumn and complex layouts for text and graphics, and they used images when they wanted to display typefaces other than Times or Helvetica.

HTML-based formatting was so misguided a concept that it was deprecated from the language less than a year after it was formally adopted in favor of cascading style sheets (CSS). CSS avoids all the problems of HTML formatting while saving time and money too. Using CSS lets you strip the HTML code down to its essential content and structure and then apply the formatting separately so that you can more easily tailor the webpage to specific devices and applications.

# HTML vs. CSS formatting

● **Note:** To save ink, screen shots in this and all subsequent lessons were taken using the lightest UI and the Classic code-coloring theme. You are free to use the default dark UI and code theme if you prefer them, or any custom setting of your own choosing. The program and lessons will perform identically in any UI color settings.

When comparing HTML-based formatting to CSS-based formatting, it's easy to see how CSS produces vast efficiencies in time and effort. In the following exercise, you'll explore the power and efficiency of CSS by editing two webpages, one formatted by HTML and the other by CSS.

1 Launch Dreamweaver CC 2021 or later, if it's not currently running.

2 If you have not done so yet, create a new site based on the lesson03 folder, using the instructions in the "Getting Started" section at the beginning of the book. Name the site **lesson03**.

3 Choose File > Open.

4 Navigate to the lesson03 folder.
Open **html-formatting.html**.

● **Note:** Code and Live view windows can be swapped top to bottom and left to right by selecting the option under the View menu. See Lesson 1, "Customizing Your Workspace," for more information.

5 Click the Split view button. If necessary, choose View > Split > Split Vertically to split Code and Live view windows vertically, side by side.

Note that each element of the content is formatted individually using the deprecated `<font>` tag. Note the attribute `color="blue"` in each `<h1>` and `<p>` element.

● **Note:** *Deprecated* means that the tag has been formally removed from future support in HTML but may still be honored by current browsers and HTML readers.

6 Replace the word "blue" with "green" in each line in which it appears. If necessary, click the mouse cursor in the Live view window to update the display.

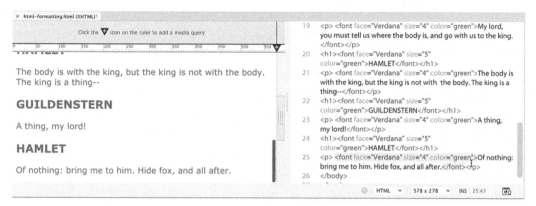

The text displays in green now in each line where you changed the color value. As you can see, formatting using the obsolete `<font>` tag is not only slow but also prone to error. Make a mistake, like typing `greeen` or `geen`, and the browser will ignore the color formatting entirely.

7 Open **css-formatting.html** from the lesson03 folder.

8 If it's not currently selected, click the Split view button.

The content of the file is identical to the previous document, except that it's formatted using CSS. The code that formats the HTML elements appears in the `<head>` section of this file. Note that the code contains only two `color:blue;` attributes.

9 In the code `h1 { color: blue; }` select the word `blue` and type `green` to replace it. If necessary, click in the Live view window to update the display.

**Note:** Dreamweaver usually defaults to Live view when you open or create a new page. If not, you may select it from the Document toolbar using the Live/Design dropdown menu.

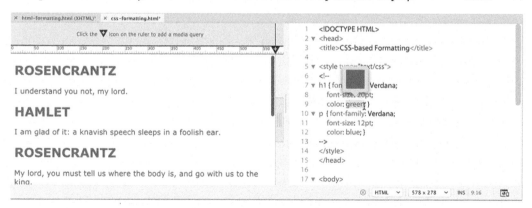

In Live view, all the heading elements display in green. The paragraph elements remain blue.

**10** Select the word `blue` in the code `p { color: blue; }` and type `green` to replace it. Click in the Live view window to update the display.

In Live view, all the paragraph elements have changed to green.

**11** Close all files and do not save the changes.

In this exercise, CSS accomplished the color change with two simple edits, whereas using the HTML `<font>` tag required you to edit every line individually. Now think how tedious it would be to go through thousands of lines of code and hundreds of pages on a site to make such a change. Is it any wonder that the W3C, the web standards organization that establishes internet specifications and protocols, deprecated the `<font>` tag and developed cascading style sheets? This exercise highlights just a small sample of the formatting power and productivity enhancements offered by CSS, unmatched by HTML alone.

## HTML defaults

Since the very beginning, HTML tags came right out of the box with one or more default formats, characteristics, or behaviors. So even if you did nothing, much of your text would already be formatted in a certain way in most browsers. One of the essential tasks in mastering CSS is learning and understanding these defaults and how they may affect your content. Let's take a look.

**1** Open **html-defaults.html** from the lesson03 folder. If necessary, select Live view to preview the contents of the file.

The file contains a range of HTML headings and text elements. Each element visually exhibits basic styling for traits such as size, font, and spacing, among others.

**2** Switch to Split view.

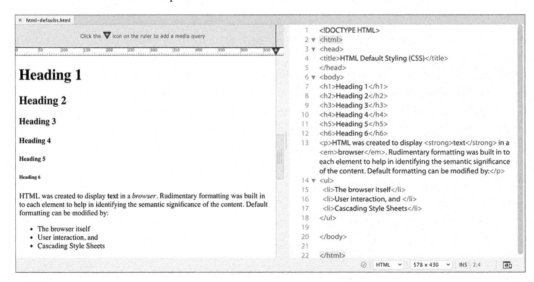

3  In the Code view window, locate the `<head>` section, and try to identify any code that may be formatting the HTML elements.

A quick look will tell you that there is no overt styling information in the file, yet the text still displays different kinds of formatting. So where does the formatting come from? And, more importantly, what are the settings being used?

The answer is: It depends. In the past, HTML 4 elements drew characteristics from multiple sources. The first place to look is the W3C. For HTML 4 it created a default style sheet, which you can find at www.w3.org/TR/CSS21/sample.html. The style sheet defines the standard formatting and behaviors of all HTML elements. The browser vendors used this style sheet to base their default rendering of HTML elements. But that was before HTML5.

4  Close **html-defaults.html** and do not save any changes.

## HTML5 defaults?

The last decade has seen a consistent movement on the web to separate "content" from its "styling." The concept of "default" formatting in HTML seems to be dead. According to specifications adopted by the W3C in 2014, there are no default styling standards for HTML5 elements. If you look for a default style sheet for HTML5 on w3.org—like the one identified earlier for HTML 4—you won't find one. As of this writing, there are no public moves to change this relationship, and browser manufacturers are still honoring and applying HTML 4 default styling to HTML5-based webpages. Confused? Join the club.

● **Note:** If the current trends continue, the lack of an HTML5 default style sheet makes the development of your own site standards even more important.

The ramifications of this trend could be dramatic and wide reaching. Someday, in the not-too-distant future, HTML elements may not display any formatting at all by default. That means that understanding how elements are currently formatted is more important than ever so that you will be ready to develop your own standards if or when the need arises.

To save time and give you a head start, I pulled together **Table 3.1**, with some of the most common defaults.

**Table 3.1** Common HTML defaults

| ITEM | DESCRIPTION |
| --- | --- |
| Background | In most browsers, the page background color is white. The background of the elements `<div>`, `<table>`, `<td>`, and `<th>` and of most other tags is transparent. |
| Headings | Headings `<h1>` through `<h6>` are bold and align to the left. The six heading tags also apply differing font size attributes, with `<h1>` the largest and `<h6>` the smallest. Apparent sizes may vary between browsers. Headings and other text elements may also display additional spacing (margins) above or below. |

| ITEM | DESCRIPTION |
| --- | --- |
| Body text | Outside of a table cell, paragraphs—`<p>`, `<li>`, `<dd>`, `<dt>`—align to the left and start at the top of the page. |
| Table cell text | Text within table cells, `<td>`, aligns horizontally to the left and vertically to the center. |
| Table header | Text within header cells, `<th>`, aligns horizontally and vertically to the center and styles the text in bold in some browsers (this is not standard across all browsers). |
| Fonts | Text color is black. Default typeface and font are specified and supplied by the browser, which in turn can be overridden by the user using the preference settings in the browser itself. |
| Margins | Spacing external to the element border/boundary is handled by margins. Many HTML elements feature some form of margin spacing. Margins are often used to insert additional space between paragraphs and to indent text, as in lists and blockquotes. The margin displayed by these elements varies among browsers. |
| Padding | Spacing within the box border is handled by padding. According to the default HTML 4 style sheet, no elements feature default padding. |

## Browser antics

The next task in developing your own styling standards is to identify the browser (and its version) that is displaying the HTML. That's because browsers frequently differ (sometimes dramatically) in the way they interpret, or render, HTML elements and CSS formatting. Unfortunately, even different versions of the same browser can produce wide variations from identical code.

Web design best practices dictate that you build and test your webpages to make sure they work properly in the browsers employed by the majority of web users in general—but especially the browsers preferred by your own visitors. The breakdown of browsers used by your own visitors can differ quite a bit from the norm. They also change over time—especially now, as more and more people abandon desktop computers in favor of tablets and smartphones. In August 2020, the W3C published the following statistics identifying the most popular browsers from the 50 million visitors they receive each year on their website.

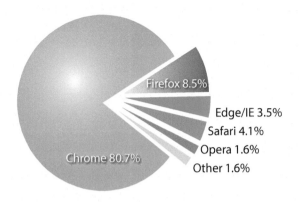

Although it's nice to know which browsers are the most popular among the general public, it's crucial that you identify the browsers your target audience uses before you build and test your pages.

Although this chart shows the basic breakdown in the browser world, it obscures the fact that multiple versions of each browser are still being used. This is important to know because older browser versions are less likely to support the latest HTML and CSS features and effects. To make matters more complicated, these statistics show trends for the internet overall, but the statistics for your own site may vary wildly.

While HTML5 is widely supported, inconsistencies between browsers may never go away. For example, some aspects of HTML 4 and CSS 1 and 2 are still not universally agreed upon to this day. It's vital that any text styling, page structures, and CSS animation be tested carefully. Occasionally, you will find that you must create custom CSS styling to contend with issues in one or more browsers.

## CSS box model

Browsers normally read the HTML code, interpret its structure and formatting, and then display the webpage. CSS does its work by stepping between HTML and the browser, redefining how each element should be rendered. It imposes an imaginary box around each element and then enables you to format almost every aspect of how that box and its contents are displayed.

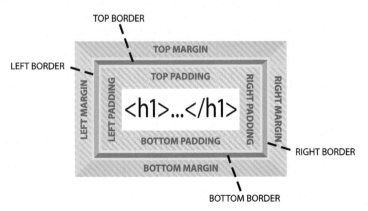

TOP BORDER

LEFT BORDER

TOP MARGIN

TOP PADDING

LEFT MARGIN

LEFT PADDING

RIGHT PADDING

RIGHT MARGIN

<h1>...</h1>

BOTTOM PADDING

BOTTOM MARGIN

RIGHT BORDER

BOTTOM BORDER

The box model is a programmatic construct imposed by HTML and CSS that enables you to format, or redefine, the default settings of any HTML element.

CSS permits you to specify fonts, line spacing, colors, borders, background shading and graphics, margins, and padding, among other things. Most of the time, these boxes are invisible, and although CSS gives you the ability to format them, it doesn't require you to do so.

1    Launch Dreamweaver (2021 release) or later.
     Open **boxmodel.html** from the lesson03 folder.

2    If necessary, switch to Split view.

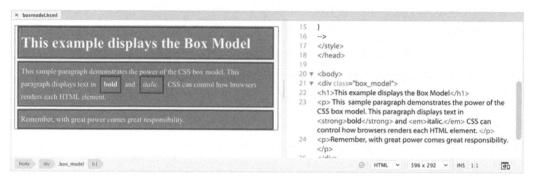

The file's sample HTML code contains a heading and two paragraphs with sample text formatted to illustrate some of the properties of the CSS box model. The text displays visible borders, background colors, margins, and padding. To see the real power of CSS, sometimes it's helpful to see what the page would look like without CSS.

● **Note:** The Style Rendering command is available only in Design view.

3    Switch to Design view.
     Choose View > Design View Options > Style Rendering > Display Styles to disable style rendering.

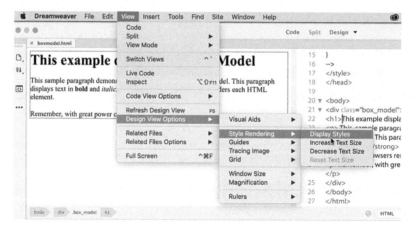

Dreamweaver now displays the page without any applied styling. A basic tenet in web standards today is the separation of the *content* (text, images, lists, and so on) from its *presentation* (formatting). Although the text now is not wholly unformatted, it's easy to see the power of CSS to transform HTML code. Whether the text is formatted or not, this illustrates the importance of the structure and *quality* of your content. Will people still be enthralled by your website if all the wonderful formatting were pulled away?

4   Choose View > Design View Options > Style Rendering > Display Styles to enable the CSS rendering in Dreamweaver again.

5   Close all files, and do not save changes.

The working specifications found at www.w3.org/TR/css3-box describe how the box model is supposed to render documents in various media.

# Applying CSS styling

You can apply CSS formatting in three ways: *inline* (on the element itself), *embedded* (in an internal style sheet), or *linked* (via an external style sheet). A CSS formatting instruction is known as a *rule*. A rule consists of two parts: a *selector* and one or more *declarations*. The selector specifies what element, or combination of elements, is to be formatted; declarations contain the styling information. CSS rules can redefine any existing HTML element, as well as define two custom element modifiers, named "class" and "id."

A rule can also combine selectors to target multiple elements at once or to target specific instances within a page where elements appear in unique ways, such as when one element is nested within another.

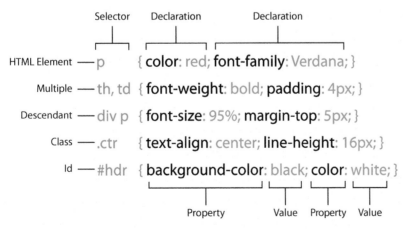

Sample CSS Rule Construction

These sample rules demonstrate some typical constructions used in selectors and declarations. The way the selector is written determines how the styling is applied and how the rules interact with one another.

Applying a CSS rule is not a simple matter of selecting some text and applying a paragraph or character style, as in Adobe InDesign or Adobe Illustrator. CSS rules can affect single words, paragraphs of text, or combinations of text and objects. Basically, anything that has an HTML tag on it can be styled, and there is even an HTML tag (span) specifically intended to style content that has no tag.

Many factors come into play in how a CSS rule performs its job. To help you better understand how it all works, the following sections illustrate four main CSS concepts, which I'll refer to as theories: cascade, inheritance, descendant, and specificity.

## Cascade theory

The cascade theory describes how the order and placement of rules in the style sheet or on the page affects the application of styling. In other words, if two rules conflict, which one wins out?

Take a look at the following rules that might appear in a style sheet:

```
p { color: red; }
p { color: blue; }
```

Both rules apply text color to the paragraph <p> tag. Since they style the same element, they both cannot win. According to the cascade theory, the rule declared last, or *closest* to the HTML code, wins. That means, in this case, the text would appear in blue.

When you try to determine which CSS rule will be honored and which formatting will be applied, browsers typically honor the following order of hierarchy, with number 4 being the most powerful:

1. Browser defaults.

2. External or embedded style sheets. If both are present, the one declared last supersedes the earlier entry when there's a conflict.

3. Inline styles (within the HTML element itself).

4. Styles with the value attribute !important applied.

# CSS rule syntax: write or wrong

CSS is a powerful adjunct to HTML. It has the power to style and format any HTML element, but the language is sensitive to even the smallest typo or syntax error. Miss a period, comma, or semicolon and you may as well have left the code out of your page entirely. Even worse, an error in one rule may cancel all the styling in subsequent rules or the entire style sheet.

For example, take the following simple rule:

```
p {  padding: 1px;
     margin: 10px; }
```

It applies both padding and margins to the paragraph `<p>` element.

This rule can also be written properly without spacing as:

```
p{padding:1px;margin:10px;}
```

The spaces and line breaks used in the first example are unnecessary, merely accommodations for the humans who may write and read the code. Removing excess spacing is known as *minification* and is often used to optimize style sheets. Browsers and other applications processing the code do not need this extra space, but the same cannot be said of the various punctuation marks sprinkled throughout the CSS.

Use parentheses ( ) or brackets [ ] instead of braces { }, and the rule (and perhaps your entire style sheet) is useless. The same goes for the use of colons : and semicolons ; in the code.

Can you catch the errors in each of the following sample rules?

```
p { padding; 1px: margin; 10px: }
p { padding: 1px; margin: 10px; ]
p { padding 1px, margin 10px, }
```

Similar problems can arise in the construction of compound selectors too. For example, putting a space in the wrong place can change the meaning of a selector entirely.

The rule `article.content { color: #F00 }` formats the `<article>` element and all its children in this code structure:

```
<article class="content"><p>...</p></article>
```

On the other hand, the rule `article .content { color: #F00 }` would ignore the previous HTML structure altogether, and format only the `<p>` element in the following code:

```
<article class="content"><p class="content">...</p></article>
```

A tiny error can have dramatic and far-reaching repercussions. To keep their CSS and HTML functioning properly, good web designers keep their eyes peeled for any little error, misplaced space, or punctuation mark. As you work through the following exercises, keep a careful eye on all the code for any similar errors. As mentioned in the "Getting Started" section, some instructions in this book may omit an expected period or other punctuation in a sentence on purpose when including it might cause confusion or possible code errors.

## Inheritance theory

The inheritance theory describes how an element can be affected by one or more rules at the same time. Inheritance can affect rules of the same name as well as rules that format *parent* elements—ones that contain other elements. Take a look at the following code:

```
<article>
    <h1>Pellentesque habitant</h1>
    <p>Vestibulum tortor quam</p>
    <h2>Aenean ultricies mi vitae</h2>
    <p>Mauris placerat eleifend leo.</p>
    <h3>Aliquam erat volutpat</h3>
    <p>Praesent dapibus, neque id cursus.</p>
</article>
```

The code contains various headings and paragraph elements and one parent element `<article>` that contains them all. If you wanted to apply blue to all the text, you could use the following set of CSS rules:

```
h1 { color: blue;}
h2 { color: blue;}
h3 { color: blue;}
p { color: blue;}
```

That's a lot of code all saying the same thing, something most web designers typically want to avoid. This is where inheritance comes into play to save time and effort. Using inheritance you can replace all four lines of code with:

```
article { color: blue;}
```

That's because all the headings and paragraphs are children of the `article` element; they each inherit the styling applied to their parent, as long as there are no other rules or presets overriding it. Inheritance can be of real assistance in economizing the amount of code you have to write to style your pages. But it's a double-edged sword. As much as you can use it to style elements intentionally, you also have to keep an eye out for unintentional effects.

Inheritance is not universally guaranteed. That's because inheriting certain properties can cause undesirable effects. Margin, padding, border, and background styling are properties that cannot be applied via inheritance. Check out the following resource to see which properties are inheritable: https://tinyurl.com/css-inheritance.

## Descendant theory

Inheritance provides a means to apply styling to multiple elements at once, but CSS also provides the means to target styling to specific elements based on the HTML structure.

The descendant theory describes how formatting can target specific elements based on their position relative to other elements. This technique involves the creation of a selector name that identifies a specific element, or elements, by combining multiple tags and, in some cases, id and class attributes.

Take a look at the following code:

```
<section><p>The sky is blue</p></section>
<div><p>The forest is green.</p></div>
```

Notice how both paragraphs contain no intrinsic formatting or special attributes, although they do appear in different parent elements. Let's say you wanted to apply blue to the first line and green to the second. You would not be able to do this using a single rule targeting the <p> tag alone. But it's a simple matter using descendant selectors, like these:

```
section p { color: blue;}
div p { color: green;}
```

See how two tags are combined in each selector? The selectors identify a specific kind of element structure, or hierarchy, to format. The first targets p tags that are children of section tags, the second targets p tags that are children of div tags. It's a common practice to combine multiple tags within a selector to tightly control how the styling is applied and to limit unintended inheritance.

In recent years, a set of special characters has been developed to hone this technique to a fine edge. For example, use a plus (+) sign like this section+p to target only the first paragraph that appears after a <section> tag. Use the tilde (~) like this h3~ul to target unordered lists that are preceded by an <h3> tag. Check out https://tinyurl.com/special-selectors to see the full set of special selector characters and wildcards and how to use them. But be careful using these special characters. Many of them were added only in the last few years and still have limited support.

## Specificity theory

Conflicts between two or more rules are the bane of most web designers' existence and can waste hours of time in troubleshooting CSS formatting errors. In the past, designers would have to spend hours manually scanning style sheets and rules one by one, trying to track down the source of styling errors.

*Specificity* describes how browsers determine what formatting to apply when two or more rules conflict. Some refer to this as *weight*—giving certain rules higher priority, or more weight, based on order (cascade), proximity, inheritance, and descendant relationships. One way to make it easier to see a selector's weight is by giving numeric values to each component in the name.

For example, each HTML tag gets 1 point, each class gets 10 points, each id gets 100 points, and inline style attributes get 1000 points. By adding up the component values within each selector, its specificity can be calculated and compared to another, and the higher specific weight wins.

## Calculating specificity

Can you do the math? Look at the following list of selectors and see how they add up. Look through the list of rules appearing in the sample files in this lesson. Can you determine the weight of each of those selectors and figure out which rule is more specific on sight?

```
* (wildcard) { } 0 + 0 + 0 + 0    =      0 points
h1           { } 0 + 0 + 0 + 1    =      1 point
ul li        { } 0 + 0 + 0 + 2    =      2 points
.class       { } 0 + 0 + 10 + 0   =     10 points
.class h1    { } 0 + 0 + 10 + 1   =     11 points
a:hover      { } 0 + 0 + 10 + 1   =     11 points
#id          { } 0 + 100 + 0 + 0  =    100 points
#id.class    { } 0 + 100 + 10 + 0 =    110 points
#id.class h1 { } 0 + 100 + 10 + 1 =    111 points
style=" "    { } 1000 + 0 + 0 + 0 =   1000 points
```

As you have learned in this lesson, CSS rules often don't work alone. They may style more than one HTML element at a time and may overlap or inherit styling from one another. Each of the theories described so far has a role to play in how CSS styling is applied through your webpage and across your site. When the style sheet is loaded, the browser will use the following hierarchy—with number 4 being the most powerful—to determine how the styles are applied, especially when rules conflict:

1. Cascade

2. Inheritance

3. Descendant structure

4. Specificity

Of course, knowing this hierarchy doesn't help much when you are faced with a CSS conflict on a page with dozens or perhaps hundreds of rules and multiple style sheets. Luckily, Dreamweaver has two powerful tools that can help you in this endeavor. The first one we'll look at is named Code Navigator.

## Code Navigator

Code Navigator is a tool within Dreamweaver that allows you to instantly inspect an HTML element and assess its CSS-based formatting. When activated, it displays all the embedded and externally linked CSS rules that have some role in formatting a selected element, and it lists them in the order of their cascade application and specificity. Code Navigator works in all Dreamweaver-based document views.

1  Open **css-basics-finished.html** from the lesson03 folder.

Since you were using Split view with the previous webpage, it should still be selected when the new file opens. One window shows Code view and the other shows Design view.

2  Select Live view in the Document toolbar.

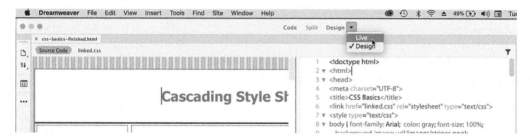

Depending on the size of your computer display, you may want to split the screen horizontally to see the entire page width at once.

3  Select View > Split > Split Horizontally.

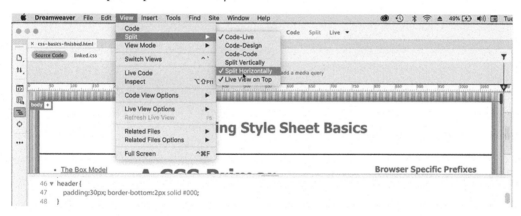

The screen shot shows the Live view window on top.

4  In Split view, observe the CSS code and the structure of the HTML content. Then, note the appearance of the text in the Live view window.

The page contains headings, paragraphs, and lists in various HTML5 structural elements, such as `article`, `section`, and `aside`, styled by CSS rules appearing in the `<head>` section of the code.

5  In Live view, insert the cursor into the heading "A CSS Primer."
Press Ctrl+Alt+N/Cmd+Opt+N.

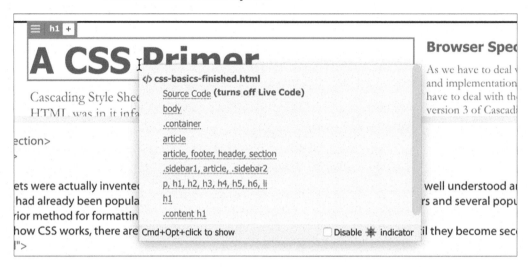

A small window appears, displaying a list of eight CSS rules that apply to this heading.

This is how you access Code Navigator in Live view. You can also right-click any element and select Code Navigator from the context menu. Code Navigator works in all document views.

If you position the pointer over each rule in turn, Dreamweaver displays any properties defined within the rule and their values. The rule with the highest specificity (most powerful) is at the bottom of the list.

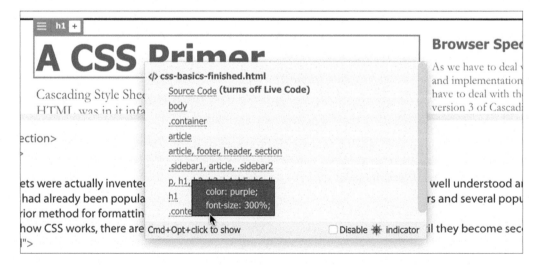

Unfortunately, Code Navigator doesn't show styling applied via inline styles, so you'll have to check for these types of properties separately and calculate the effect of inline styles in your head. Otherwise, the sequence of rules in the list indicates both their cascade order and their specificity.

When rules conflict, rules farther down in the list override rules that are higher up. Remember that elements may inherit styling from one or more rules and be influenced by default styling, and all can play a role in the final presentation. Unfortunately, Code Navigator doesn't show what, if any, default styling characteristics may still be in effect. You have to figure that out for yourself.

In this case, the `.content h1` rule appears at the bottom of the Code Navigator window, indicating that its specifications are the most powerful ones styling this element. But many factors can influence which of the rules may win. Sometimes the specificity of two rules is identical; then, it's simply the order (cascade) in which rules are declared in the style sheet that determines which one is actually applied.

As described earlier, changing the order of rules can often affect how the rules work. There's a simple exercise you can perform to determine whether a rule is winning because of cascade or specificity.

6  In the Code view window, locate the `.content h1` rule (around line 13) and click the line number.

Clicking the line number selects all the code on that line.

7  Press Ctrl+X/Cmd+X to cut the line.

8  Insert the cursor at the beginning of the style sheet (line 8). Press Ctrl+V/Cmd+V to paste the line at the top of style sheet.

```
7 ▼  <style type="text/css">
8 ▼  body { font-family: Arial;  color: gray; font-size: 100%;
9        background-image: url(/images/stripes.png);
10       background-color:#acd8b6; }
11     p, h1, h2, h3, h4, h5, h6, li { margin: 10px 0px; }
12     header { padding:30px; border-bottom:2px solid #000; text-align:center; }
13 ▼  .content h1 { color: purple; font-size: 300%; }
14     p { font-family: Garamond; }
```

```
7 ▼  <style type="text/css">
8    .content h1 { color: purple; font-size: 300%; }
9 ▼  body { font-family: Arial;  color: gray; font-size: 100%;
10       background-image: url(/images/stripes.png);
11       background-color:#acd8b6; }
12     p, h1, h2, h3, h4, h5, h6, li { margin: 10px 0px; }
13     header { padding:30px; border-bottom:2px solid #000; text-align:center; }
14     p { font-family: Garamond; }
```

9  Click in the Live view window to refresh the display, if necessary.

The styling did not change.

10  Click the text of the heading "A CSS Primer" to select it and activate Code Navigator, as you did in step 5.

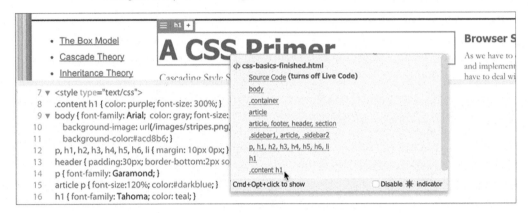

▶ **Tip:** Code Navigator may be disabled by default. To have it display automatically, deselect the Disable option in the Code Navigator window when it's visible.

Although the rule was moved to the top of the style sheet—the weakest position—the order of the rules in Code Navigator did not change. In this case, cascade was not responsible for the power of the rule. The `.content h1` selector has a specificity higher than either the body or h1 selector. In this instance, it would win no matter where it was placed in the code. But you can change its specificity by simply modifying the selector.

11  Select and delete the ~~.content~~ class notation from the `.content h1` selector.

● **Note:** Don't forget to delete the leading period indicating the class name.

12  Click in the Live view window to refresh the display, if necessary.

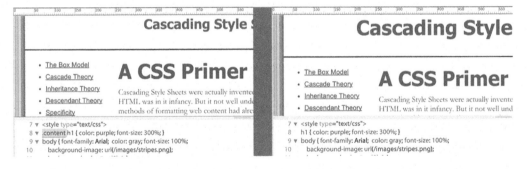

Did you notice how the styling changed? The "A CSS Primer" heading reverted to the color teal, and the other h1 headings scaled to 300 percent. Do you know why this happened?

13 Click the heading "A CSS Primer" to select it and activate Code Navigator.

Because you removed the class notation from its selector, it now has equal value to the other h1 rule, but since it is the first one declared, it loses precedence by virtue of its cascade position.

14 Using Code Navigator, examine and compare the rules applied to the headings "A CSS Primer" and "Creating CSS Menus."

Code Navigator shows the same rules applied to both.

● **Note:** Code Navigator doesn't display inline CSS rules. Since most CSS styling is not applied this way, it's not much of a limitation, but you should still be aware of this blind spot as you work with Code Navigator.

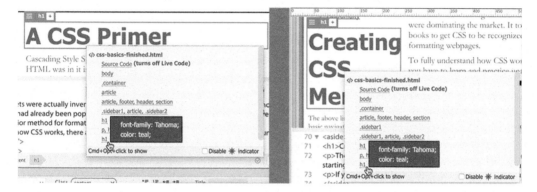

Because the .content class was removed from the selector, the rule no longer targets only h1 headings in the <article class="content"> element; it's now styling all h1 elements on the page.

15 Choose Edit > Undo to restore the .content class to the h1 selector. Refresh the Live view display.

All the headings return to their previous styling.

16 Insert the pointer in the heading "Creating CSS Menus" and activate Code Navigator.

The heading is no longer styled by the properties in the .content h1 rule.

Is it starting to make more sense? Don't worry, it will—over time. Until that time, just remember that the rule appearing last in Code Navigator has the most influence on any particular element.

## CSS Designer

Code Navigator was introduced a while ago and has been an invaluable aid for troubleshooting CSS formatting. Yet a newer tool in Dreamweaver's CSS arsenal is much more than a good troubleshooting tool. CSS Designer not only displays all the rules that pertain to any selected element but also allows you to create and edit CSS rules at the same time.

When you use Code Navigator, it shows you the relative importance of each rule, but you still have to access and assess the effect of all the rules to determine the final effect. Since some elements can be affected by a dozen or more rules, this can be a daunting task for even a veteran web coder. CSS Designer eliminates this pressure altogether by computing the final CSS display for you. And best of all, unlike Code Navigator, CSS Designer can even compute the effects of inline styles too.

1  If necessary, open **css-basics-finished.html** in Split view.

2  If you do not see the panel, choose Window > CSS Designer to display the panel.

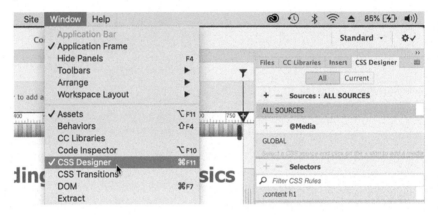

The CSS Designer panel features four panes: Sources, @Media, Selectors, and Properties. Feel free to adjust the heights and widths of the panes as needed. The panel is also responsive—it will take advantage of any extra screen space by splitting into two columns if you increase the panel's width.

3  If you do not see two columns in the CSS Designer, drag the left edge of the panel to the left to increase its width.

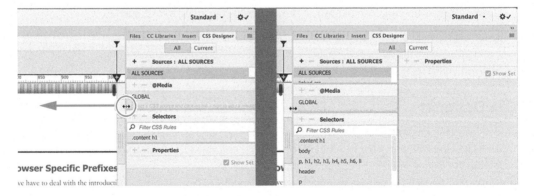

The CSS Designer will split into two columns, displaying the Sources, @Media, and Selectors panes on the left and the Properties pane on the right. Each of the panels specializes in one aspect of the styling applied to the page: style sheets, media queries, rules, or properties.

By selecting the items listed in each panel, CSS Designer enables you to inspect and even edit the existing styling. This functionality is helpful when trying to identify a pertinent rule or troubleshoot a styling issue, but some pages may have hundreds or thousands of rules styling them.

Trying to pinpoint one rule or property on such a page could be a daunting task. Fortunately, CSS Designer provides features that are designed just for this situation.

4   Select the heading "A CSS Primer" in Live view.

The Element Display now appears around the heading in the Live view window. The simple action of selecting tells Dreamweaver you want to work with this specific element.

▶ **Tip:** Sometimes when you first try to select an element in a document, Dreamweaver may highlight the wrong element first. If so, click an element in a different part of the page and then try again.

5   If necessary, deselect the Show Set checkbox in the CSS Designer.

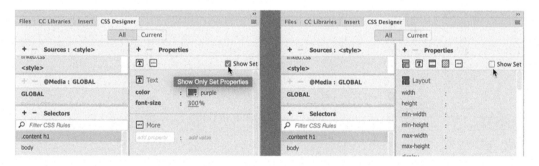

Show Set is disabled by default when Dreamweaver is installed, and if you are a beginner with CSS you may want leave it disabled until you become more comfortable with the language. When it's deselected, the CSS Designer displays a list of the major properties available in CSS, such as width, height, margins, padding, borders, background, and so on. It is not all the possible options, but certainly the most common. If a property you want is not visible in the pane, you can enter it manually.

Dreamweaver integrates the entire interface into the job of creating and styling your webpage. It's important to understand how this works. It starts by selecting the element you want to inspect or format.

You could try to find the rules formatting the heading by going through the list of rules in the Selectors pane, but that could take hours. There's a better way.

CSS Designer has two basic modes: *All* and *Current.* When All mode is engaged, the panel allows you to review and edit all existing CSS rules as well as create new rules. In Current mode, the panel allows you to identify and edit the rules and styling already applied to a selected element.

6  If necessary, click the Current button in the CSS Designer panel.

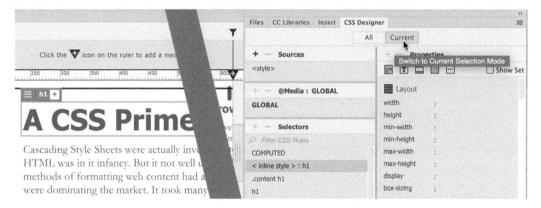

When Current mode is active, the panel displays only the CSS rules that are affecting the selected heading. In CSS Designer, the most powerful rules appear at the top of the Selectors window, the opposite of Code Navigator.

7  Click the rule `.content h1` in the Selectors panel.

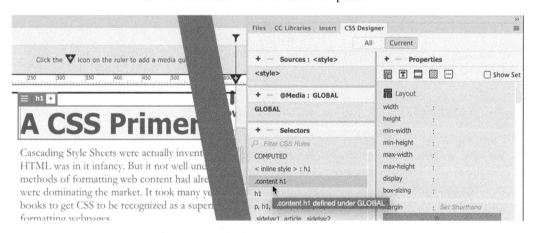

When Show Set is deselected, the Properties pane shows a seemingly endless list of properties. This is helpful when you are first styling the element, but it can be confusing as well as inefficient when inspecting or troubleshooting existing styles. For one thing, it makes it difficult to differentiate the properties that are assigned from those that aren't. Luckily, CSS Designer allows you to limit the display to only the properties currently applied to the selected element.

8  Click the Show Set option in the CSS Designer panel menu to enable it.

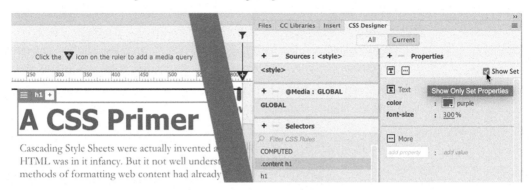

When Show Set is enabled, the Properties panel shows only the properties that have been set in that rule. In this instance, only the color and font size are actually styled by the rule.

9  Select each rule that appears in the Selectors window, and observe the properties of each.

Some rules may set the same properties, whereas others will set different properties. To weed out the conflicts and see the expected result of all the rules combined, Dreamweaver provides a COMPUTED option.

The COMPUTED option analyzes all the CSS rules affecting the element and generates a list of properties that should be displayed by browsers or HTML readers. By displaying a list of pertinent CSS rules and then computing how the CSS should render, CSS Designer does Code Navigator one step better. But it doesn't even stop there.

Although Code Navigator allows you to select a rule and then edit it in Code view, CSS Designer lets you edit the CSS properties right inside the panel itself. Best of all, CSS Designer can even compute *and* edit inline styles.

10  Select COMPUTED in the Selectors window.

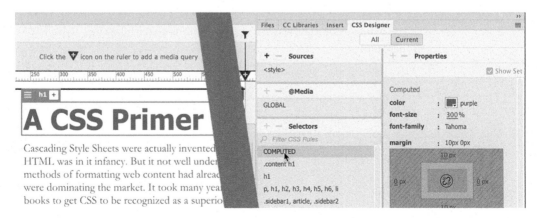

The Properties pane displays only the styles actually formatting the selected element. By using these features, you have eliminated hours of manual effort inspecting and comparing rules and properties.

But the functionality still doesn't end there. CSS Designer also allows you to edit the properties.

11 In the Properties window, select the color property purple. Enter red in the field, and press Enter/Return to complete the change.

You should now see the heading displayed in red in the layout. What you may not have noticed is that the change you made was actually entered directly in the CSS rule itself.

12 In the Code view window, scroll to the embedded style sheet, and examine the .content h1 rule.

As you can see, the color was changed within the code and added to the proper rule.

13 Close all files and do not save any changes.

▶ **Tip:** Click to edit the text-based color name. You can also select colors by using the color picker.

In upcoming exercises, you'll get the chance to experience all aspects of CSS Designer as you learn more about cascading style sheets.

# Multiples, classes, and ids, oh my!

By taking advantage of the cascade, inheritance, descendant, and specificity theories, you can target formatting to almost any element anywhere on a webpage. But CSS offers a few more ways to optimize and customize the formatting and increase your productivity even further.

## Applying formatting to multiple elements

To speed things up, CSS allows you to apply formatting to multiple elements at once by listing each in the selector, separated by commas. For example, the formatting in these rules:

```
h1 { font-family:Verdana; color:gray; }
h2 { font-family:Verdana; color:gray; }
h3 { font-family:Verdana; color:gray; }
```

can also be expressed like this:

```
h1, h2, h3 { font-family:Verdana; color:gray; }
```

## Using CSS shorthand

Although Dreamweaver will write most of the CSS rules and properties for you, at times you will want, or need, to write your own. All properties can be written out fully, but many can also be written using a shorthand method. Shorthand does more than make the job of the web designer easier; it reduces the total amount of code that has to be downloaded and processed. For example, when all properties of margins or padding are identical, such as:

```
margin-top:10px;
margin-right:10px;
margin-bottom:10px;
margin-left:10px;
```

the rule can be shortened to `margin:10px;`

When the top and bottom and left and right margins or padding are identical, like this:

```
margin-top:0px;
margin-right:10px;
margin-bottom:0px;
margin-left:10px;
```

it can be shortened to `margin:0px 10px;`

But even when all four properties are different, like this:

```
margin-top:20px;
margin-right:15px;
margin-bottom:10px;
margin-left:5px;
```

● **Note:** Margin and padding are specified clockwise starting at the top of the box model.

they can still be shortened to `margin:20px 15px 10px 5px;`

In these three examples, you can see clearly how much code can be saved using shorthand. There are far too many references and shorthand techniques to cover here. Check out **tinyurl.com/shorten-CSS** to get a full description.

Throughout the book I'll use common shorthand expressions wherever possible; see if you can identify them as we go.

## Creating class attributes

So far, you've learned that you can create CSS rules that format specific HTML elements and ones that can target specific HTML element structures or relationships. In some instances, you may want to apply unique formatting to an element that is already formatted by one or more existing rules. To accomplish this, CSS allows you to make your own custom attributes named *class* and *id*.

Class attributes may be applied to any number of elements on a page, whereas individual id attributes can appear only once per page. If you are a print designer, think of classes as being similar to a combination of Adobe InDesign's paragraph, character, table, and object styles all rolled into one.

Class and id names can be a single word, an abbreviation, any combination of letters and numbers, or almost anything, but they may not contain spaces. In HTML 4, ids could not start with a number. There don't seem to be any similar restrictions in HTML5. For backward compatibility, you should probably avoid starting class and id names with numbers.

Although there's no strict rule or guideline on how to create them, classes should be more general in nature, and ids should be more specific. Everyone seems to have an opinion, but at the moment there is no absolutely right or wrong answer. However, most agree that they should be descriptive, such as `"co-address"` or `"author-bio"` as opposed to `"left-column"` or `"big-text"`. This will especially help improve your site analytics. The more sense Google and other search engines can make of your site's structure and organization, the higher your site will rank in the search results.

To declare a CSS class selector, insert a period before the name within the style sheet, like this:

```
.content
.sidebar1
```

Then, apply the CSS class to an entire HTML element as an attribute, like this:

```
<p class="intro">Type intro text here.</p>
```

Or to individual characters or words using the `<span>` tag, like this:

```
<p>Here is <span class="copyright">some text formatted
differently</span>.</p>
```

## Creating id attributes

HTML designates `id` as a unique attribute. Therefore, any id should be assigned to no more than one element per page. In the past, many web designers used id attributes to style or identify specific components within the page, such as the header, the footer, or specific articles. With the advent of new HTML5 elements—`header`, `footer`, `aside`, `article`, and so on—the use of `id` and `class` attributes for this purpose has become less necessary. But ids can still be used to identify specific text elements, images, and tables to assist you in building powerful hypertext navigation within your page and site. You will learn more about using ids this way in Lesson 10, "Working with Navigation."

To declare an id attribute in a CSS style sheet, insert a number sign, or hash mark, before the name, like this:

```
#cascade
#box_model
```

Here's how you apply the CSS `id` to an entire HTML element as an attribute:

```
<div id="cascade">Content goes here.</div>
<section id="box_model">Content goes here.</section>
```

Or to a portion of an element:

```
<p>Here is <span id="copyright">some text</span> formatted
differently.</p>
```

## CSS3 features and effects

CSS3 has more than two dozen new features. Many have been implemented in all modern browsers and can be used today; others are still experimental and are supported less fully. Among the new features, you will find

- Rounded corners and border effects
- Box and text shadows
- Transparency and translucency
- Gradient fills
- Multicolumn text elements

You can implement all these features and more via Dreamweaver today. The program will even assist you in building vendor-specific markup when necessary. To give you a quick tour of some of the coolest features and effects brewing, I've provided a sample of CSS3 styling in a separate file.

1   Open **css3-demo.html** from the lesson03 folder.

Display the file in Split view and observe the CSS and HTML code.

Some of the new effects can't be previewed directly in Design view. You'll need to use Live view or an actual browser to get the full effect.

2   If necessary, activate Live view to preview all the CSS3 effects in the Live view window.

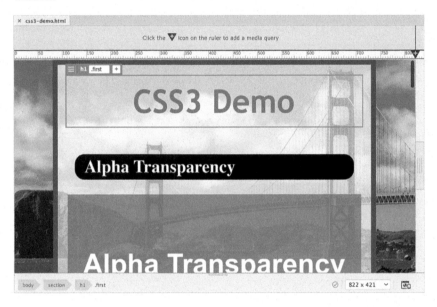

● **Note:** When writing new CSS3 properties that still require vendor prefixes today, place standard properties last. That way, when the subject browser finally supports the standard specifications, their cascade position will allow them to supersede the other settings.

The file contains a hodgepodge of features and effects that may surprise and even delight you—but don't get too excited. Although many of these features are already supported in Dreamweaver and will work fine in modern browsers, a lot of older hardware and software out there can turn your dream site into a nightmare. And there's at least one additional twist.

Even now, some of the new CSS3 features have not been fully standardized and certain browsers may not recognize the default markup generated by Dreamweaver. In these instances, you may have to include specific vendor commands to make them work properly, such as moz, ms, and webkit.

As you examine the new features demonstrated in the code of the demo file, can you think of ways of using some of them in your own pages?

# CSS3 overview and support

The internet doesn't stand still for long. Technologies and standards are evolving and changing constantly. The members of the W3C have been working diligently to adapt the web to the latest realities, such as powerful mobile devices, large flat-panel displays, and HD images and video—all of which seem to get better and cheaper every day. This is the urgency that currently drives the development of HTML5 and CSS3.

Many of these new standards have not been officially defined yet, and browser vendors are implementing them in varying ways. But don't worry. This version of Dreamweaver, as always, has been updated to take advantage of the latest changes. This includes ample support for the current mix of HTML5 elements and CSS3 properties. As new features and capabilities are developed, you can count on Adobe to add them to the program as quickly as possible using Creative Cloud.

As you work through the lessons that follow, you will be introduced to and actually implement many of these new and exciting techniques in your own sample pages.

## Additional CSS support

CSS formatting and application is so complex and powerful that this short lesson can't cover all aspects of the subject. For a full examination of CSS, check out the following books:

- *CSS3: The Missing Manual (4th Edition)*, David Sawyer McFarland (O'Reilly Media, 2015) ISBN: 978-1-491-91801-2

- *CSS Secrets: Better Solutions to Everyday Web Design Problems*, Lea Verou (O'Reilly Media, 2015) ISBN: 978-1-449-37263-7

- *HTML5 & CSS3 for the Real World (2nd Edition)*, Alexis Goldstein, Louis Lazaris, and Estelle Weyl (SitePoint Pty. Ltd., 2015) ISBN: 978-0-987-46748-5

- *Stylin' with CSS: A Designer's Guide (3rd Edition)*, Charles Wyke-Smith (New Riders Press, 2012) ISBN: 978-0-321-85847-4

# Review questions

1 Should you use HTML-based formatting?

2 What does CSS impose on each HTML element?

3 True or false? If you do nothing, HTML elements will feature no formatting or structure.

4 What four "theories" affect the application of CSS formatting?

5 True or false? All CSS3 features are experimental, and you shouldn't use them at all.

# Review answers

1 No. HTML-based formatting was deprecated in 1997, when HTML 4 was adopted. Industry best practices recommend using CSS-based formatting instead.

2 CSS imposes an imaginary box on each element. This box, and its content, can then be styled with borders, background colors and images, margins, padding, and other types of formatting.

3 False. Even if you do nothing, many HTML elements feature default formatting.

4 The four theories that affect CSS formatting are cascade, inheritance, descendant, and specificity.

5 False. Most CSS3 features are already supported by modern browsers and can be used right now.

# 4 WORKING WITH CODE

## Lesson overview

In this lesson, you'll learn how to work with code and do the following:

- Write code using code hinting and Emmet shorthand.
- Set up a CSS preprocessor and create SCSS styling.
- Use multiple cursors to select and edit code.
- Collapse and expand code entries.
- Use Live Code view to test and troubleshoot dynamic code.
- Use Inspect mode to identify HTML elements and associated styling.
- Access and edit attached files using the Related Files interface.

 This lesson will take about 90 minutes to complete. To get the lesson files used in this lesson, download them from the webpage for this book at www.adobepress.com/DreamweaverCIB2021. For more information, see "Accessing the lesson files and Web Edition" in the "Getting Started" section at the beginning of this book.

Dreamweaver's claim to fame is as a visually based HTML editor, but its code-editing features don't take a back seat to its graphical interface, and they offer few compromises to professional coders and developers.

# Creating HTML code

● **Note:** If you have not already down-loaded the project files for this lesson to your computer from your Account page, make sure to do so now. See "Getting Started" at the beginning of the book.

As one of the leading WYSIWYG HTML editors, Dreamweaver allows users to create elaborate webpages and applications without touching or even seeing the code that does all the work behind the scenes. But for many designers, working with the code is not only a desire but a necessity.

Although Dreamweaver has always made it as easy to work with a page in Code view as it is in Design view or Live view, some developers believe that the code-editing tools took a back seat to the visual design interface. Although in the past this was partially true, Dreamweaver CC (2021 release) is fully invested in the vastly improved tools and workflows for coders and developers that were brought to the program in the previous version. In fact, Dreamweaver can now unify your entire web development team as never before by providing a single platform that can handle almost any task.

● **Note:** Some tools and options are available only when Code view is active.

You'll often find that a specific task is actually easier to accomplish in Code view than in Live view or Design view alone. In the following exercises, you'll learn more about how Dreamweaver makes working with the code an effortless and surprisingly enjoyable task.

## Writing code manually

As you complete this and the next eight lessons, you will have numerous opportunities to view and edit code by hand. But for anyone jumping directly to this lesson, this exercise will provide a quick overview of the topic. One way to experience Dreamweaver's code-writing and editing tools is to create a new file.

1  Define a site based on the lesson04 folder downloaded from your account page, as described in the "Getting Started" section at the beginning of the book.

2  Select Developer from the Workspace menu.

All the code-editing tools work identically in either workspace, but the Developer workspace focuses on the Code view window and provides a better experience for the following exercises.

**3**  Choose File > New.

The New Document dialog appears.

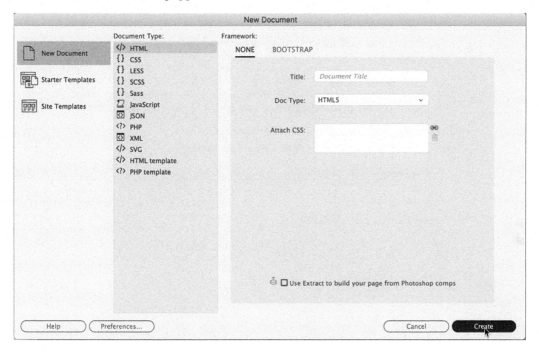

**4**  Choose New Document > HTML > None.
Click Create.

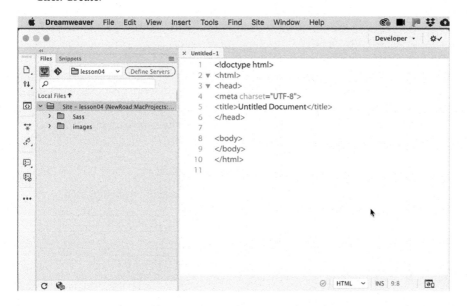

● **Note:** In all screen shots, we use the Classic color theme, which can be selected in Preferences. See the "Getting Started" section at the beginning of the book for more details.

Dreamweaver creates the basic structure of a webpage automatically. The cursor will probably appear at the beginning of the code.

As you can see, Dreamweaver provides color-coded tags and markup to make it easier to read, but that's not all. It also offers code hinting for ten different web development languages, including but not limited to HTML, CSS, JavaScript, and PHP.

5  Choose File > Save.

6  Name the file **myfirstpage.html** and save it in the lesson04 folder.

7  Insert the cursor after the <body> tag.
   Press Enter/Return to create a new line. Type <

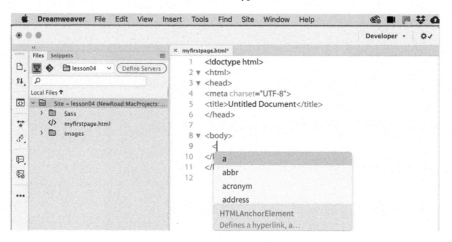

● **Note:** Line breaks, indenting, and other whitespace is not required in HTML and is used only to make the code easier to read and edit.

A code-hinting window appears, showing you a list of HTML-compatible codes you can select from.

8  Type **d**

The code-hinting window filters to code elements that start with the letter *d*. You can continue to type the tag name directly or use this list to select the desired element. By using the list, you can eliminate simple typing errors.

9  Press the Down Arrow key.

The dd tag in the code-hinting window is highlighted.

10 Continue pressing the Down Arrow key until the tag div is highlighted.
   Press Enter/Return.

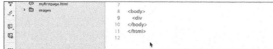

The tag name `div` is inserted in the code. The cursor remains at the end of the tag name, waiting for your next input. For example, you could complete the tag name or enter various HTML attributes. Let's add an `id` attribute to the `div` element.

**Note:** Depending on the settings in your program, tags may close automatically and you may have to move the cursor to complete the next step. This behavior can be turned off or adjusted in the Code Hints section of Preferences.

11 Press the spacebar to insert a space.

The hinting menu opens again, displaying a different list; this time the list contains various appropriate HTML attributes.

12 Type `id` and press Enter/Return.

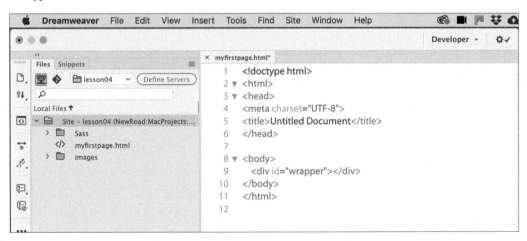

Dreamweaver creates the `id` attribute, complete with equals sign and quotation marks. Note that the cursor appears within the quotation marks, ready for your entry.

**Note:** In HTML5, quotation marks are no longer required for tag attributes. However, older browsers and applications may not display the code properly without them. It does no harm to use them, so continue to add them to your code.

13 Type `wrapper` and press the Right Arrow key once.

The cursor moves outside the closing quotation mark.

**Note:** If your tag closed automatically, you can skip step 14.

14 Type `></`

When you type the backslash (`/`), Dreamweaver closes the `div` element automatically. As you see, the program can provide a lot of help as you write code manually. But it can help you write code automatically too.

15 Choose File > Save.

## Writing code automatically

*Emmet* is a web-developer toolkit that was added to a previous version of Dreamweaver and enables you to supercharge your code-writing tasks. When you enter shorthand characters and operators, Emmet enables you to create whole blocks of code with just a few keystrokes. To experience the power of Emmet, try this exercise.

1 If necessary, open **myfirstpage.html**.

2 In Code view, insert the cursor within the `div` element and press Enter/Return to create a new line.

Emmet is enabled by default and works whenever you are typing in Code view. In the original site mockup, the navigation menu appears at the top of the page. HTML5 uses the `<nav>` element as the foundation of site navigation.

3 Type **nav** and press Tab.

```
 8 ▼ <body>
 9       <div id="wrapper">
10          nav</div>
11     </body>
12   </html>
13
```

```
 8 ▼ <body>
 9       <div id="wrapper">
10          <nav></nav></div>
11     </body>
12   </html>
13
```

Dreamweaver creates the opening and closing tags all at once. The cursor appears inside the `nav` element, ready for you to add another element, some content, or both.

HTML navigation menus are usually based on an unordered list, which consists of a `<ul>` element with one or more child `<li>` elements. Emmet allows you to create multiple elements at the same time, and by using one or more operators, you can specify whether the subsequent elements follow the first (+) or are nested one within the other (>).

4 Type **ul>li** and press Tab.

```
 8 ▼ <body>
 9       <div id="wrapper">
10          <nav>ul>li</nav></div>
11     </body>
12   </html>
13
```

```
 8 ▼ <body>
 9 ▼     <div id="wrapper">
10 ▼        <nav><ul>
11             <li></li>
12          </ul></nav></div>
13     </body>
14   </html>
```

A `<ul>` element containing one list item appears. The greater-than symbol (>) is used to create the parent–child structure you see here. By adding another operator, you can create several list items.

5 Choose Edit > Undo.

The code reverts to the `ul>li` shorthand. It's easy to adapt this shorthand markup to create a menu with five items.

**6** Edit the existing shorthand phrase as highlighted—ul>li**5**—and press Tab.

```
 8 ▼ <body>                                    8 ▼ <body>
 9     <div id="wrapper">                       9 ▼   <div id="wrapper">
10       <nav>ul>li*5</nav></div>             10 ▼     <nav><ul>
11     </body>                                11           <li></li>
12   </html>                                  12           <li></li>
13                                            13           <li></li>
                                              14           <li></li>
                                              15           <li></li>
                                              16         </ul></nav></div>
                                              17     </body>
                                              18   </html>
                                              19
```

A new unordered list appears, this time with five <li> elements. The asterisk (*) is the mathematical symbol for multiplication, so this latest change says "<li> times 5."

To create a proper menu, you also need to add a hyperlink to each menu item.

**7** Press Ctrl+Z/Cmd+Z or choose Edit > Undo.

The code reverts to the ul>li*5 shorthand.

**8** Edit the existing shorthand phrase as highlighted:

ul>li*5>a

If you guessed that adding the markup >a would create a hyperlink child element for each link item, you are correct. Emmet can also create placeholder content. Let's use it to insert some text in each link item.

**9** Edit the shorthand phrase as highlighted:

ul>li*5>a{Link}

Adding text within braces passes it to the final structure of the hyperlink, but we're not done yet. You can also increment the items, such as Link 1, Link 2, Link 3, and so on, by adding a variable character ($).

**10** Edit the shorthand phrase as highlighted—ul>li*5>a{Link $}—and press Tab.

● **Note:** The cursor must be outside the brace before you press Tab.

```
 8 ▼ <body>                                    8 ▼ <body>
 9     <div id="wrapper">                       9 ▼   <div id="wrapper">
10       <nav>ul>li*5>a{Link $}</nav></div>   10 ▼     <nav><ul>
11     </body>                                11           <li><a href="">Link 1</a></li>
12   </html>                                  12           <li><a href="">Link 2</a></li>
13                                            13           <li><a href="">Link 3</a></li>
                                              14           <li><a href="">Link 4</a></li>
                                              15           <li><a href="">Link 5</a></li>
                                              16         </ul></nav></div>
                                              17     </body>
                                              18   </html>
                                              19
```

**Note:** Adding the new line makes the code easier to read and edit, but it has no effect on how it operates.

The new menu appears fully structured, with five link items and hyperlink placeholders incremented 1 through 5. The menu is nearly complete. The only thing missing are targets for the href attributes. You could add them now using another Emmet phrase, but let's save that change for the next exercise.

11 Insert the cursor after the closing </nav> tag.

Press Enter/Return to create a new line.

Let's see how easy it is to use Emmet to add a header element to your new page.

12 Type **header** and press Tab.

As with the <nav> element you created earlier, the opening and closing header tags appear, with the cursor positioned to insert the content. We will model the header after one you will use in Lesson 6, "Creating a Page Layout." You need to add two text components: an <h2> for the company name and a <p> element for the motto. Emmet provides a method for adding not only the tags but also the content.

13 Type **h2{Favorite City Tour}+p{Travel with a purpose}** and press Tab.

```
 8 ▼ <body>
 9 ▼    <div id="wrapper">
10 ▼        <nav><ul>
11              <li><a href="">Link 1</a></li>
12              <li><a href="">Link 2</a></li>
13              <li><a href="">Link 3</a></li>
14              <li><a href="">Link 4</a></li>
15              <li><a href="">Link 5</a></li>
16          </ul></nav>
17          <header>h2{Favorite City Tour}+p{Travel with a
                purpose} </header></div>
18      </body>
19  </html>
```

```
 8 ▼ <body>
 9 ▼    <div id="wrapper">
10 ▼        <nav><ul>
11              <li><a href="">Link 1</a></li>
12              <li><a href="">Link 2</a></li>
13              <li><a href="">Link 3</a></li>
14              <li><a href="">Link 4</a></li>
15              <li><a href="">Link 5</a></li>
16          </ul></nav>
17          <header><h2>Favorite City Tour</h2>
18              <p>Travel with a purpose</p></header></div>
19      </body>
20  </html>
```

The two elements appear complete and contain the company name and motto. Note how you added the text to each item using braces. The plus (+) sign designates that the <p> element should be added as a peer to the heading.

14 Insert the cursor after the closing </header> tag.

**Note:** The entire phrase may wrap to more than one line in Code view, but make sure there are no spaces or line breaks within the markup.

15 Press Enter/Return to insert a new line.

As you can see, Emmet enables you to quickly build complex multifaceted parent–child structures like the navigation menu and the header, but it doesn't stop there. As you string together several elements with placeholder text, you can even add id and class attributes. To insert an id, start the name with the hash symbol (#); to add a class, start the name with a dot (.). It's time to push your skills to the next level.

**16** Type `main#content>aside.sidebar1>p(lorem)^article>` `p(lorem100)^aside.sidebar2>p(lorem)` and press Tab.

```
 8 ▼  <body>                              18      <p>Travel with a purpose</p></header>
 9 ▼    <div id="wrapper">                19 ▼  <main id="content">
10 ▼      <nav><ul>                       20 ▼    <aside class="sidebar1">
11           <li><a href="">Link 1</a></li>   21      <p>Lorem ipsum dolor sit amet, consectetur
12           <li><a href="">Link 2</a></li>            adipisicing elit. Similique dignissimos
13           <li><a href="">Link 3</a></li>            nostrum voluptates assumenda? Dolor
14           <li><a href="">Link 4</a></li>            enim ex ipsum dignissimos! Asperiores
15           <li><a href="">Link 5</a></li>            dolor minus ab placeat fuga neque vero
16         </ul></nav>                               suscipit aspernatur nihil doloribus!</p>
17         <header><h2>Favorite City Tour</h2>  22      </aside>
18         <p>Travel with a purpose</p></header>  23 ▼    <article>
19         main#content>aside.sidebar1>p(lorem)^article>p(lo   24      <p>Lorem ipsum dolor sit amet, consectetur
           rem100)^aside.sidebar2>p(lorem)</div>            adipisicing elit. In repudiandae iusto nisi
20      </body>                                          quasi, soluta architecto. Ea, quaerat
21    </html>                                            voluptatum. Unde omnis incidunt
22                                                       architecto sunt, pariatur possimus? Ipsam
                                                         nostrum, assumenda recusandae quia
```

A `<main>` element is created with three child elements (`aside`, `article`, `aside`), along with `id` and `class` attributes. The caret (`^`) symbol in the shorthand is used to ensure that the `article` and `aside.sidebar2` elements are created as siblings of `aside.sidebar1`. Within each child element, you should see a paragraph of placeholder text.

Emmet includes a *Lorem* generator to create blocks of placeholder text automatically. When you add `lorem` in parentheses after an element name, such as `p(lorem)`, Emmet will generate 30 words of placeholder content. To specify a larger or smaller amount of text, just add a number at the end, such as `p(lorem100)` for 100 words.

Let's finish up the page with a `footer` element containing a copyright statement.

**17** Insert the cursor after the closing `</main>` tag.
Create a new line.
Type `footer{Copyright 2021 Favorite City Tour.` `All rights reserved.}` and press Tab.

```
         explicabo sit quia rerum optio cum magni           explicabo sit quia rerum optio cum magni
         nostrum fuga.</p>                                   nostrum fuga.</p>
28      </aside>                             28      </aside>
29    </main>footer{Copyright 2021 Favorite City Tour. All   29    </main><footer>Copyright 2021 Favorite City Tour.
      rights reserved.}  </div>                              All rights reserved.</footer>  </div>
30    </body>                               30    </body>
31    </html>                               31    </html>
```

**18** Save the file.

Using a few shorthand phrases, you have built a complete webpage structure and some placeholder content. You can see how Emmet can supercharge your code-writing tasks. Feel free to use this amazing toolkit at any time to add a single element or a complex, multifaceted component. It's there anytime you need it.

This exercise has barely scratched the surface of what Emmet can do. It is simply too powerful to fully describe in just a few pages. But you got a good peek at its capabilities.

Check out http://emmet.io to learn more about Emmet. Check out http://docs.emmet.io/cheat-sheet/ for a handy Emmet shorthand cheat sheet.

# Working with multicursor support

Have you ever wanted to edit more than one line of code at a time? Another code-editing feature in Dreamweaver CC (2021 release) is multicursor support. This feature allows you to select and edit multiple lines of code at once to speed up a variety of mundane tasks. Let's take a look at how it works.

1   If necessary, open **myfirstpage.html** as it appears at the end of the previous exercise.

The file contains a complete webpage with `header`, `nav`, `main`, and `footer` elements. The content features classes and several paragraphs of placeholder text. The `<nav>` element includes five placeholders for a navigation menu, but the `href` attributes are empty. For the menu and links to appear and behave properly, you need to add a filename, URL, or placeholder element to each link. The hash mark (#) is used as placeholder content until the final link destinations can be added.

## Customizing the Common toolbar

Some of the code-editing exercises in this lesson require tools that may not appear in the interface by default. The Common toolbar was previously called the Coding toolbar and appeared only in Code view. The new toolbar appears in all views, but some tools may be visible only when the cursor is inserted directly in the Code view window.

If the exercise calls for a tool that is not visible, even with the cursor in the proper position, you may need to customize the toolbar yourself. This can be done by first clicking the Customize Toolbar icon ••• and then enabling the tools within the Customize Toolbar dialog. At the same time, feel free to disable tools you don't use.

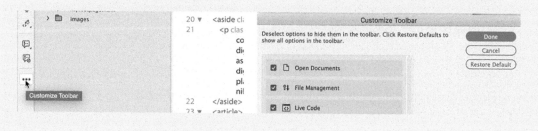

2  Insert the cursor between the quotation marks in the `href=""` attribute in Link 1.

Normally, you would have to add a hash mark (#) to each attribute individually. Multicursor support makes this task much easier, but don't be surprised if it takes you a little practice. Note that all the link attributes are aligned vertically on consecutive lines.

3  Hold the Alt key (Windows) or Option key (macOS) and drag the mouse down through all five links.

Using the Alt/Option key enables you to select code or insert cursors in consecutive lines. Be careful to drag down in a straight line. If you slip a little to the left or right, you may select some of the surrounding markup. If that happens, you can just start over. When you are finished, you should see a cursor flashing in the `href` attribute for each link.

4  Type #
The hash mark (#) appears in all five attributes at the same time.

```
 8 ▼ <body>                                     8 ▼ <body>
 9 ▼ <div id="wrapper">                         9 ▼ <div id="wrapper">
10 ▼     <nav><ul>                              10 ▼     <nav><ul>
11        <li><a href="">Link 1</a></li>        11        <li><a href="#">Link 1</a></li>
12        <li><a href="">Link 2</a></li>        12        <li><a href="#">Link 2</a></li>
13        <li><a href="">Link 3</a></li>        13        <li><a href="#">Link 3</a></li>
14        <li><a href="">Link 4</a></li>        14        <li><a href="#">Link 4</a></li>
15        <li><a href="">Link 5</a></li>        15        <li><a href="#">Link 5</a></li>
16     </ul></nav>                              16     </ul></nav>
```

The Ctrl/Cmd key enables you to select code or insert cursors in nonconsecutive lines of code.

5  Hold the Ctrl/Cmd key and click to insert the cursor between the p and the > bracket in each of the three opening `<p>` tags in the `<main>` element.

6  Press the spacebar to insert a space, and type `class="first"`

```
20 ▼     <aside class="sidebar1">               20 ▼     <aside class="sidebar1">
21        <p>Lorem ipsum dolor sit amet, consectetur   21        <p class="first">Lorem ipsum dolor sit amet,
          adipisicing elit. Similique dignissimos              consectetur adipisicing elit. Similique
          nostrum voluptates assumenda? Dolor                 dignissimos nostrum voluptates
          enim ex ipsum dignissimos! Asperiores               assumenda? Dolor enim ex ipsum
          dolor minus ab placeat fuga neque vero              dignissimos! Asperiores dolor minus ab
          suscipit aspernatur nihil doloribus!</p>            placeat fuga neque vero suscipit aspernatur
22     </aside>                                                nihil doloribus!</p>
23 ▼     <article>                              22     </aside>
24        <p>Lorem ipsum dolor sit amet, consectetur   23 ▼     <article>
          adipisicing elit. In repudiandae iusto nisi  24        <p class="first">Lorem ipsum dolor sit amet,
          quasi, soluta architecto. Ea, quaerat               consectetur adipisicing elit. In repudiandae
          voluptatum. Unde omnis incidunt                     iusto nisi quasi, soluta architecto. Ea,
```

The attribute appears simultaneously in all three `<p>` tags.

7  Save the file.

Multicursor support can save tons of time in repetitive code-editing tasks.

# Commenting your code

Comments allow you to leave notes within the code—invisible in the browser—to describe the purpose of certain markup or provide important information to other coders. Although you can add comments manually at any time, Dreamweaver has a built-in feature that can speed up the process.

1 Open **myfirstpage.html** and switch to Code view, if necessary.

2 Insert the cursor after the opening tag
`<aside class="sidebar1">`.

3 Click the Apply Comment icon 🗨.

A pop-up menu appears with several comment options. Dreamweaver supports comment markup for various web-compatible languages, including HTML, CSS, JavaScript, and PHP.

4 Choose Apply HTML Comment.

An HTML comment block appears, with the text cursor positioned in the center.

5 Type `Insert customer testimonials into Sidebar 1`

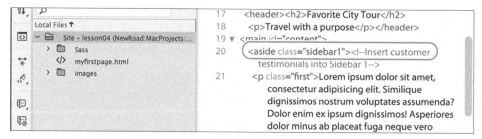

The comment appears in gray between the `<!--` and `-->` markup. The tool can also apply comment markup to existing text.

6 Insert the cursor after the opening tag
`<aside class="sidebar2">`.

7 Type `Sidebar 2 should be used for content related to the tour or product`

8 Select the text created in step 7.
Click the Apply Comment icon 🗨.

A pop-up menu opens.

**9** Select Apply HTML Comment.

Dreamweaver applies the `<!--` and `-->` markup to the selection. If you need to remove existing comment markup from a selection, click the Remove Comment icon 🔖 in the toolbar.

**10** Save all files.

You've created a basic webpage complete with placeholder text. The next step is to style the page. Dreamweaver CC (2021 release) supports CSS preprocessors for LESS, Sass, and SCSS. In the next exercise, you'll learn how to set up and create CSS styling using a preprocessor.

# Working with CSS preprocessors

One of the biggest additions to Dreamweaver was support for LESS, Sass, and SCSS. These industry-standard CSS preprocessors are scripting languages that enable you to extend the capabilities of cascading style sheets with a variety of productivity enhancements that can then be compiled in a standard CSS file. These languages provide a variety of benefits for designers and developers who prefer to write their code by hand, including speed, ease of use, reusable snippets, variables, logic, calculations, and much more. No other software is needed to work in these preprocessors, but Dreamweaver also supports other frameworks, such as Compass and Bourbon.

In this exercise, you'll get a taste of how easy it is use preprocessors with Dreamweaver as well as what advantages they offer compared to a regular CSS workflow.

## Enabling a preprocessor

Support for CSS preprocessors is site-specific and must be enabled for each site defined in Dreamweaver, as desired. To enable LESS, Sass, or SCSS, you first define a site and then enable the CSS Preprocessors option within the Site Definition dialog.

**1** Select Site > Manage Sites.
The Manage Sites dialog appears.

2   Select **lesson04** in the Manage Sites window.

Click the Edit icon ✐ at the bottom of the Manage Sites window.

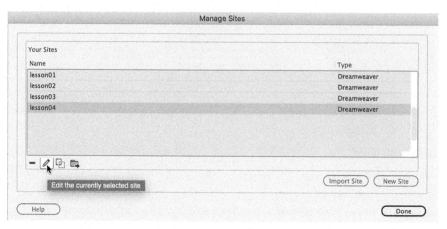

The Site Definition dialog for lesson04 appears.

3   Select the **CSS Preprocessors** option in the Site Definition dialog.

The CSS Preprocessors option contains six subcategories, including General, Source & Output, and options for various Compass and Bourbon frameworks. You can check out the Dreamweaver Help topics for more information on these frameworks. For this exercise, you need only the features that are built into the program itself.

4   Select the General category.

When selected, this category features the on/off switch for the LESS, Sass, or SCSS compiler, as well as various options for how the languages operate. For our purposes, the default settings will work fine.

5   Select the Enable Auto Compilation On File Save checkbox to enable the pre-processor compiler, if necessary.

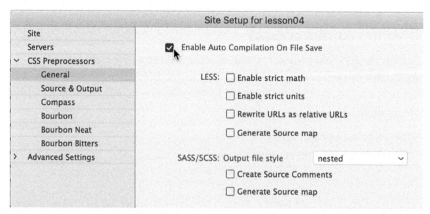

When this is enabled, Dreamweaver will automatically compile your CSS from your LESS, Sass, or SCSS source files whenever they are saved. Some designers and developers use the root folder of the site for compilation. In this case, we'll separate the source and output files in distinct folders.

## LESS or Sass—the choice is yours

LESS and Sass offer similar features and functions, so which one should you choose? That's hard to say. Some think that LESS is easier to learn but that Sass offers more powerful functionality. Both make the chore of writing CSS by hand faster and easier and, more importantly, provide significant advantages for maintaining and extending your CSS over time. There are lots of opinions on which preprocessor is better, but you'll find that it comes down to personal preference.

Before you decide, check out the following links to get some informed perspectives:

- blog.udemy.com/less-vs-sass/
- css-tricks.com/sass-vs-less/
- keycdn.com/blog/sass-vs-less

Dreamweaver provides two syntaxes for Sass. In this lesson, we use SCSS (Sassy CSS), which is a form of Sass that is written like and looks more like regular CSS.

6 Select the Source & Output category.

This category enables you to designate the source and output folders for your CSS preprocessor. The default option targets the folder where the source file is saved.

7 Select the Define Output Folder option.

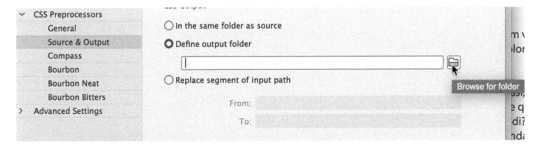

8 Click the Browse For Folder icon 📁.

A file browser dialog appears.

9 Navigate to the Site Root folder, if necessary.
Create a new folder.

**10** Name the new folder **css**.
Click Create.

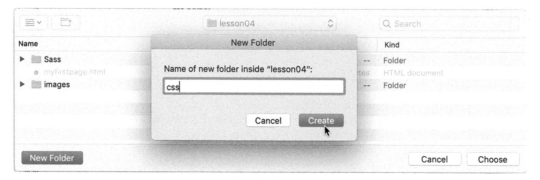

**11** Select the css folder and click Select Folder/Choose.

**12** Click the Browse For Folder icon ▣ beside the Source Folder field.

**13** Navigate to the Site Root folder.

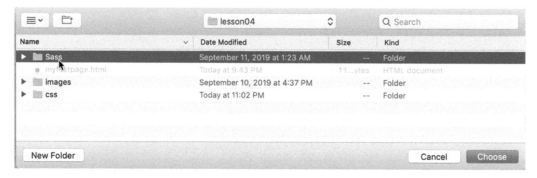

Select the existing Sass folder, and
click Select Folder/Choose.

**14** Save the changes and click Done to return to your site.

The CSS preprocessor is enabled, and the source and output folders are now designated. Next, you'll create the CSS source file.

## Creating the CSS source file

When using a preprocessor workflow, you do not write the CSS code directly. Instead, you write rules and other code in a source file that is then compiled to the output file. For the following exercise, you'll create a Sass source file and learn some of the functions of that language.

**1** Select Standard from the Workspace menu.

**2** Choose Window > Files to display the Files panel, if necessary.

Select lesson04 from the Site List dropdown menu, if necessary.

3  If necessary, open **myfirstpage.html** and switch to Split view.

The webpage is unstyled at the moment.

4  Choose File > New.

The New Document dialog appears. This dialog allows you to create all types of web-compatible documents. In the Document Type section of the dialog, you will see the LESS, Sass, and SCSS file types.

5  Choose New Document > SCSS.
Click the Create button.

A new blank SCSS document appears in the document window. SCSS is a flavor of Sass that uses a syntax similar to regular CSS that many users find easier to learn and work with.

6  Save the file as **favorite-styles.scss** in the Sass folder you targeted as the Source folder in the previous exercise.

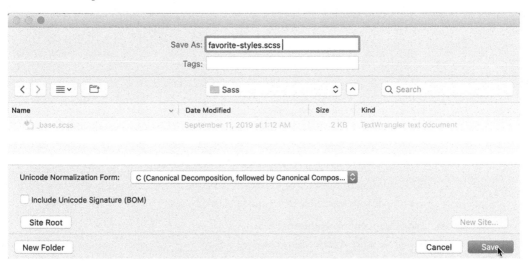

There's no need to create the CSS file; the compiler in Dreamweaver will do that for you. You're all set to start working with Sass. The first step is to define variables. Variables are programmatic constructs that enable you to store CSS specifications you want to use multiple times, such as colors in your site theme.

By using a variable, you have to define it only once. If you need to change it in the future, you can edit one entry in the style sheet and all the instances of the variable will update automatically.

7 Insert the cursor into line 2 of **favorite-styles.scss**.
Type `$logoyellow: #ED6;` and press Enter/Return.

You've created your first variable. This is the main green color of the site theme. Let's create the rest of the variables.

8 Type `$darkyellow: #ED0;`
`$lightyellow: #FF3;`
`$logoblue: #069;`
`$darkblue: #089;`
`$lightblue: #08A;`
`$font-stack: "Trebuchet MS", Verdana, Arial, Helvetica,`
`sans-serif;`
and press Enter/Return to create a new line.

Entering the variables on separate lines makes them easier to read and edit but does not affect how they perform. Just make sure you add a semicolon (`;`) at the end of each variable.

Let's start the style sheet with the base or default styling of the body element. SCSS markup in most cases looks just like regular CSS, except in this case you'll use one of your variables to set the font family.

9 Type `body` and press the spacebar.
Type `{` and press Enter/Return.

When you typed the opening brace (`{`), Dreamweaver created the closing brace automatically. When you created the new line, the cursor was indented by default, and pressing Enter/Return moved the closing brace to the following line. You can also use Emmet to enter the settings more quickly.

**10** Type `ff$font-stack` and press Tab.

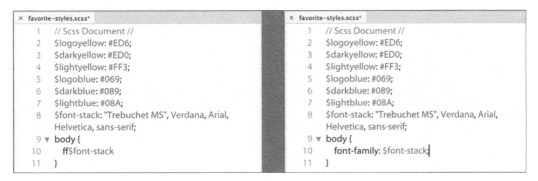

The shorthand expands to `font-family: $font-stack;`.

**11** Press Enter/Return to create a new line.

Type `c` and press Tab.

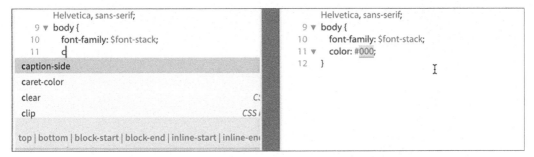

The shorthand expands to `color: #000;`. The default color is acceptable.

**12** Hold the Alt/Cmd key and press the Right Arrow key to move the cursor to the end of the current line of code.

**13** Press Enter/Return to create a new line.

Type `m0` and press Tab.

```
        Helvetica, sans-serif;                          Helvetica, sans-serif;
  9 ▼  body {                                      9 ▼  body {
 10        font-family: $font-stack;              10        font-family: $font-stack;
 11        color: #000;                           11        color: #000;
 12        m0|                                     12        margin: 0;
 13    }                                           13    }
```

The shorthand expands to `margin: 0;`, completing the basic styling for the body element. Before you save the file, this is a good time to see how preprocessors do their work.

## Compiling CSS code

You have completed the specifications for the body element. But you have not created the styling directly in a CSS file. Your entries were made entirely in the SCSS source file. In this exercise, you will see how the compiler that is built into Dreamweaver generates the CSS output.

1  Display the Files panel, if necessary, and expand the list of site files.

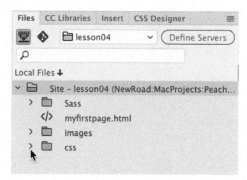

The site consists of one HTML file and three folders: Sass, images, and css.

● **Note:** The **favorite-styles.css** file should have been created automatically in the previous exercise when the SCSS file was saved. If you do not see the .css file, you may need to shut down and relaunch Dreamweaver.

2  Expand the view of the css and Sass folders.

The Sass folder contains **favorite-styles.scss** and **_base.scss**. The css folder contains **favorite-styles.css**. This file did not exist when you started the lesson. It was generated automatically when you created the SCSS file and saved it into the site folder defined as the Source folder. At the moment, the CSS file should contain no CSS rules or markup. It's also not referenced in the sample webpage.

3  Select the document tab for **myfirstpage.html**.

Select View > Split > Code-Live.

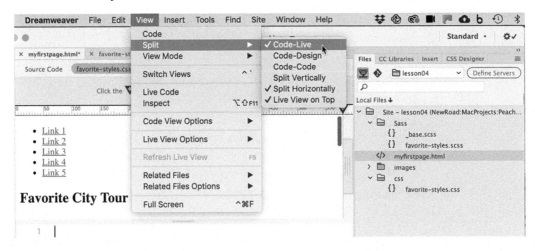

The page shows only default HTML styling.

4  In the Code view window, insert the cursor after the opening `<head>` tag and press Enter/Return to insert a new line.

5  Type `<link` and press the spacebar.

The hinting menu appears. You'll link the webpage to the generated CSS file.

6  Type `href` and press Enter/Return.

The complete `href=""` attribute appears, and the hinting menu changes to display the Browse command and a list of pathnames to folders available in the site.

7  Press the Down Arrow key to select the path `css/` and press Enter/Return.

The hinting menu now displays the path and filename to **favorite-styles.css**.

8  Press the Down Arrow key to select
css/favorite-styles.css and press Enter/Return.

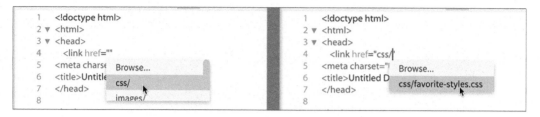

The URL to the CSS output file appears in the attribute. The cursor is moved outside the closing quotation mark and is ready for the next entry. For the style sheet reference to be valid, you need to create one more attribute.

9  Press the spacebar, type rel, and then press Enter/Return.

Select stylesheet from the hinting menu.

10  Move the cursor outside the closing quotation mark. Type > to close the link.

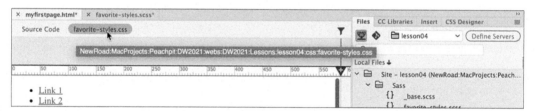

The CSS output file is now referenced by the webpage. In the Live view window, there should be no difference in the styling, but you should now see **favorite-styles.css** displayed in the Related Files interface.

● **Note:** If you accidentally saved the SCSS file before this step, you may see styling in the HTML file and another filename in the Related Files interface.

11  Select **favorite-styles.css** in the Related Files interface.

Code view displays the contents of **favorite-styles.css,** which is empty at the moment. An asterisk appears next to the filename in the document tab for **favorite-styles.scss**, indicating that the file has been changed but not saved.

**12** Choose Window > Arrange > Tile.

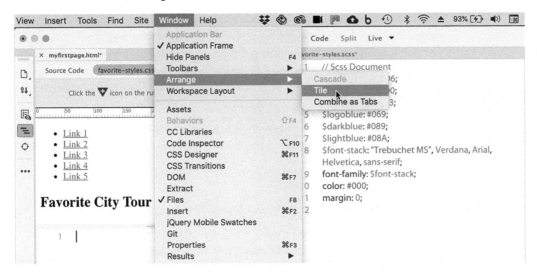

The webpage and the source file appear side by side in the program window.

**13** Insert the cursor anywhere in the **favorite-styles.scss** document window and choose File > Save All.

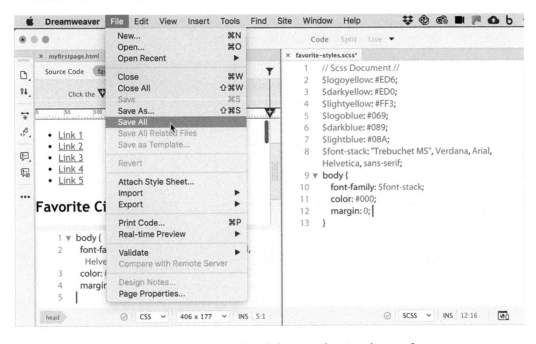

After a moment, the display of **myfirstpage.html** changes, showing the new font and margin settings. The Code view window also updates to display the new contents of **favoritestyles.css**. Each time you save the SCSS source file, Dreamweaver will update the output file.

## Nesting CSS selectors

Targeting CSS styling to one element without accidentally affecting another is a constant challenge for web designers everywhere. Descendant selectors are one method for ensuring that the styling is applied correctly. But creating and maintaining the correct descendant structure becomes more difficult as the site and style sheets grow in size. All preprocessor languages offer some form of nesting for selector names.

● **Note:** Make sure you are working in the SCSS file.

In this exercise, you will learn how to nest selectors while styling the navigation menu. First, you'll set the basic styling for the <nav> element itself.

1　In the **favoritestyles.scss** window, insert the cursor after the closing brace (}) on line 13 for the body rule.

2　Create a new line; type `nav {` and press Enter/Return.

The nav selector and declaration structure are created and ready for your entry. Emmet provides shorthand entries for all CSS properties.

3　Type `bg$logoyellow` and press Tab.
Press Enter/Return.

The shorthand expands to `background: $logoblue`, which is the first variable you created in the SCSS source file. This will apply the color #069 to the nav element.

4　Type `ta:c` and press Tab. Press Enter/Return.

The shorthand expands to `text-align: center`.

5　Type `ov:a` and press Tab. Press Enter/Return.

The shorthand expands to `overflow: auto`.

6　Save the source file.

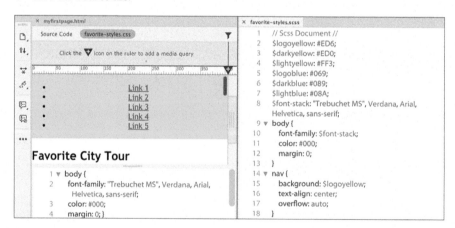

The <nav> element in **myfirstpage.html** displays the color #069. The menu doesn't look like much yet, but you've only just begun. Next, you'll format the

`<ul>` element. Note that the cursor is still within the declaration structure for the nav selector.

7　Type `ul {` and press Enter/Return.

The new selector and declaration are created within the nav rule.

8　Create the following properties:

`list-style: none; margin: 5px;`

These properties reset the default styling of the unordered list, removing the bullet and indent. Next, you'll override the styling of the list items.

9　Press Enter/Return and type `li {`
Press Enter/Return again.

As before, the new selector and declaration are fully within the ul rule.

10　Create the property `display: inline-block;` and press Enter/Return.

This property will display all the links in a single row, side by side. The last element to style is the `<a>` for the link itself.

11　Type `a {` and press Enter/Return.
Create the following properties:

```
margin: 0;
padding: 10px 15px;
color: $logoblue;
text-decoration: none;
background: $lightyellow;
```

The rule and declaration for a appear entirely within the li rule. Each of the rules styling the navigation menu has been nested one inside the other in a logical, intuitive manner and will result in an equally logical and intuitive CSS output.

12　Save the file.

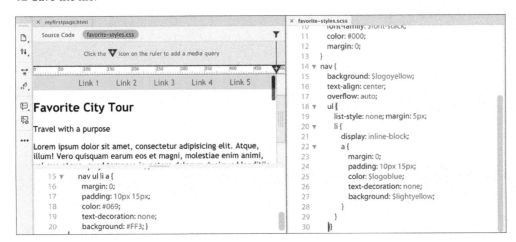

The navigation menu in **myfirstpage.html** is reformatted to display a single line of links, side by side. The CSS output file displays several new CSS rules. The new rules are not nested as in the source file. They are separate and distinct. And more surprisingly, the selectors have been rewritten to target the descendant structures of the menu, such as nav ul li a. As you can see, nesting rules in the SCSS source file eliminates the chore of writing complex selectors.

## Importing other style sheets

To make CSS styling more manageable, many designers split their style sheets into multiple separate files, such as one for navigation components, another for feature articles, and still another for dynamic elements. Large companies may create an overall corporate standard style sheet and then allow various departments or subsidiaries to write custom style sheets for their own products and purposes. Eventually, all these CSS files need to be brought together and called by the webpages on the site, but this can create a big problem.

Every resource linked to a page creates an HTTP request that can bog down the loading of your pages and assets. This is not a big deal for small sites or lightly traveled ones. But popular, heavily traveled sites with tons of HTTP requests can overload a web server and even cause pages to freeze in a visitor's browser. Too many experiences like this can cause visitors to flee.

Reducing or eliminating superfluous HTTP calls should be the goal of any designer or developer, but especially those working on large enterprise or highly popular sites. One important technique is to cut down on the number of individual style sheets called by each page. If a page needs to link to more than one CSS file, it's usually recommended that you designate one file as the main style sheet and then simply import the other files into it, creating one large universal style sheet.

In a normal CSS file, importing multiple style sheets would not produce any benefit, because the import command creates the same type of HTTP request that you're trying to avoid in the first place. But since you are using a CSS preprocessor, the import command happens *before* any HTTP request occurs. The various style sheets are imported and combined. Although this makes the resulting style sheet larger, this file is downloaded only once by the visitor's computer and then cached for their entire visit, speeding up the process overall.

Let's see how easy it is to combine multiple style sheets in one file.

1  Open **myfirstpage.html** and switch to Split view, if necessary.

   Open **favoritestyles.scss** and choose Window > Arrange > Tile.

   The two files are displayed side by side to make it easier to edit the CSS and see the changes as they occur.

2  In **myfirstpage.html,** click **favoritestyles.css** in the Related Files interface.

   Code view displays the content of **favoritestyles.css**. It contains the output of rules written in the SCSS source file.

**3** In **favoritestyles.scss**, insert the cursor before the body rule.

Type `@import "_base.scss";` and press Enter/Return to insert a new line.

This command imports the contents of the file `_base.scss` stored in the Sass folder. The file was created ahead of time to style other portions of your page. At the moment, nothing has changed, because **favorite-styles.scss** has not been saved yet.

**4** Save **favoritestyles.scss** and observe the changes in **myfirstpage.html**.

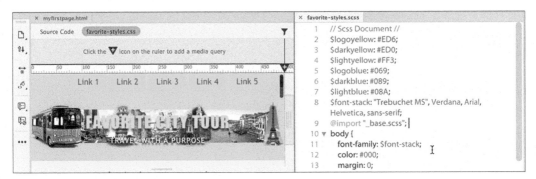

If you correctly followed the instructions on how to create the HTML structure earlier in this lesson, the page should be entirely formatted now. If you examine **favoritestyles.css**, you will see that several rules were inserted before the body rule. Imported content will be added starting at line 2, the position of the `@import` command. Once the content has been imported, normal CSS precedence and specificity take effect. Just make sure that all rules and file references appear after the variables; otherwise, the variables won't work.

**5** Save and close all files.

In this section, you created an SCSS file and learned how to work with a CSS preprocessor. You experienced various productivity enhancements and advanced functionality and have glimpsed just a bit of the breadth and scope of what is possible.

## Learning more about preprocessors

Check out the following books to learn more about CSS preprocessors and supercharging your CSS workflow:

*Beginning CSS Preprocessors: With SASS, Compass.js, and Less.js*, by Anirudh Prabhu, Apress (2015), ISBN: 978-1484213483

*Instant LESS CSS Preprocessor How-to*, by Alex Libby, Packt Publishing (2013), ISBN: 978-1782163763

*Jump Start Sass: Get Up to Speed with Sass in a Weekend*, by Hugo Giraudel and Miriam Suzanne, SitePoint (2016), ISBN: 978-0994182678

## Using linting support

Dreamweaver CC (2021 release) provides live code error checking. Linting support is enabled by default in Preferences, which means the program monitors your code writing and flags errors in real time.

1 Open **myfirstpage.html**, if necessary, and switch to Code view.
   If necessary, select Source Code in the Related Files interface.

2 Insert the cursor after the opening `<article>` tag and press Enter/Return to create a new line.

● **Note:** Dreamweaver may create the opening and closing tags at once. If so, delete the closing `</h1>` tag before proceeding to step 4.

3 Type `<h1>Insert headline here`

4 Save the file.

   You failed to close the `<h1>` element in step 3. When an error occurs, a red X will appear at the bottom of the document window whenever you save the page.

5 Click the X ⊗ icon.

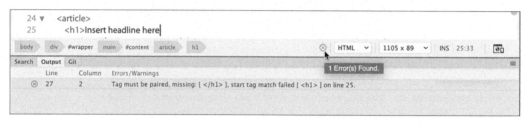

● **Note:** You may need to click the Refresh button to display the Linting report.

The Output panel opens automatically and displays the coding errors. In this case, the message says that the tag must be paired and identifies what line it thinks the error occurs on. The message erroneously targets line 27, but this can happen because of the nature of HTML tags and structures.

6 Double-click the error message.

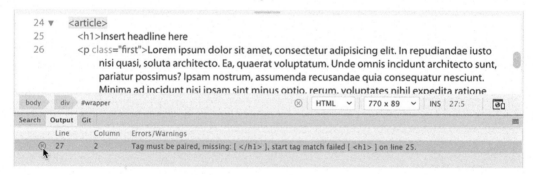

Dreamweaver focuses on the article in the Code view window that it identifies as containing the error. Since Dreamweaver is looking for the closing tag for the `<h1>` element, the first closing tag it encounters is `</article>` and flags it, which is incorrect. This behavior will get you close to the error, but often you will have to track down the actual issue yourself.

7　Insert the cursor at the end of the code
　　`<h1>Insert headline here.` Type `</`

> ● **Note:** If your heading closed automatically in step 3, typing `</` will probably not close the tag. Check your preference settings for code rewriting and adjust them as desired.

Dreamweaver should close the `<h1>` tag automatically. If not, go ahead and finish it properly.

8　Save the file.

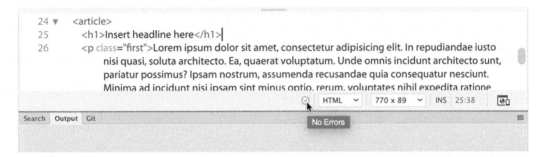

Once the error is corrected, the red X is replaced by a green checkmark ⊘.

9　Right-click the Output panel tab and select Close Tab Group from the context menu.

It's important to be alert for this icon as you save your work. No other error message will pop up indicating any problems, and you'll want to catch and correct any errors before uploading your pages to the web server.

# Selecting code

Dreamweaver provides several methods for interacting with and selecting code in Code view.

## Using line numbers

You can use your cursor to interact with the code in several ways.

1　Open **myfirstpage.html**, if necessary, and switch to Code view.

2　Scroll down and locate the `<nav>` element (around line 11).

3　Drag the cursor across the entire element, including the menu items.

Using the cursor in this way, you can select any portion of the code or its entirety. However, using the cursor in this way can be prone to error, causing you to miss vital portions of the code. At times, using line numbers to select whole lines of code is easier.

4   Click the line number beside the <nav> tag.

The entire line is selected within the window.

5   Drag down the line numbers to select the entire <nav> element.

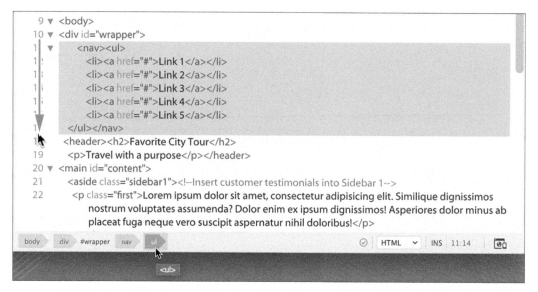

Dreamweaver completely highlights all seven lines. Using line numbers can save a lot of time and avoid errors during selection, but it doesn't take into account the actual structure of the code elements, which may begin and end in the middle of a line. Tag selectors provide a better way to select logical code structures.

## Using tag selectors

One of the easiest and most efficient ways to select code is to use the tag selectors, as you will frequently do in upcoming lessons.

1   Scroll down and locate the following code:
```
<a href="#">Link 1</a>
```

2   Insert the cursor anywhere in the text Link 1.
Examine the tag selectors at the bottom of the document window.

The tag selectors in Code view display the <a> tag and all its parent elements, the same way they do in Live or Design view.

3  Select the <a> tag selector.

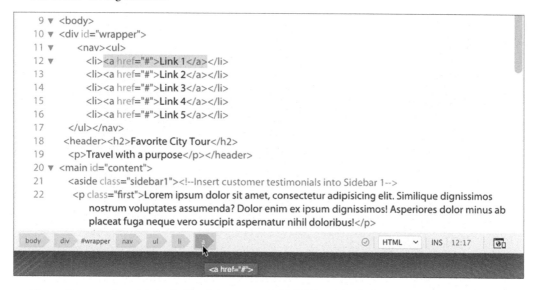

```
 9 ▼ <body>
10 ▼ <div id="wrapper">
11 ▼    <nav><ul>
12 ▼       <li><a href="#">Link 1</a></li>
13          <li><a href="#">Link 2</a></li>
14          <li><a href="#">Link 3</a></li>
15          <li><a href="#">Link 4</a></li>
16          <li><a href="#">Link 5</a></li>
17      </ul></nav>
18      <header><h2>Favorite City Tour</h2>
19      <p>Travel with a purpose</p></header>
20 ▼ <main id="content">
21      <aside class="sidebar1"><!--Insert customer testimonials into Sidebar 1-->
22      <p class="first">Lorem ipsum dolor sit amet, consectetur adipisicing elit. Similique dignissimos
            nostrum voluptates assumenda? Dolor enim ex ipsum dignissimos! Asperiores dolor minus ab
            placeat fuga neque vero suscipit aspernatur nihil doloribus!</p>
```

body   div   #wrapper   nav   ul   li   a          ⊘   HTML ∨   INS   12:17

<a href="#">

The entire <a> element, including its content, is highlighted in Code view. It
can now be copied, cut, moved, or collapsed. The tag selectors clearly reveal the
structure of the code, even without referring to the Code view display. The <a>
is a child of the <li> element, which is a child of <ul>, which is in turn a child
of <nav>, which is a child of <div#wrapper>, and so on.

The tag selectors make it a simple chore to select any part of the code structure.

4  Select the <ul> tag selector.

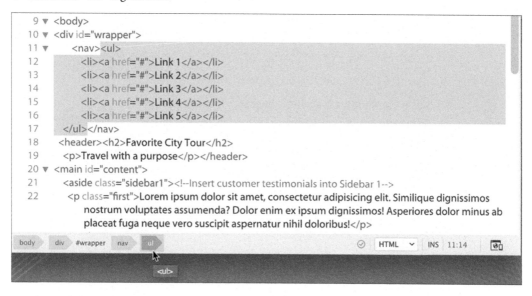

```
 9 ▼ <body>
10 ▼ <div id="wrapper">
11 ▼    <nav><ul>
12          <li><a href="#">Link 1</a></li>
13          <li><a href="#">Link 2</a></li>
14          <li><a href="#">Link 3</a></li>
15          <li><a href="#">Link 4</a></li>
16          <li><a href="#">Link 5</a></li>
17      </ul></nav>
18      <header><h2>Favorite City Tour</h2>
19      <p>Travel with a purpose</p></header>
20 ▼ <main id="content">
21      <aside class="sidebar1"><!--Insert customer testimonials into Sidebar 1-->
22      <p class="first">Lorem ipsum dolor sit amet, consectetur adipisicing elit. Similique dignissimos
            nostrum voluptates assumenda? Dolor enim ex ipsum dignissimos! Asperiores dolor minus ab
            placeat fuga neque vero suscipit aspernatur nihil doloribus!</p>
```

body   div   #wrapper   nav   ul          ⊘   HTML ∨   INS   11:14

<ul>

The code for the unordered list is entirely selected.

5  Select the `<nav>` tag selector.

The code for the entire menu is selected.

6  Select the `<div#wrapper>` tag selector.

```
 9 ▼ <body>
10 ▼ <div id="wrapper">
11 ▼    <nav><ul>
12          <li><a href="#">Link 1</a></li>
13          <li><a href="#">Link 2</a></li>
14          <li><a href="#">Link 3</a></li>
15          <li><a href="#">Link 4</a></li>
16          <li><a href="#">Link 5</a></li>
17       </ul></nav>
18       <header><h2>Favorite City Tour</h2>
19          <p>Travel with a purpose</p></header>
20 ▼    <main id="content">
21          <aside class="sidebar1"><!--Insert customer testimonials into Sidebar 1-->
22          <p class="first">Lorem ipsum dolor sit amet, consectetur adipisicing elit. Similique dignissimos
                 nostrum voluptates assumenda? Dolor enim ex ipsum dignissimos! Asperiores dolor minus ab
                 placeat fuga neque vero suscipit aspernatur nihil doloribus!</p>
```

body  div  #wrapper                                                    ⊘  HTML ∨  INS  10:1        

<div id="wrapper">

The code for the entire page is now selected. Using the tag selectors allows you to identify and select the structure of any element on your page, but it requires you to identify and select the parent tag yourself. Dreamweaver offers another tool that can do it for you automatically.

## Using parent tag selectors

Using the parent tag selector in the Code view window makes the job of selecting the hierarchical structure of your page even simpler.

1  Choose Window > Toolbars > Common to display the Common toolbar, if necessary.

● **Note:** The Select Parent Tag icon may not be displayed by default in the Common toolbar. Click the Customize Toolbar icon ••• and enable the tool before proceeding to step 3, if necessary.

2  Insert the cursor anywhere in the text `Link 1`.

3  In the Common toolbar, click the Select Parent Tag icon 🔾 .

```
{}  favorite-styles.scss
{}  _base.scss
</>  myfirstpage.html
Select Parent Tag  es
    ∨ 🗁  css
       {}  favorite-styles.css
```

```
 5    <meta charset="UTF-8">
 6    <title>Untitled Document</title>
 7    </head>
 8
 9 ▼  <body>
10 ▼  <div id="wrapper">
11 ▼     <nav><ul>
12 ▼        <li><a href="#">Link 1</a></li>
13          <li><a href="#">Link 2</a></li>
14          <li><a href="#">Link 3</a></li>
15          <li><a href="#">Link 4</a></li>
16          <li><a href="#">Link 5</a></li>
17       </ul></nav>
18       <header><h2>Favorite City Tour</h2>
19          <p>Travel with a purpose</p></header>
```

The entire `<a>` element is highlighted.

4   Click the Select Parent Tag icon ⬚ again or press Ctrl+[/Cmd+[ (left bracket).

The entire <li> element is selected.

5   Click the Select Parent Tag icon ⬚.

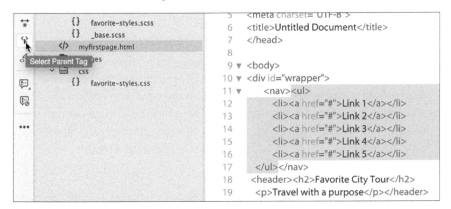

The entire <ul> element is selected.

6   Press Ctrl+[/Cmd+[ until <div#wrapper> is selected.

Each time you click the icon or press the shortcut key, Dreamweaver selects the parent element of the current selection. Once you've selected it, you may find working with long sections of code unwieldy. Code view offers other handy options to collapse long sections to make them easier to work with.

## Collapsing code

Collapsing code is a productivity tool that makes a simple process out of copying or moving large sections of code. Coders and developers also collapse code sections when they are looking for a particular element or section of a page and want to temporarily hide unneeded sections from view. Code can be collapsed either by selection or by logical element.

1   Select the first three Link items in the <nav> element.

Note the Collapse icon ▼ along the left edge of Code view; it indicates that the selection is currently expanded.

2   Click the Collapse icon ▼ to collapse the selection.

The selection collapses, showing only the first <li> element and a snippet of text from it.

You can also collapse code based on logical elements, like <ul> or <nav>. Notice that each line that contains an opening element tag also displays a Collapse icon.

3  Click the Collapse icon ▼ beside the line for the <nav> element.

The entire <nav> element collapses in the Code window, showing only an abbreviated snippet of the entire element. In either instance, the code hasn't been deleted or damaged in any way. It still functions and operates as expected. Also, the collapse functionality appears only in Code view in Dreamweaver; on the web or in another application, the code will appear normally. To expand the code, just reverse the process, as described in the following section.

## Expanding code

When the code is collapsed, you can still copy, cut, or move it like you would any other selected element. You can then expand elements one at a time or all at once.

1  Click the Expand icon ▶ beside the line for the <nav> element.

The <nav> element expands, but the three <li> elements collapsed in the previous exercise are still collapsed.

2  Click the Expand icon ▶ beside the line for the <li> elements.

All collapsed elements are now expanded. Note that the Expand icon for the three <li> elements disappears altogether.

## Accessing Split Code view

Why should coders be denied the ability to work in two windows at the same time? Split Code view enables you to work in two different documents or two different sections of the same document at once. Take your pick.

1  If necessary, switch to Code view.

2  Choose View > Split > Code-Code.

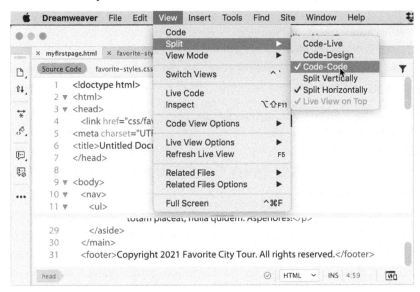

The document displays two Code view windows, both focusing on
**myfirstpage.html**.

3  Insert the cursor in the top window and scroll down to the `<footer>` element.

Split Code view enables you to view and edit two different sections of the
same file.

4  Insert the cursor in the bottom window and scroll to the `<header>` element.

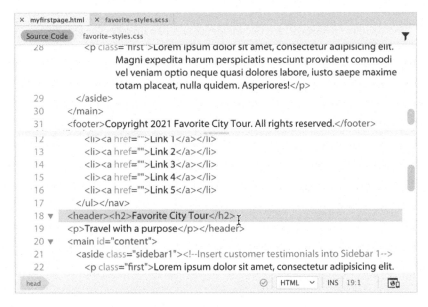

You can also view and edit the contents of any related file.

5   In the Related Files interface, select **favoritestyles.css**.

The window loads the style sheet into one of the windows. You can work in either window and save your changes in real time. Dreamweaver displays an asterisk (*) on any filename in the interface that has been changed but not saved. If you select File > Save or press Ctrl+S/Cmd+S, Dreamweaver saves the changes in the document where your cursor is inserted. Since Dreamweaver can make changes to documents even when they are not open, this feature allows you to edit and update even the files that are closed but linked to your webpage.

## Previewing assets in Code view

Although you may be a diehard coder or developer, there's no reason you can't feel the love from Dreamweaver's graphical display too. The program provides visual previews of graphic assets and certain CSS properties in Code view.

1   Open **myfirstpage.html.** Select Code view.

In Code view, you see only the HTML. The graphical assets are simply references that appear in the CSS file **favoritestyles.css**.

2   Click **favoritestyles.css** in the Related Files interface.

The style sheet appears in the window. Although it's fully editable, don't waste your time making any changes to it. Since the file is the output of the SCSS source file, any changes you make will be overwritten the next time the file compiles.

3   Locate the header rule (around line 6).

The header consists of two text elements and two images. You should be able to see the image references in the background property.

4   Position the cursor over the markup url(../images/favcity-logo.jpg) in the background property (line 8).

A miniature preview of the company logo appears below the cursor.

5  Position the cursor over the markup `background-color: #ED6;` in the background property.

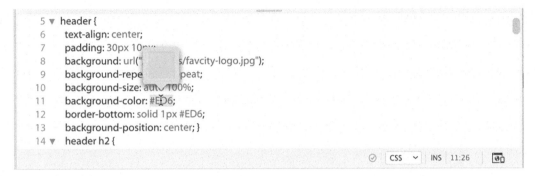

```
 5 ▼  header {
 6       text-align: center;
 7       padding: 30px 10
 8       background: url("        s/favcity-logo.jpg");
 9       background-repe         peat;
10       background-size: auto 100%;
11       background-color: #ED6;
12       border-bottom: solid 1px #ED6;
13       background-position: center; }
14 ▼  header h2 {
```

⊘  [ CSS  ∨ ]  INS  11:26        [⊡]

A small color chip appears, displaying the color specified. The preview functions the same way for all color models. You no longer have to guess what image or color you specified before you can see it in Live view or the browser.

In this lesson, you learned a number of techniques to make working with code easier and more efficient. You learned how to write code manually using hinting and auto-code completion and how to write code automatically using Emmet shorthand. You learned how to check code construction using built-in linting support. You learned how to select, collapse, and expand code, as well as how to create HTML comments and view code in different ways.

Overall, you learned that whether you are a visual designer or a hands-on coder, you can rely on Dreamweaver to offer vital features and power that will allow you to create and edit HTML and CSS code without compromises. Remember these techniques as you work through the book and use any of them whenever appropriate.

# Review questions

1 In what ways does Dreamweaver assist you in creating new code?

2 What is Emmet, and what functionality does it provide to users?

3 What do you have to install to create a LESS, Sass, or SCSS workflow in Dreamweaver?

4 What feature in Dreamweaver reports code errors when you save a file?

5 True or false: Collapsed code will not appear in Live view or the browser until it is expanded.

6 What Dreamweaver feature provides instant access to files linked or referenced within the document?

## Review answers

1 Dreamweaver provides code hinting and auto-completion for HTML tags, attributes, and CSS styling as you type, along with support for ColdFusion, JavaScript, and PHP, among other languages.

2 Emmet is a scripting toolkit that creates HTML code by converting shorthand entries into complete elements, placeholders, and even content.

3 No additional software or services are needed to use LESS, Sass, or SCSS. Dreamweaver supports these CSS preprocessors out of the box. You merely have to enable the compiler in the Site Definition dialog.

4 Linting checks the HTML code and structure every time you save a file, and then displays a red X icon at the bottom of the document window when an error is detected.

5 False. Collapsing code has no effect on the display or operation of the code outside of Dreamweaver.

6 The Related Files interface appears at the top of the document window and enables users to instantly access and review CSS, JavaScript, and other compatible file types linked to the webpage. In some cases, a file displayed in the interface will be stored on a remote resource on the internet. While the Related Files interface enables you to view the contents of all the files displayed, you will be able to edit only ones stored on your local hard drive.

# 5 WEB DESIGN BASICS

## Lesson overview

In this lesson, you'll learn the following:

- The basics of webpage design.
- How to create page thumbnails and wireframes.

 This lesson will take about 30 minutes to complete. To get the lesson files used in this lesson, download them from the webpage for this book at www.adobepress.com/DreamweaverCIB2021. For more information, see "Accessing the lesson files and Web Edition" in the "Getting Started" section at the beginning of this book.

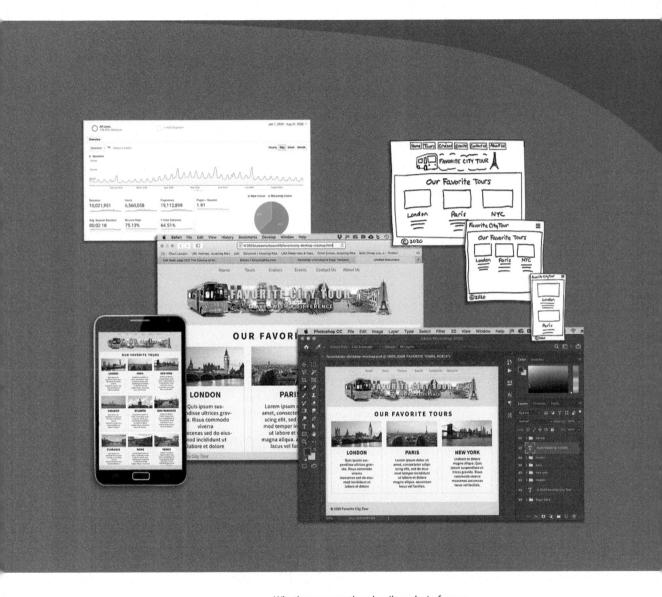

Whether you use thumbnails and wireframes, Photoshop, or just a vivid imagination, Dreamweaver can quickly turn your design concepts into complete, standards-based CSS layouts.

# Developing a new website

Before you begin any web design project for yourself or for a client, you need to answer three important questions:

- What is the purpose of the website?
- Who is the audience?
- How do they get here?

## What is the purpose of the website?

Will the website sell or support a product or service? Is your site for entertainment or games? Will you provide information or news? Will you need a shopping cart or database? Do you need to accept credit card payments or electronic transfers?

Knowing the purpose of the website tells you what type of content you'll be developing and working with and what types of technologies you'll need to incorporate.

## Who is the audience?

Is the audience adults, children, seniors, professionals, hobbyists, men, women, everyone? Knowing *who* your audience will be is vital to the overall design and functionality of your site. A site intended for children probably needs animation, interactivity, and bright, engaging colors. Adults will want serious content and in-depth analysis. Seniors may need larger type and other accessibility enhancements.

A good first step is to check out the competition. Is there an existing website performing the same service or selling the same product? Are they successful? You don't have to mimic others just because they're doing the same thing. Look at Google and Yahoo—they perform the same basic service, but their site designs couldn't be more different from one another.

Google and Yahoo provide basically the same service but do so with dramatically different methods.

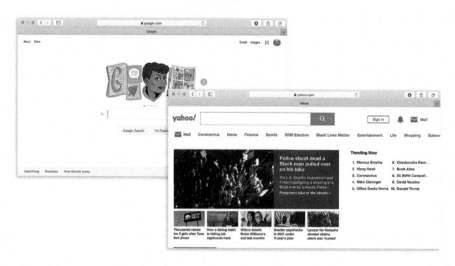

## How do they get here?

This sounds like an odd question when speaking of the internet. But just as with a brick-and-mortar business, your online customers can come to you in a variety of ways. For example, are they accessing your site on a desktop computer, laptop, tablet, or smartphone? Are they using high-speed internet, wireless, or dial-up service? What browser are they most likely to use, and what is the size and resolution of the display?

These answers will tell you a lot about what kind of experience your customers will expect. Dial-up and smartphone users may not want to see a lot of graphics or video, whereas users with large flat-panel displays and high-speed connections may demand as much bang and sizzle as you can send at them.

So where do you get this information? Some you'll have to get through painstaking research and demographic analysis. Some you'll get from educated guesses based on your own tastes and understanding of your market. But a lot of it is actually available on the internet itself. W3Schools, for one, keeps track of tons of statistics regarding access and usage, all updated regularly:

- https://w3schools.com/browsers/default.asp provides information about browser statistics.

- https://w3schools.com/browsers/browsers_os.asp gives the breakdown on operating systems. In 2011, W3Schools started to track the usage of mobile devices on the internet.

- https://w3schools.com/browsers/browsers_display.asp lets you find out the latest information on the resolution, or size, of screens using the internet.

If you are redesigning an existing site, your web-hosting service itself may provide valuable statistics on historical traffic patterns and even the visitors themselves. If you host your own site, you can incorporate third-party tools, such as Google Analytics or Adobe Analytics, into your code to do the tracking for you for free or for a small fee.

As of the summer of 2020, Windows desktop computers still dominated the internet (74 percent), with most browser users favoring Google Chrome (81 percent), followed by Firefox (9.2 percent), and with various versions of Edge/Internet Explorer (3.3 percent) a distant third. The vast majority of desktop browsers (98 percent) are set to a resolution higher than 1280 pixels by 800 pixels.

These statistics would be great news for most web designers and developers if it weren't for the dominance of tablets and smartphones on the internet today. But designing a website that can look good and work effectively on both flat-panel desktop displays and smartphones is a tall order.

Analytics provides comprehensive statistics on the visitors to your site. Google Analytics, pictured here, is a popular choice.

## Scenario

For the purposes of this book, you'll be working to develop a website for Favorite City Tour, a fictitious travel and tour organization. This website will offer a variety of tours and services and require a broad range of webpage types, including dynamic pages using technologies such as jQuery, which is a form of JavaScript.

Your customers come from a demographic that includes ages from young adult to senior citizens with disposable income and higher educational levels. They are people who are looking for a new experience and a different, edgier take on travel and tourism.

Your marketing research indicates that most of your customers still use desktop computers or laptops, connecting via high-speed internet services. You can expect to get 20 to 30 percent of your visitors exclusively via smartphone and other mobile devices, and much of the rest will be using mobile from time to time, especially when traveling.

To simplify the process of learning Dreamweaver, we'll focus on creating a site based on one of the program's pre-built starter layouts, where you will learn how to adapt your design theme to the existing framework.

## Working with thumbnails and wireframes

After you have nailed down the answers to the three questions about your website purpose, customer demographic, and access model, the next step is to determine how many pages you'll need, what they will do, and what they will look like.

# Responsive web design

Each day, more people are using smartphones and other mobile devices to access the internet. Some people may use them to access the internet more frequently than they use desktop computers. This presents several nagging challenges to web designers. For one thing, smartphone screens are a fraction of the size of even the smallest flat-panel display. How do you cram a two- or three-column page design into a meager 3- to 4-inch screen?

Until the last five years or so, web design usually required that you target an optimum size (height and width in pixels) for a webpage and then build the entire site on these specifications. Today, that scenario is becoming a rare occurrence. Now, you are presented with the decision to build a site that either can scale to any size display (responsive) or can morph to support a few target display types for desktop and mobile users (adaptive).

Your own decision will be based in part on the content you want to provide and on the capabilities of the devices accessing your pages. Building an attractive website that supports video, audio, and other dynamic content is hard enough without throwing in a panoply of different display sizes and device capabilities. The term *responsive web design* was coined, in a book of the same name (2011), by a Boston-based web developer named Ethan Marcotte. In the book, he describes the notion of designing pages that can adapt to multiple screen dimensions automatically. Along with more standard techniques, you will learn many techniques for responsive web design and implement them in your site and asset design later in this book.

Many of the concepts of print design are not applicable to the web, because you are not in control of the user's experience. For example, print designers know in advance the page size for which they are designing. The printed page and its content don't change when you rotate it from portrait to landscape. On the other hand, a page carefully designed for a typical flat panel is basically useless on a smartphone.

## Creating thumbnails

Many web designers start by drawing thumbnails with pencil and paper. Think of thumbnails as a graphical shopping list of the pages you'll need to create for the website. Thumbnails can help you work out the basic navigation structure for the site. Draw lines between the thumbnails showing how the site navigation will connect them.

Thumbnails list the pages that need to be built and how they are connected to each other.

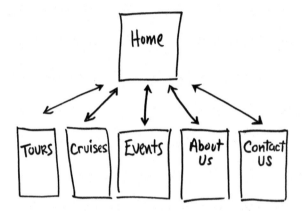

Most sites are divided into levels. Typically, the first level starts with the home page and includes all the pages in your main navigation menu—the ones a visitor can reach directly from the home page. The second level includes pages you can reach only through specific actions or from specific locations, say from a shopping cart or a product detail page.

## Creating a page design

Once you've figured out what your site needs in terms of pages, products, and services, you can then turn to what those pages will look like. Make a list of components you want or need on each page, such as headers and footers, navigation, and areas for the main content and the sidebars (if any). Put aside any items that won't be needed on every page. What other factors do you need to consider? If mobile devices are going to be an important consideration of your design identity, will any of the components be required (as opposed to optional) for these devices? Although many components can simply be resized for mobile screens, some will have to be completely redesigned or reimagined.

Identifying the essential components for each page helps you create a page design and structure that will meet your needs.

1. Horizontal navigation (for internal reference, i.e., Home, About Us, Contact Us)
2. Header (includes banner and logo)
3. Footer (copyright info)
4. Main content (one column with chance of two or more)

Do you have a company logo, business identity, graphic imagery, or color scheme you want to match or complement? Do you have existing or proposed publications, brochures, or advertising campaigns you want to emulate? Often, these materials precede the construction of the website. It helps to gather them all in one place so you can see everything all at once on a desk or conference table. If you're lucky, a theme will rise organically from this collection. In some cases, the print identity and publications will evolve from the web design.

### Desktop or mobile

Once you've created your checklist of the components that you'll need on each page, sketch out several rough layouts that work for these components. Depending on your target visitor demographics, you may decide to focus on a design that's optimized for desktop computers or one that works best on tablets and smartphones.

Most designers settle on one basic page design that is a compromise between flexibility and sizzle. Some site designs may naturally lean toward using more than one basic layout. But resist the urge to design each page separately. Minimizing the number of page designs may sound like a major limitation, but it's key to producing a professional-looking site that's easy to manage. It's the reason why some professionals, such as doctors and airline pilots, wear uniforms. Using a consistent page design, or template, conveys a sense of professionalism and confidence to your visitor. While you're figuring out what your pages will look like, you'll have to address the size and placement of the basic components. Where you put a component can drastically affect its impact and usefulness.

In print, designers know that the upper-left corner of a layout is considered one of the "power positions," a place where you want to locate important aspects of a design, such as a logo or title. This is because in western culture we read from left to right, top to bottom. The second power position is the lower-right corner because this is the last thing your eyes will see when you're finished reading.

Unfortunately, in web design this theory doesn't hold up for one simple reason: You can never be certain how the user is seeing your design. Are they on a 20-inch flat panel or a 3-inch-wide smartphone?

In most instances, the only thing you can be certain of is that the user can see the upper-left corner of any page. Do you want to waste this position by slapping the company logo here? Or make the site more useful by slipping in a navigational menu? This is one of the key predicaments of the web designer. Do you go for design sizzle, workable utility, or something in between?

## Creating wireframes

After you pick the winning design, wireframing is a fast way to work out the structure of each page in the site. A wireframe is like a thumbnail, but bigger, that sketches out each page and fills in more details about the components, such as actual link names and main headings, but with minimal design or styling. This step helps to anticipate problems before you smack into them when working in code. What might take you hours or days to produce digitally can be sketched out in minutes by hand.

Wireframes allow you to experiment with page designs quickly and easily without wasting time with code.

Once the basic concepts are worked out, many designers take an extra step and create a full-size mockup or "proof of concept" using a program such as Photoshop or even Adobe Illustrator. It's a handy thing to do because you'll find that some clients just aren't comfortable giving approvals or authorizing budgets based only on pencil sketches. The advantage here is that these programs allow you to export the results to full-size images (JPEG, GIF, or PNG) that can be viewed in a browser as if they were finished webpages. Such mockups are as good as seeing the real thing but may take only a fraction of the time to produce.

The wireframe for the final design should identify all components and include specific information about content, color, and dimensions.

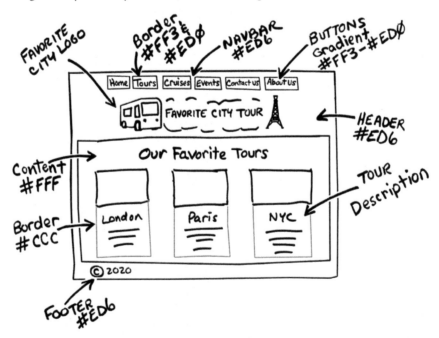

To demonstrate how a graphics program could be used to build such a mockup, I created a sample webpage layout using Photoshop and saved it into the Lesson 5 resources folder. Let's take a look.

1 Launch Photoshop CC or higher.

2 Open **favoritecity-desktop-mockup.psd** from the lesson05/resources folder.

The Photoshop file contains a mockup of the Favorite City Tour site design geared for desktop computers using flat-panel displays. It is composed of various vector-based design components as well as image assets stored in separate layers. Note the use of colors and gradients in the design. Feel free to experiment with the layers and various components to see how they were created.

In addition to creating graphical mockups, Photoshop has tricks geared specifically for web designers.

## Designing for mobile devices

Depending on the needs and demographics of your desired audience, you will also have to contend with visitors accessing your site via smartphones and tablets. These devices can range in size from just a few hundred pixels to nearly the size of a desktop display. For many sites, mobile users may be your main target audience. If this is the case with your site, you may want to consider using a mobile-first strategy.

*Mobile-first* focuses on design requirements for phones and tablets over those of desktop users. By making the design and environment optimal for these visitors, you create a welcoming experience, which should therefore translate to increased traffic and revenue.

● **Note:** You should be able to open the sample file with any version of Photoshop CC or higher. Be aware that if you use a version different from the one pictured, the panels and menu options may appear different.

● **Note:** The mockup uses fonts from Typekit, Adobe's online font service. To view the final design properly in Photoshop, you will need to download and install these fonts. Typekit fonts are included in your subscription to Creative Cloud.

● **Note:** If you do not have access to Photoshop you can open the HTML file of the same name.

Since phones and many tablets provide much less real estate, you have to rethink common design practices. For example, many designers try to emphasize graphics and photos, maximizing their size and composition on large landscape flat-panel displays. But this strategy can backfire on small vertically oriented phones, where a bold and dramatic landscape may be displayed only a few inches wide.

In turn, headlines and text that can be seen and read all at once on a large display may require the visitor to scroll several screens to read on a phone. Writing effectively for mobile users presents a daunting challenge at the least. In some cases, companies actually provide customized content for different types of visitors. By using various dynamic schemes based on programming languages such as PHP, ASP, and JavaScript, the site can determine what type of device is viewing it and then serve content specifically geared for that display size.

## The third way

The third option is to design the site to compromise between desktop and mobile visitors. You'll find that many visitors will alternate between desktop and mobile devices, sometimes on the same day. They will use their computers or laptops at home and work and then jump on their phones and tablets when they are on the road or running around town.

This is the easiest and least expensive strategy. It doesn't require any special programming or development, and it's the one I use throughout the book. To show how this can work, I've created mockups of the site design for mobile users too.

1 Open **favoritecity-tablet-mockup.psd** from the lesson05 folder.

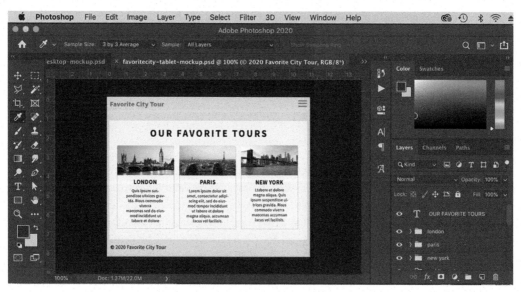

This file contains the mockup for the site design on tablets.

2   Open **favoritecity-phone-mockup.psd**.

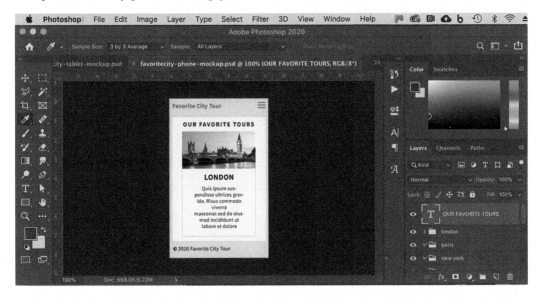

This file contains the mockup for the site design on a smartphone.

All three mockups should be open in Photoshop or Dreamweaver. You can alternate between them by clicking the tabs at the top of the document window. Switch between the layouts and compare and contrast them. Notice how each design features the same content, only resized and reformatted for the specific environment.

The mockup of the Favorite City Tour site design is composed of various vector-based design components as well as image assets stored in separate layers. Note the use of colors and gradients in the design. Feel free to experiment with the layers and various components to see how they were created.

In addition to creating graphical mockups, Photoshop has tricks geared specifically for web designers. Adobe Generator is a feature that allows you to create image assets in real time as you work in Photoshop. To learn more about Adobe Generator, check out the following link:

https://tinyurl.com/generate-photoshop

To learn how to use the Adobe Generator, see this tutorial:
https://preview.tinyurl.com/generate-tutorial

In the next lesson you will learn how to modify a built-in Dreamweaver template to match the site design mockup.

**Note:** If you do not have access to Photoshop, you can open the HTML files of the same name.

## Review questions

1 What three questions should you ask before starting any web design project?

2 What is the purpose of using thumbnails and wireframes?

3 Why is it important to create a design that takes into account smartphones and tablets?

4 What is responsive design, and why should Dreamweaver users be aware of it?

5 Why would you use Photoshop and Illustrator, or other programs, to create design mockups for a website?

## Review answers

1 What is the purpose of the website? Who is the audience? How did they get here? These questions, and their answers, are essential in helping you develop the design, content, and strategy of your site.

2 Thumbnails and wireframes are quick techniques for roughing out the design and structure of your site without having to waste lots of time coding sample pages.

3 Mobile device users are one of the fastest-growing demographics on the web. Many visitors will use a mobile device to access your website on a regular basis or exclusively. Webpages designed for desktop computers often display poorly on mobile devices, making the websites difficult or impossible to use for these mobile visitors.

4 Responsive design is a method for making the most effective use of a webpage, and its content, by designing it to adapt to various types of displays and devices automatically.

5 Using Photoshop and Illustrator you can produce page designs and mockups much faster than when designing in code with Dreamweaver. Designs can even be exported as web-compatible graphics that can be viewed in a browser to get client approval.

# 6 CREATING A PAGE LAYOUT

## Lesson overview

In this lesson, you'll learn how to work faster, make updating easier, and be more productive. You'll learn how to do the following:

- Evaluate basic page structure from design mockups.
- Create a layout based on a predefined starter layout.
- Upload a Photoshop mockup as a Creative Cloud asset.
- Extract styling, text, and image assets from a Photoshop mockup.
- Apply extracted styles, text, and image assets to a starter layout in Dreamweaver.

This lesson will take about 2 hours to complete. To get the lesson files used in this lesson, download them from the webpage for this book at www.adobepress.com/DreamweaverCIB2021. For more information, see "Accessing the lesson files and Web Edition" in the "Getting Started" section at the beginning of this book.

Dreamweaver provides powerful tools with which to apply styling, text, and image assets created in other Adobe applications, such as Photoshop.

# Evaluating page design options

In the previous lesson, you went through the process of identifying the pages, components, and structures you would need for a specific website. The selected design balances those needs against a variety of other factors, such as the types of visitors that may come to the site and their means of connecting to it. In this lesson, you will learn how to implement those structures and components in a basic layout.

Since there are almost unlimited ways to build a design, we'll concentrate on building a simple structure that uses the minimum number of HTML5 semantic elements. This will produce a page design that is easy to implement and maintain. Let's start by taking a look at the mockup introduced in Lesson 5, "Web Design Basics."

1  In Dreamweaver, open **favoritecity-mockup.html** from the lesson06 folder.

   This HTML file contains an image depicting the final mockup of the Favorite City Tour site design that you saw in Lesson 5. The design can be broken into basic components: header, footer, navigation, and main content elements.

   Once you have the skills to build your own page layouts, you can use Dreamweaver to execute any design from scratch. Until then, one option is to fall back on the handy webpage layouts provided by Dreamweaver itself.

2  Close **favoritecity-mockup.html** and do not save any changes.

In the next exercise, you will examine Dreamweaver's starter layouts and pick one to jumpstart the web design process.

# Working with predefined layouts

Dreamweaver has always tried to offer the latest tools and workflows to all web designers regardless of their skill level. For example, over the years, the program has provided a selection of predefined templates, various page components, and code snippets to make the task of building and populating webpages fast and easy.

Often, the first step of building a website was to see whether one of its predefined layouts matched your needs or whether your needs could be adapted to one of the available designs.

Dreamweaver CC (2021 release) continues this tradition by providing sample CSS layouts and web frameworks that you can adapt to many popular types of projects. You can access these samples from the File menu.

1 Choose File > New.

The New Document dialog appears. Dreamweaver allows you to build a wide spectrum of web-compatible documents besides those built using HTML, CSS, and JavaScript. The New Document dialog displays many of these document types, including PHP, XML, and SVG. Predefined layouts, templates, and frameworks can also be accessed from this dialog. Let's check out the options.

2 In the New Document dialog, choose Starter Templates > Basic Layouts.

The Starter Templates window of the New Document dialog displays three choices: Multi Column, Simple Grid, and Single Page.

At the time of this writing, Dreamweaver CC (2021 release) offers three basic layouts, six Bootstrap templates, four email templates, and three responsive starter layouts. The exact number and features of these layouts may change over time through automatic updates via Creative Cloud. The changes to this list may occur without notice or fanfare, so keep your eyes peeled for new options in this dialog.

All the featured layouts are responsive designs built using HTML5-compatible structures and will help you gain valuable experience with this evolving standard. Unless you need to support older browsers (such as IE5 and IE6), there's little to worry about when using these newer designs.

3 If necessary, select **Basic – Multi Column**.
Observe the preview image in the dialog.

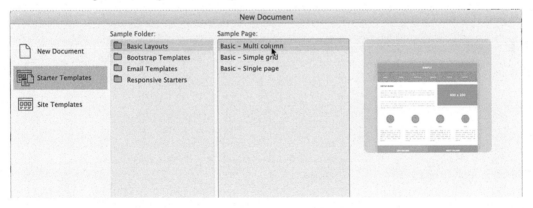

A preview image shows the design of a multicolumn webpage.

4   Select Basic – Simple Grid.

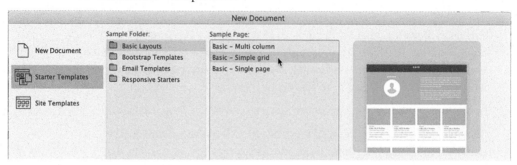

The preview image changes to depict the new grid-based design.

5   Select each of the categories and design options in turn.
Observe each preview image in the dialog.

Each template offers a design appropriate for specific applications. After reviewing all the sample layouts, only the Bootstrap eCommerce template is close to the design of the Favorite City Tour mockup.

6   Choose Bootstrap Templates > Bootstrap eCommerce.

7   Click Create.

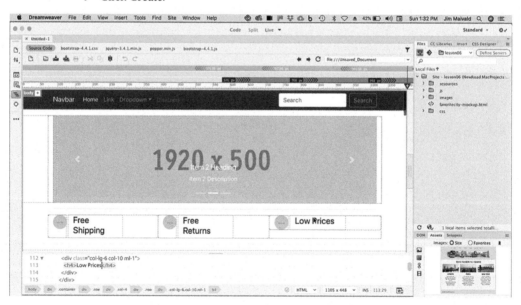

The file contains a one-column layout with navigation, body content, and footer components. Before we proceed, it's a good idea to save the file.

8   Select File > Save.

The first time you save a new file, the Save and Save As commands are identical. Once a file is saved, use the Save As command to save a file under a new name or in a different folder.

9   Name the file **mylayout.html** and save it in the root of the lesson06 folder.

► **Tip:** If necessary, click the Site Root button to navigate to the home folder of lesson06.

When the file is saved, it may not be obvious, but Dreamweaver automatically adds various resources—image placeholders, CSS, and JavaScript libraries—to the site folder to support the Bootstrap functionality of the template. You can see these new assets in the Files panel.

● **Note:** The Files panel will update automatically, but it may take a few moments.

If you examine the new webpage, you can see it has some similarities to the site mockup viewed earlier. In the following exercises, you will learn how to adapt this layout to make it match that design and to create the site template in Lesson 7, "Working with Templates."

## Styling a predefined layout

Once you get the skills under your belt, it will be simple to build a webpage layout from scratch. For now, the Dreamweaver starter layouts provide a great place to jumpstart the process of building your site template.

1   If necessary, open **mylayout.html** from the lesson06 folder. Make the Dreamweaver document as large as the computer display will allow (at least 1200 pixels).

This webpage is based on a fully responsive Bootstrap starter template. The styling you see will change based on the width and orientation of the document window in Dreamweaver. To ensure you are obtaining the same results shown in this lesson, make sure the document window is at least 1200 pixels in width unless otherwise directed within the exercise. Check out Lesson 1, "Customizing Your Workspace" to learn how to resize the window.

The first step is to make this generic layout take on some of the personality of the proposed design. Normally, you would have to do that the old-fashioned way, by editing the CSS by hand. But since the layout was mocked up in Adobe Photoshop, Dreamweaver has a built-in feature called Extract that can use the site mockup to create some of the desired styling for you.

Extract was added to Dreamweaver a few versions ago. It is a feature hosted by Creative Cloud and accessed through a panel in the program.

● **Note:** Before accessing the Extract panel, you must have the Creative Cloud desktop app running and be logged in to your account.

2  Select Window > Extract.

The Extract panel appears. The panel connects to your Creative Cloud account and will display any Photoshop files in your assets. To use the site mockup, you first have to upload it to the Creative Cloud server.

3  Click the option Upload PSD.

A file dialog appears.

4  Select **favoritecity-mockup.psd** in the lesson06/resources folder and click Open.

The file is copied to your Creative Cloud Files folder on your computer, which is then synced to your Creative Cloud remote storage. Once the file is uploaded, it should be visible in the Extract panel.

5   Click to load **favoritecity-mockup.psd** in the Extract panel.

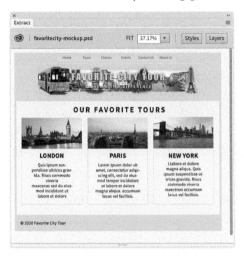

The mockup loads and fills the entire panel. Extract enables you to access and derive styling information, image assets, and even text from the mockup.

# Styling elements using the Extract panel

The Extract panel can obtain image assets and styling data from the Photoshop file. In this exercise, we're interested only in the styling data. Let's start at the top and work down the page. First, we'll grab the background color.

1   In the Extract panel, click the yellow background of the page.

When you click in the preview image, a pop-up window appears. The pop-up window allows you to select the data you want to obtain from the mockup.

The buttons at the top of the pop-up indicate what data is available from the selected component, such as CSS, text, and image assets. Notice that the Copy CSS and Extract Asset buttons are selectable, indicating that styling and image assets are available. The Copy Text option is grayed out, indicating that no text content is available to be downloaded.

The window displays the CSS styling as a list with checkboxes. When you select a checkbox, those specifications will be copied to program memory. The CSS styling that is displayed includes properties for width, height, and background color. You can select all the settings or only the ones you want to use.

2   If necessary, deselect width and height.
    Select background-color.

3   Click the Copy CSS button.

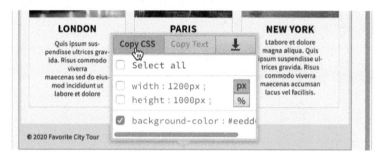

Once you've copied the settings, you can then apply them directly to the layout in Dreamweaver. The easiest way to use this data is via the CSS Designer.

4   Select Window > CSS Designer to open or display the panel and enable the Show Set option.
    Click the All button, if necessary.

First, we want to apply the specifications to the top navigation menu in the current layout. You can target the menu by selecting the appropriate rule in the Selectors pane or by selecting the actual element in Live view.

The current layout is fully responsive so that the styles are applied based on the width and sometimes the orientation of the document window. To obtain the correct styling, you have to make sure the document window is showing the full desktop version of the design at a minimum of 1200 pixels.

5   In Live view, click to select the top navigation menu.

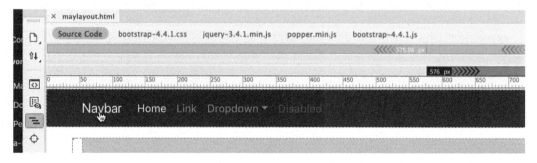

In some cases, when you select an element in the document window, Dreamweaver does not select the desired one first. To ensure the proper element is targeted, you should use the tag selector interface.

6   Select nav in the tag selector interface.

The Element Display will appear targeting the <nav> element. There are four classes assigned to the element: .navbar, .navbar-expand-lg, .navbar-dark, and .bg-dark. CSS Designer will display all the CSS rules defined in the site. This will include the style affecting the navbar, but it may be hard to find them.

When tracking down the current styling of an element, be aware that it can be applied directly to the <nav> element, applied to any one of the individual classes assigned to it, or divvied up between two or more rules. Part of your job in this instance is to figure out where the styling is coming from and then to either replace or override it.

7   In the CSS Designer, click the Current button.

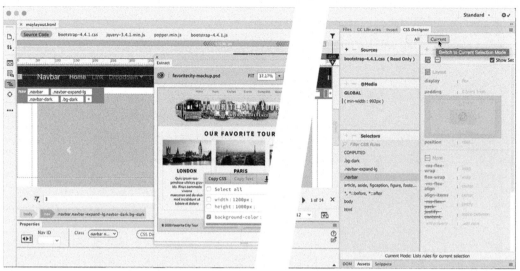

As you learned in Lesson 3, "CSS Basics," the Current button displays any styling set on the element selected in the layout. The Selectors pane in the CSS Designer displays the rules applied to the current navigation menu. The CSS rules listed include `.bg-dark`, `.navbar-expand-lg`, and `.navbar`.

One of these rules is applying the background color to the `nav` element. By clicking the selectors, you can inspect the properties assigned to it. In CSS Designer, the rule at the top of the list is the most powerful. If there are any conflicts with it and any other rule, the properties in the first rule will override the others.

8   Select `.bg-dark` and examine the Properties pane.

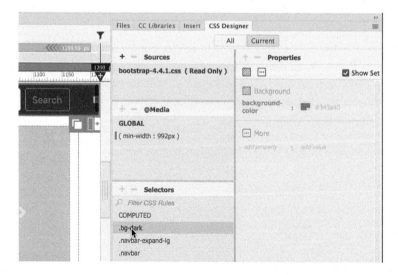

The rule applies a background color of #343a40. If the rule were contained in a normal style sheet, you could use the background color from the mockup to replace the existing color. But the style sheet applied to this page was created by the Bootstrap framework and is marked as Read Only in CSS Designer. You can see that the rules and properties are grayed out in CSS Designer. To override the existing styling, you will have to create a new separate style sheet. All the styles you create from this point on should be added to this new style sheet.

● **Note:** Some Windows users have reported that the Bootstrap style sheet is not marked Read Only. Either way, I recommend that you leave the Bootstrap CSS as is and follow the directions as written.

## Reading, no writing

The Bootstrap style sheet is formatted as a read-only file to prevent you from making accidental changes to the framework's complex styling. From time to time as you work in your pages, a warning message may appear at the top of the screen indicating that the file is read-only and prompting you to make it *writable*.

⚠ 'bootstrap–4.3.1.css' is read only. Make writable                                          ⊗

You can dismiss the message by clicking the Close icon ⊗ on the right side. It also provides an option to make the file writable. You're advised to resist the temptation to make the Bootstrap style sheet editable.

9   In the Sources pane of CSS Designer, click the Add CSS Source icon ✚.

A dropdown menu appears that allows you to create a new CSS file, attach an existing CSS file, or define a style sheet embedded within the page code.

10  Choose **Create A New CSS File** from the dropdown menu.

The Create A New CSS File dialog appears.

11  Type **favorite-styles.css** in the Create A New CSS File dialog. Click OK to create the style sheet reference.

● **Note:** It is essential to note here that the CSS file has not been created yet, and will not be until you create a CSS rule and save the file. If Dreamweaver crashes before that happens, you will have to re-create the file in a separate operation.

When you click OK, a reference to the new style sheet is added to the CSS Designer Sources pane. The CSS file has not actually been created yet, but a link has been added to the <head> section of the page, and the file will be created automatically as soon as you create your first custom rule and save the file.

Another thing you may not have noticed in the process is that Dreamweaver automatically switched to the All button in CSS Designer and selected the new style sheet. This is important because when the Current button is selected, you cannot create new selectors or properties.

12 If necessary, click **favorite-styles.css** in the Sources panel.

The @Media and Selectors panes are both empty. This means there are no CSS rules or media queries defined in this file. You have a blank slate on which you can make any design additions or modifications. Since you will not change the Bootstrap CSS directly, this style sheet will be the means you use to make its structure and content bend to your wishes.

The rule applying the current background color to the nav element was .bg-dark. To override that styling, you need to create an identical rule in the new style sheet.

13 In the Selectors pane, click the Add Selector icon ➕.

A field appears in the Selectors panel that enables you to create a new selector name. Dreamweaver even jumpstarts the process by generating a sample name for you based on the element selected in the document window. In this case, the selector name uses all four classes assigned to the nav element. Since the rule setting the background color uses only one of the classes, the new rule should be identical to avoid any unintended consequences.

14 Type .bg

Since the automatic selector was highlighted, it is completely replaced by the new text. Don't forget to start with the initial period (.) that defines a class name in CSS. A hinting menu appears listing any classes used within the HTML or selectors defined within the CSS that match the entered text. You should see .bg-dark in the list.

15 Select .bg-dark in the hinting menu and press Enter/Return to complete the selector name.

The .bg-dark selector now appears in the **favorite-styles.css** style sheet. Note that there are no properties defined yet. Once the selector is created, you can apply the styling extracted from the mockup.

16 Move the cursor over and right-click the .bg-dark selector.

A context menu appears, providing options to interact with the rule by editing, copying, or pasting the CSS specifications. In this case, you want to *paste* the styles derived from the Extract panel.

17 Select Paste Styles from the context menu.

The background color properties of the mockup now appear in the new CSS rule. But there is a problem. The navbar is still showing a dark background. Conflicts between rules and other style sheets is a common issue on the web. Knowing how to troubleshoot styling problems is an important skill in a web designer. Fortunately, Dreamweaver has some great troubleshooting tools.

# Troubleshooting CSS conflicts

Although this is the first CSS conflict you may have encountered, it certainly won't be the last. There are a variety of tools in Dreamweaver that make sussing out these errors a relatively simple task.

1 Select the Current button in CSS Designer.

2 Click the nav tag selector.

The Selectors pane displays a list of rules formatting some aspect of the navbar or its parent structure. The first selector in the pane is .bg-dark.

> **Tip:** If the *nav* tag selector is not visible, you may have to first select the navbar or one of its components in the document window.

3   Click `.bg-dark` in the Selectors pane and examine its properties.

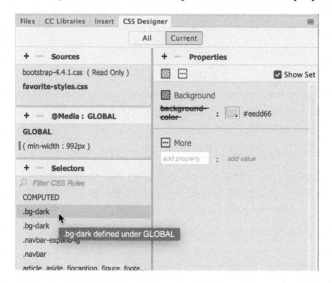

The Properties pane displays the rule `.bg-dark` first in the list with the `background-color` property you just added. This usually indicates that the rule has a higher specificity and should override any other styling. But in this case, the property has a black line through it. Dreamweaver is showing you that the rule is disabled for some reason. Fortunately, the built-in troubleshooting doesn't stop there.

4   Move the cursor over the `background-color` property in CSS Designer.

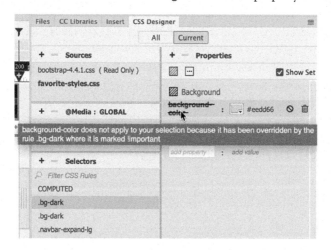

A tool tip appears reporting that `background-color` is being disabled because the specification in the Bootstrap template is marked `!important`. This CSS attribute is usually only used in emergencies to override conflicting styling that can't be fixed any other way.

There are two ways to fix the issue. You can remove the !important attribute or add !important to the new property. Since the Bootstrap style sheet is formatted as Read Only, you will have to use the latter solution.

5  Right-click the rule .bg-dark.
   Select Go To Code in the context menu.

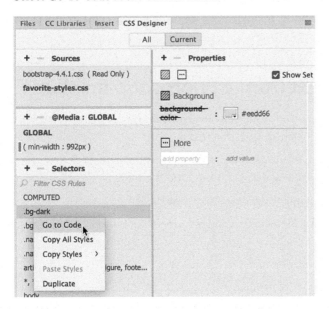

The document window splits horizontally, showing the Code view window at the bottom focused on the new **favorite-styles.css** style sheet and the .bg-dark rule.

6  Insert the cursor after the color value #eedd66 but before the semicolon (;).

7  Press the spacebar to insert a space.
   Type !

● **Note:** The space is not required for the attribute to function. It just makes the code easier to read and edit.

Dreamweaver should autocomplete the !important attribute. As soon as the attribute appears in the style sheet, the navbar reformats to match the styling shown in the mockup.

As you may have noticed, the `!important` attribute has no representation anywhere in CSS Designer. Keep this in mind when you troubleshoot other CSS issues in the future.

8  Choose File > Save All.

By using Save All, you have saved the changes to the webpage and created the **favorite-styles.css** file in the site folder. The Extract panel also enables you to pick up the text content in the mockup.

## Extracting text from a Photoshop mockup

The Extract panel enables you to pick up formatting for text as well as the text itself. In this exercise, you will pick up both from the mockup.

1  If necessary, open **mylayout.html** from the lesson06 folder in Live view. The document window should be displayed at a width of 1200 pixels or wider.

▶ **Tip:** The Extract panel may obscure part of the page you need to work on. Feel free to reposition or dock the panel at any time.

2  If necessary, select Window > Extract to display the Extract panel.

The mockup should still be displayed in the panel. If not, simply select it in the list of assets.

3  Examine the top navigation menu in the mockup.

The navigation bar has six menu items: *Home, Tours, Cruises, Events, Contact Us,* and *About Us.* The navigation bar in the Bootstrap layout is completely different. It has four menu items, one of which is a dropdown menu with additional options of its own, and a search box with a button.

When working with a third-party template, it's a good idea to remove items that you don't need or want as soon as possible so they don't get in the way.

The first item in the Bootstrap menu is the text *Navbar.* This item is a hyperlink, but it's not part of the menu. Nothing like it appears in the site mockup, but there is a text element in the tablet and phone designs. This text element will replace the header and logo image on smaller screens.

4  Select the *Navbar* element.

An orange border appears around the element. This indicates the text can be edited.

5  Double-click the word *Navbar.*

The entire word is highlighted.

**6** Type `Favorite City Tour`

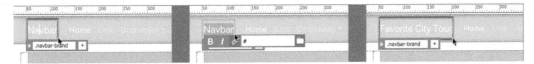

The company name will appear on phones and tablets but will be hidden for desktop visitors. We'll leave it visible for the time being.

Take a close look at the *Home* menu item. You may notice that it's formatted differently than the other items. When you see odd formatting like this, it's usually because of a CSS class not assigned to the other items.

**7** Select the *Home* menu item.

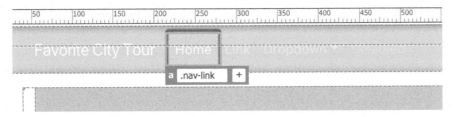

The Element Display appears focused on the a tag. Notice the orange border around the element.

There's nothing special about this element. Let's check the `<li>` element. To change the focus of the Element Display, you can use the tag selectors, the mouse, or the keyboard. Let's use the keyboard.

**8** Press the Esc key.

The border color on the `<a>` element changes to blue. You can also use the keyboard to change the focus within the document window.

**9** Press the up arrow key.

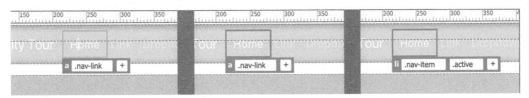

The Element Display focus changes to the li element. Notice that this link has two classes assigned to it: `.nav-link` and `.active`.

● **Note:** Pressing the up or down arrows when the blue border is visible will change the Element Display, focusing on elements as they appear in the document object model (DOM).

**10** Position the cursor over the class `.active`.
Click the Remove Class/ID icon ☒ on the `.active` class.

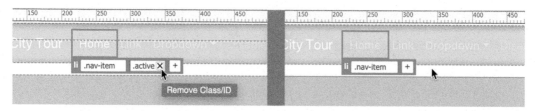

Once the `.active` class is removed, the *Home* menu item is formatted the same as the *Link* item.

The next item in the menu mockup is *Tours*. The Extract panel enables you to pull text content as well as CSS from the mockup.

**11** In the Extract panel, select the second item: *Tours*.
Make sure you select the text and not the button.

The pop-up window appears. Notice that all three buttons at the top of the Extract panel window are active. This indicates that you can extract styling, text, and image assets from this selection.

**12** Click the Copy Text button.

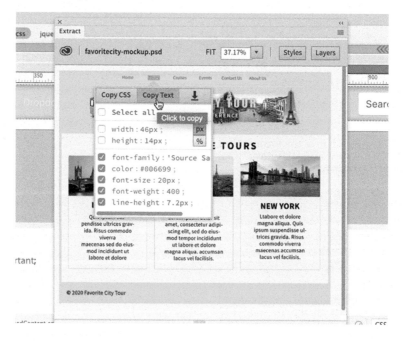

13 In **mylayout.html** double-click *Link* in Live view.

The text is highlighted and an orange box appears around the text, indicating you are in text-editing mode.

14 Right-click the selected text.

The context menu appears, giving you options for cutting, copying, and pasting the text.

15 Select Paste from the context menu.

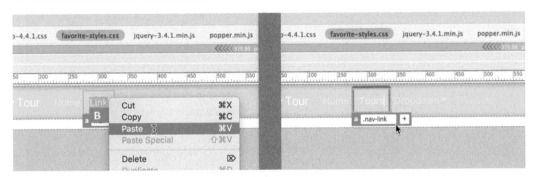

*Tours* replaces the text *Link*.

The next item in the Bootstrap menu is a dropdown menu. The mockup does not show such an item, so there's no reason to keep it.

▶ **Tip:** The text extraction feature is really intended for longer passages of text. Feel free to type the menu items by hand if you prefer.

# Deleting components and attributes from a template

If you see unneeded components in a template, feel free to delete them. When deleting components, it's important that you delete the entire element and not leave any part of its HTML code behind.

1 Select the *Dropdown* menu item in the document window.

The Element Display will appear on the *Dropdown* item. In most cases, the display will focus on the <a> element of the item.

Most navigation menus are constructed of unordered lists, using three main HTML elements: ul, li, and a. A dropdown menu is usually built using any unordered list as a child of one of the list items.

To get rid of the dropdown menu, you can either delete that child list or delete the parent containing it. The simplest method is just to delete the parent. Whenever you want to delete elements in a layout, always use the tag selectors to ensure you get all the markup.

2   Select the li tag selector for the *Dropdown* item.

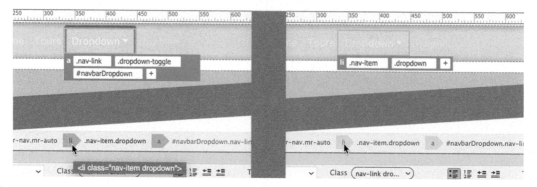

The Element Display should now focus on the li element. Note the orange border around the element. This color indicates that the element content can be edited directly. This behavior highlights a major change in the functionality of Dreamweaver's Live view.

In previous versions of Dreamweaver, Live view allowed you to delete elements immediately, but you had to double-click them to enter edit mode. In this version of Dreamweaver, you can edit elements immediately, but you have to select them a second time to delete them.

3   Click the Element Display focused on the li element for the *Dropdown* item.

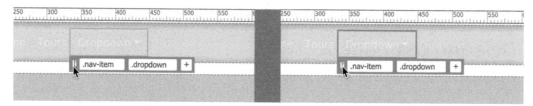

Note that the element border changes to blue. This means the element is selected instead of the content.

4   Press Delete.

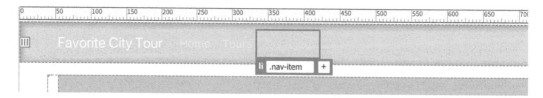

The *Dropdown* menu item and its child markup are deleted entirely from the page. Once the selected element is gone, the Element Display automatically highlights the *Disabled* menu item. A blue border appears around the element.

Note that this menu item is a lighter color than the other items. This is due to a special `.disabled` class applied to it. If you delete the class, the element's formatting will conform to the rest of the menu items.

The `.disabled` class is applied to the `<a>` element. But that element is not visible in Live view or in the tag selectors. There are several ways to select a child element in Live view when it doesn't appear in the interface. If you see the blue border in Live view, you can use the DOM selection method we used earlier.

5  Press the down arrow on the keyboard.

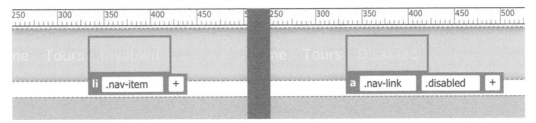

The focus of the Element Display changes to target the `<a>` element. Now you can see the `.disabled` class in the Element Display.

6  Click the Remove Class/ID icon ✕ for the `.disabled` class in the Element Display.

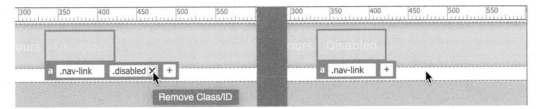

Once the class is removed, the formatting of the *Disabled* menu item conforms to the others.

7  Double-click the text *Disabled*.
   Type `Cruises`

This third menu item is now complete. Before we create any of the missing menu items, let's clean up the rest of the navbar. The mockup doesn't contain a search box, so you might as well get rid of it.

8  Select the Search button.

By examining the tag selectors, you can see that the button is part of a larger component. It's composed of three HTML elements: `form`, `input`, and `button`. The `form` element is the parent.

9  Select the `form` tag selector.

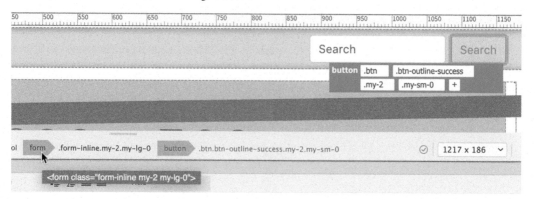

The Element Display appears focused on the `form` element, with an orange border.

10  Click the Element Display.

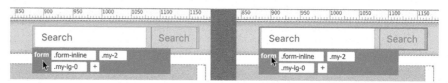

The border changes to blue.

11  Press Delete.

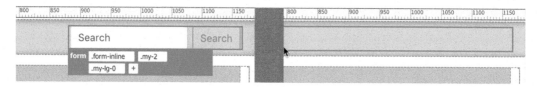

The entire Search form is deleted.

You have deleted the search component and created three menu items; you have three more to go. Let's finish the menu by creating the missing items.

## Inserting new menu items

As you learned in the previous exercise, the horizontal menu is composed of an unordered list. Adding new menu items is simple in Dreamweaver.

1  Select the third menu item, *Cruises*, in the document window.

In most cases, when you select an item in a menu like this, Dreamweaver will focus on the `<a>` element and display an orange border. Note the `.navlink` class assigned to it.

2  Press the Esc key.

The focus of Live view changes from the content of the selection to the element itself. To create a new menu item, you have to duplicate the current HTML structure.

3  Press the up arrow.

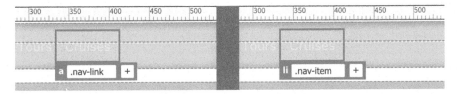

The Element Display now focuses on the li element. Note the .nav-item assigned to it.

Dreamweaver provides several ways to create new menu items.

4  Select Insert > List Item.

The Position Assist dialog appears.

5  Select After.

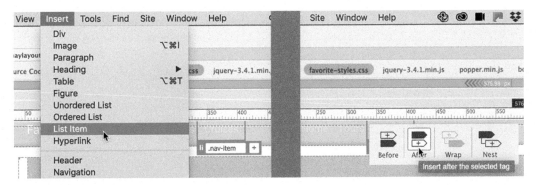

A new menu item appears with placeholder text.

6  Select the placeholder text *Content for li Goes Here.*
   Type Events

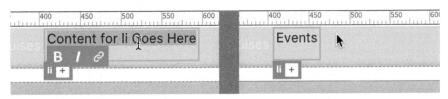

This menu item doesn't look like any of the others at the moment, but that can be quickly rectified. The other menu items are assigned a class of .nav-item.

7   Click the Add Class/ID icon ⊞ in the Element Display.

8   Type `.nav-item` and press Enter/Return.

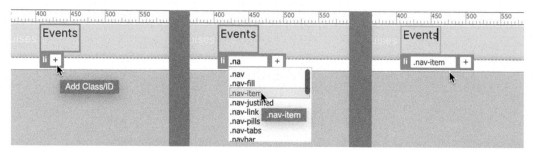

As you type, the hinting menu will display classes that are already defined in the document or style sheets. Feel free to select the proper class when you see it in the list.

The new menu item doesn't match the formatting of the other items. It's still missing a component—the menu item needs a hyperlink. Although there's nothing to link the item to, you can use the hash (#) symbol to create a link placeholder.

9   Select the text *Events*.

The Text Display appears. This dialog enables you to apply bolding, italics, and hyperlinks to a selection.

10  Click the Add Link icon ✐.
    Type # and press Enter/Return.

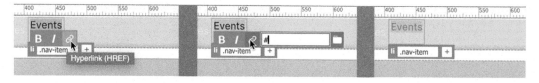

The Element Display should focus on the new <a> element. If not, you will have to select it.

11  Click the text *Events* to select the <a> element.
    Click the Add Class/ID icon in the Element Display.

**12** Type `.nav-link` and press Enter/Return.

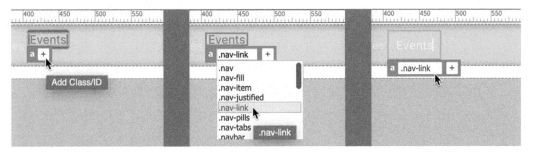

Once the class is applied, the new link matches the appearance of the other links.

You can also create new menu items using the DOM panel.

# Creating new elements with the DOM panel

The DOM panel depicts the entire HTML structure of the page, including classes and ids, but ignores the content. The functionality doesn't stop there. It also enables you to manipulate the page structure by editing, moving, deleting, and even creating new elements.

**1** If necessary, choose Window > DOM.

The DOM panel focuses on the element selected in the document window. The menu item for the *Events* `<a>` element should be highlighted from the last exercise. To insert another item, you first have to select the `<li>` element.

**2** Select the last `<li>` element in the panel.

**Note:** The instructions assume you are continuing directly from the previous exercise. If you are starting fresh, you will need to select the **Events** menu item in the Live view document window before proceeding.

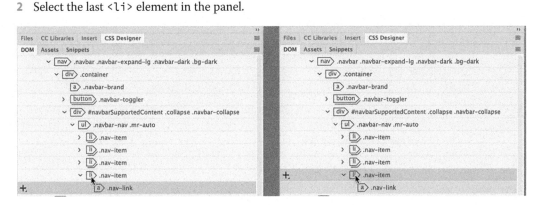

**3** Click the Add Element icon ➕ in the DOM panel.

4  Select Insert After.

A new `<div>` element appears in the DOM panel. The item is highlighted and still editable. If you press Enter/Return, the new element will be created. But we need an `<li>` element instead.

5  Type `li` and press Tab.

The `div` is replaced by `li`. The cursor moves to the attribute field.

The DOM panel allows you to create HTML elements as well as classes and ids.

6  Type `.nav-item` and press Enter/Return.

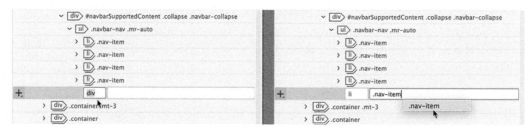

The new menu item with placeholder text appears in the document window.

7  Select the placeholder text.

Type `Contact US`

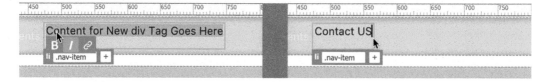

8  Select the text *Contact US*.

The Text Display appears.

9  Click the Link icon 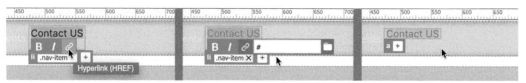.

Type `#` and press Enter/Return.

**10** Apply the class `.nav-link` to the `<a>` element.

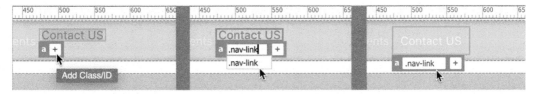

The *Contact Us* item is fully formatted. There's one item left to make. By far the easiest method for creating menu items is using copy and paste.

# Creating menu items with copy and paste

As you can see, there are a lot of tedious steps to creating a new menu item. By using copy and paste, you can cut the grunge work dramatically.

**1** Select the *Contact Us* menu item.

**2** Select the `li` tag selector.

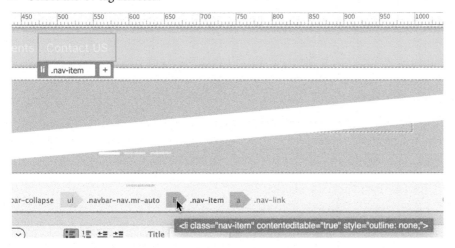

The Element Display appears focused on the `li`, with an orange border around the element.

**3** Press the Esc key.

▶ **Tip:** If the Esc key does not switch the border to blue, you can click on the Element Display.

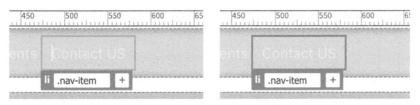

The border changes from orange to blue, indicating that the element is now selected.

4   Right-click the *Contact Us* Element Display.
Choose Copy from the context menu.

  ● **Note:** Make sure the cursor is over the Element Display label when using the context menu. Sometimes the focus can change to the <a> element and will cause an error when you paste.

When an element is selected in the document window, the Paste command inserts the new element directly after the selection as a sibling.

5   Right-click the *Contact Us* Element Display.
Choose Paste from the context menu.

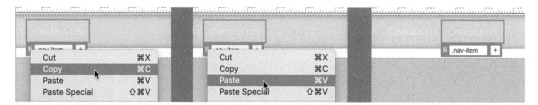

● **Note:** As before, make sure the cursor is over the Element Display label when you select Paste from the context menu.

A copy of the *Contact Us* menu item appears beside the original and is identically formatted.

6   Double-click the word *Contact* in the new menu item.

7   Type **About** and press the Esc key.

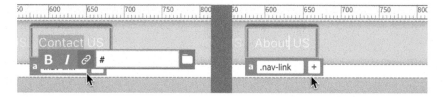

The final menu item is complete.

8   Choose File > Save All.

Now that the content of the menu is finished, you can concentrate on formatting the text and buttons in the menu.

## Extracting text styling

The text appearing in the navbar is formatted in white. This color was fine when the navbar had a black background, but white is not as effective on top of yellow. In this exercise, you will learn how to use the Extract panel to pick up from the mockup the text styling as well as the formatting for the buttons themselves.

Before you can apply any styling from the mockup, you need to have someplace to paste it. The Bootstrap style sheet is read-only, which means you'll have to create the rules before you can bring over the CSS.

1 If necessary, open **mylayout.html**. Make sure the document window is at least 1200 pixels wide.

2 Select one of the text items in the navigation menu.

The menu is composed of five types of HTML elements: `nav`, `div`, `ul`, `li`, and a. Text styling can be applied to any of these elements or even to all five at once. The goal is to have the styling from the mockup override the settings from the Bootstrap style sheet.

**Note:** When selecting the text, make sure that Dreamweaver focuses on the `<a>` element. Often, it takes two or more clicks to get the focus on the correct element.

3 Click the Current button in the CSS Designer.

The Selectors pane displays the CSS rules that affect the selected text. The rule at the top of the list is the most powerful. That's the one you usually want to target.

Notice that the Sources pane shows **bootstrap-4.3.1.css** in bold, which means that all the rules formatting the selected element are stored therein.

**Note:** The version of Bootstrap may change without notice.

Although the rule at the top of the Selectors pane is the most powerful, it's not necessarily the one formatting the selected element. Dynamic elements, such as navigation menus, by default have four separate states formatted by CSS: link, visited, hover, and active. You'll learn more about this in Lesson 10, "Working with Navigation." For now, you need to extract the default, or link, state of the menu items.

4 Right-click the selector
`.navbar-dark .navbar-nav .nav-link`.

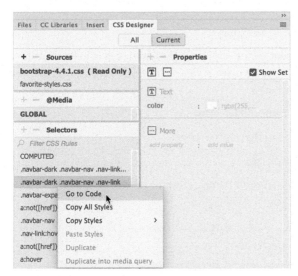

The context menu appears showing several commands, most of which are grayed out. If the Bootstrap style sheet were not read-only, you could use Duplicate to reproduce the needed selector in **favorite-styles.css**. Instead, we'll work around this limitation to achieve the same result.

**5** Choose Go To Code from the context menu.

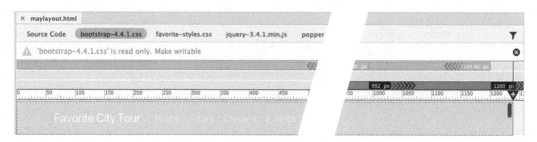

● **Note:** Some
Windows users report
that the Bootstrap style
sheet is not marked
Read Only.

The document window splits horizontally, displaying the Bootstrap style sheet in a Code view window at the bottom and focusing on the targeted rule. You may need to scroll up a bit to see the selector. At the top of the document window, a message appears indicating that the Bootstrap style sheet is locked. It provides an option to make the style sheet writeable.

**6** Select and copy the selector name.

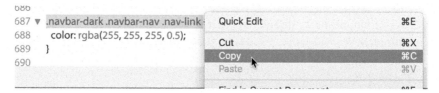

You have copied the selector that formats the default state of the menu items. Now you need to re-create it in **favorite-styles.css**.

**7** Click the All button in CSS Designer.

The focus of the document window is on Code view, which is looking at the Bootstrap style sheet. To see **favorite-styles.css** in CSS Designer, you'll have to set the focus back to Live view.

**8** Select any of the menu items in Live view.

**9** Select **favorite-styles.css** in the Sources pane.

**10** Click the Add Selector icon **+**.

A field opens for the new selector name. A sample selector appears automatically.

**11** Press Ctrl+V/Cmd+V to replace the selector.

The selector copied in step 6 appears in the field.

**12** Press Enter/Return to complete the selector.

Now you're ready to bring over the text formatting from the mockup.

**13** In the Extract panel, select any of the text items in the navigation menu.

The pop-up window appears, showing extraction options for the selection.

**14** If necessary, deselect all specifications except `font-family` and `color`.

**15** Click the Copy CSS button.

Once the CSS specifications are copied from the mockup, you have to identify the rules in the template that format the text in the menu items. This can be tricky because text styling can be very complex. Often, several rules may affect a single text element. This doesn't mean you can't successfully format an item; it just means you have to be especially vigilant when applying the new styling.

**16** Right-click and select Paste Styles on the rule created in step 12.

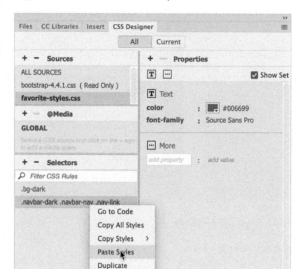

The Properties pane displays the specifications for font-family and color. The text styling in the six menu items now matches the mockup. The next task is to format the menu buttons.

# Creating a gradient background using Extract

Although you might not be able to discern this from the tiny Extract panel preview, the buttons in the navbar have a gradient background. The gradient shows darker yellow at the top, changing to a lighter yellow at the bottom.

As with the menu text, you have to identify the rules that create any type of background color for the menu items. In most cases, such formatting will be applied to the <li> or <a> elements.

**1** If necessary, open **mylayout.html** from the lesson06 folder in Live view. Make sure the document window is at least 1200 pixels wide.

**2** Select any of the items in the horizontal menu.

Typically, the <a> element will be selected by default. Since the <a> element is the child of the <li>, you can inspect all the styles applied to a menu item by selecting that element.

3  Click the a tag selector.

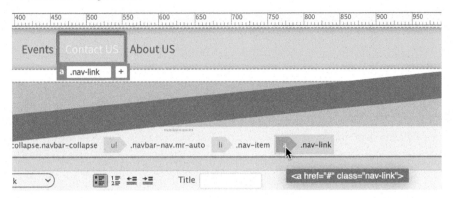

4  Click the Current button.

5  Choose Show Set in CSS Designer, if necessary.

6  Click each of the rules starting at the top of the Selectors pane.

As you inspect each rule, the Properties pane displays any style applied to the menu structure. It starts on the `<a>` element but will eventually show you styles applied to the `<li>` and `<ul>` elements too. Look for any background properties.

After examining each rule, you will discover that no background properties are set on any of the menu elements. You can use either the `<li>` or `<a>` elements. Let's apply the button styling to the `<li>`.

The first step is to create a rule to which you can apply the style. Use the following procedure to ensure the new rule is created properly.

7  Click the `li` tag selector.

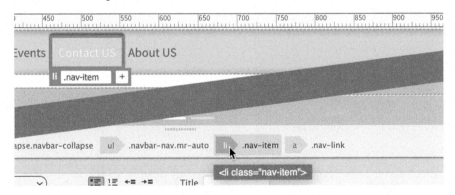

8  Click the All button in CSS Designer.

9  In the Sources pane, select **favorite-styles.css**.

**10** Click the Add Selector icon ➕.

The selector field opens, populated by a custom selector written by Dreamweaver. By default, these names are very specific. By pressing the up and down arrows on the keyboard, you can change the specificity. Although you want the selector to target the menu items, it doesn't need to be overly long.

**Note:** In some instances, you may have to press the down arrow to achieve the desired selector.

**11** Press the up arrow until the following selector appears:
`.navbar-nav.mr-auto .nav-item`

**12** Edit the selector to `.navbar-nav .nav-item` and press Enter/Return.

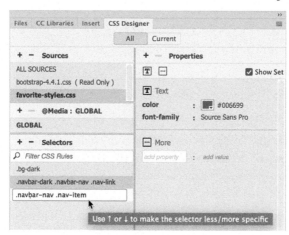

The rule is now ready for the button formatting.

**13** If necessary, choose Window > Extract.
Select **favoritecity-mockup.psd**.

**14** Select any of the menu buttons in the mockup.

You will bring over the background and border styling.

**15** If necessary, select width but deselect height in the pop-up window.

**16** Click the Copy CSS button.

**17** Right-click the rule `.navbar-nav .nav-item` and choose Paste Styles from the context menu.

The styles copied from the mockup appear in the Properties pane. The individual menu items display a gradient background, a distinct border, and a consistent width that appear similar to the mockup. But the buttons still need a bit of tweaking.

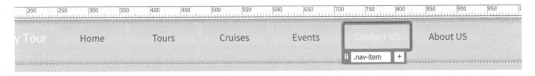

**18** In CSS Designer, deselect the Show Set option.

When Show Set is deselected, the Properties pane shows a full list of CSS properties you can apply to an element. The rule `.navbar-nav .nav-item` should still be selected.

The mockup shows a bit of space between the buttons, but that kind of styling isn't supported by Photoshop. You'll have to create it yourself.

**19** Click the Layout icon 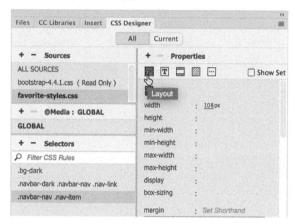.

**20** Insert **4px** in the left and right margin properties.

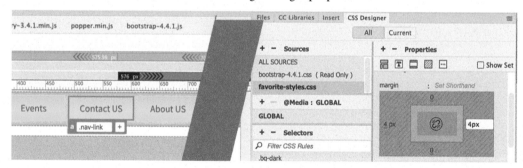

**21** Click the Text icon **T**.

**22** Choose `text-align: center`.

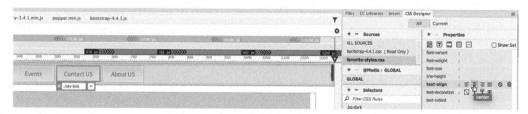

The text aligns to the center within the buttons.

**23** Choose File > Save All.

The navigation menu is done for now. The next component of the mockup is the logo image. Typically, such images are inserted in a `<header>` element. Since the Bootstrap template doesn't have one, you'll have to add it yourself.

## Extracting image assets from a mockup

The company logo appears below the navigation menu. You will extract the image from the mockup and create a new `<header>` element to contain it.

1   In the Extract panel, select the logo image.

Although the logo image is selected, don't assume Extract will export only the image. If the image is part of a Photoshop group that includes the text or other effects, it will export those as well. It's a good idea to check how the image is constructed. Don't worry, you don't need Photoshop to discover the composition of the selected element. Extract can read and display the contents of the layers in the Photoshop file.

2   Click the Layers button.

Note the selected layer in the panel. The logo is part of the *Header* layer, which includes the company name and motto. If the Header layer is selected, Extract will create an image that would include the text too. In some cases, that would be desirable, but not here. By inserting the text in the webpage, search engines can index it and perhaps improve your result ranking.

3 If necessary, select the *favcity-logo* layer.

4 Click the Extract Asset icon ⬇ in the layer.

● **Note:** If you set up the default images folder in the advanced settings of the Site Definition dialog, the site image folder will already be targeted.

A pop-up window appears in the Extract panel that enables you to name the image, choose what type of image you want to create, and choose where you want it to be saved. In Lesson 9, "Working with Images," you will learn all about web-compatible images and how to work with them. For this exercise, you will create a JPEG file.

5 If necessary, in the pop-up window Folder field, select the lesson06 images folder.

The Save As name field in the pop-up window should show `favcity-logo`. The name comes from the Photoshop layer. If the field shows any other name, make sure you don't have the wrong layer selected.

6 Click the JPG button.

● **Note:** The Extract panel is able to create only PNG and JPEG image types.

**7** If necessary, set the Optimize option to `80`.

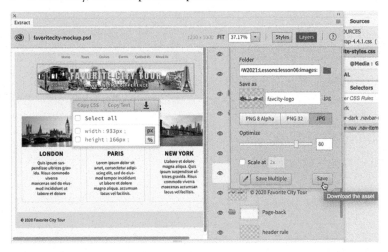

**8** Click Save.

If you set up the images folder when defining the lesson06 site, the logo image will be saved to it automatically. Now you're ready to create the `<header>` element.

# Creating new Bootstrap structures

As you can see from the mockup, the header, like the navbar, stretches across the entire screen. The other page components don't. Bootstrap uses a row and column metaphor to divide up the screen. By adding another row to the navbar, the header would automatically assume the same width.

Dreamweaver makes adding new rows to Bootstrap components a simple point-and-click process.

**1** Select any of the menu items in the navbar.

**2** Select the `nav` tag selector.

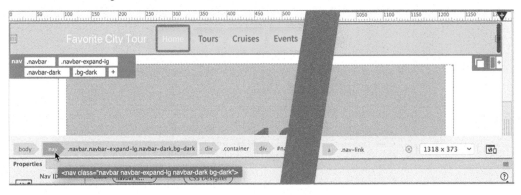

The Element Display appears focused on the `nav` element.

3   Click the Element Display or press the Esc key.
    Choose Window > Insert.

    The Insert panel appears.

4   In the Insert panel, select Bootstrap Components from the dropdown menu.

    The Bootstrap category enables you to add a variety of components to your layouts. All of them are designed to support desktops, tablets, and phones right out of the box.

5   Click Grid Row With Column.

    The Position Assist dialog appears.

6   Click After.
    In the No. Of Columns To Add field, enter 1

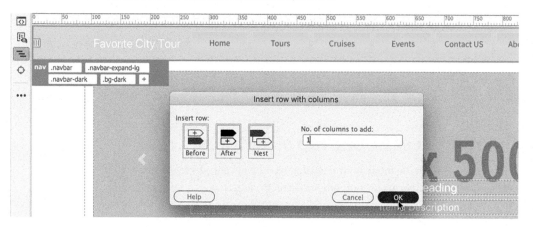

7   Click OK.

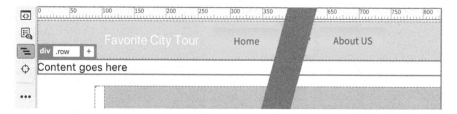

    A new `div.row` element appears below the navbar with placeholder text.

    Although a `<div>` is a perfectly acceptable element, there's a slight semantic value in using the HTML5 `header` element.

8   Press Ctrl+T/Cmd+T.

    The Quick Tag Editor appears.

9  Replace `div` with **header** and press Enter/Return.

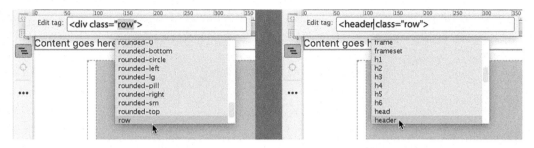

The `div.row` is now `header.row`.

10  Select the placeholder text.
Type `FAVORITE CITY TOUR`

The text has no HTML element applied to it. Semantically, the company name should be formatted as a heading. Best practices say that pages should have only one `h1` heading, and it should be reserved for the main page heading. So for the company name, you'll use an `h2` instead. The easiest way to format text is using the Property inspector.

11  Choose Window > Properties.
In the Properties panel Format field, select `Heading 2`.

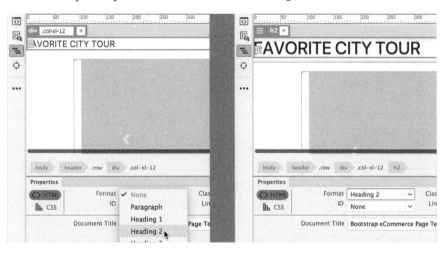

● **Note:** If the Property inspector appears as a floating panel, feel free to dock it to the bottom of the document window.

12  In the Extract panel, click the Layers button to close the Layers panel and select the company name.

**13** Deselect `font-weight` and `line-height`.
Click the Copy CSS button.

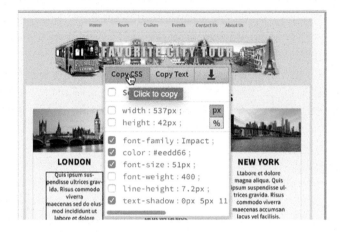

Once the styles are copied, you need to create a rule for the company name.

**14** In CSS Designer, select **favorite-style.css**.
Create a new selector: `header h2`
Paste the styles copied in step 13.

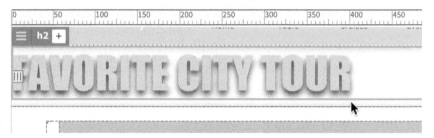

The text is formatted nicely but aligned to the left.

**15** If necessary, select the rule `header h2`.

**16** In CSS Designer, click the Text icon.

**17** Choose `text-align: center`.

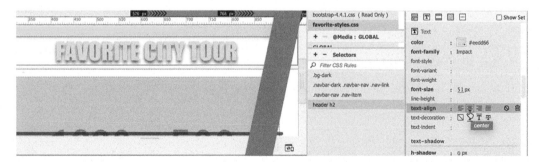

18 In the Extract panel, select the motto TRAVEL WITH A DIFFERENCE. Deselect `line-height` and copy the CSS.

19 Insert the cursor at the end of the company name.

20 Press Enter/Return to create a new line.

21 Type `TRAVEL WITH A DIFFERENCE`

22 Create a new rule: `header p`

23 Paste the styles on the new rule.
Add the property `text-align: center`

The text in the header is complete. It may need some tweaking, but let's move on for now.

24 Choose File > Save **All**.

Next you will apply the company logo as a background image.

## Adding a background image to the header

The company name and motto cannot appear in the same space unless the text is added to the image itself or unless the image is inserted as a background property. Backgrounds can be composed of one or more images and at least one overall color. When layering more than one effect, you have to make sure you order the properties correctly.

1 If necessary, open **mylayout.html** in Live view and make sure the document window is at least 1200 pixels wide.

2 In CSS Designer, make sure the All button is selected. Deselect Show Set, if necessary.

3 Create the following rule: `header`

4 Click the Background icon ▨ in the new rule.

5  Click the `background-color` color picker.
   Enter `#ED5` in the `color` field.
   Press Enter/Return.

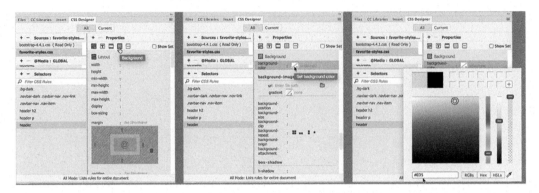

The `<header>` displays a background color matching the navbar. Let's add the logo image now.

6  Click the Browse icon 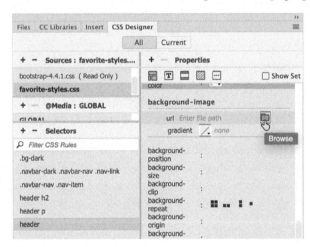 in the `background-image` property.

7  Select **favcity-logo.jpg** from the lesson06 images folder. Click Open.

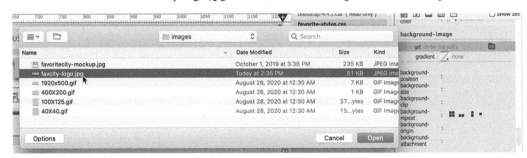

The logo image appears in the header, but it's cut off at the bottom and is repeating horizontally. By default, background images repeat horizontally and vertically. In some cases, a repeating background is desirable, but not here. A few CSS tweaks should make the background look great.

8  In the rule `header` add the following properties:

```
background-position: center center
background-repeat: no-repeat
background-size: 80% auto
```

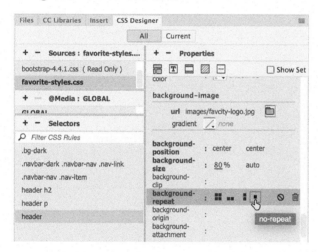

The background image looks better, but it's still cut off at the top and bottom.

9  Click the Layout icon 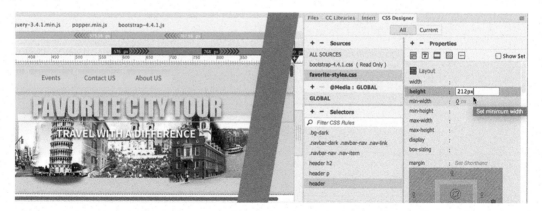.

10  In rule `header` add the following property:

```
height: 212px
```

The header expands to display the logo fully. The company name and motto are not centered vertically over the background image. Another tweak to the text elements and the `header` will be complete for now.

**11** In the rule `header h2` edit or add the following properties:

```
margin-top: 1em
font-size 350%
line-height: 1em
letter-spacing: 0.12em
```

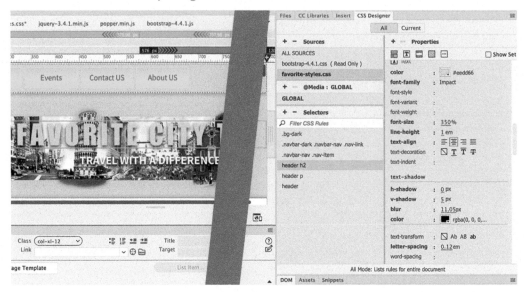

These specifications bring the company name more into alignment with the mockup. A further tweak to the motto should finish the job.

**12** In the rule `header p` edit or add the following properties:

```
font-size: 150%
line-height: 1em
letter-spacing: 0.4em
```

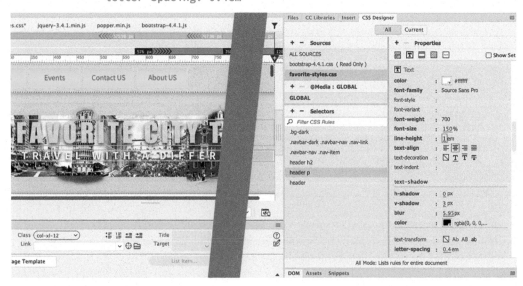

The motto appears over the background image and is spaced out as it appears in the mockup. There's one last chore to take care of to finish the header.

In the mockup, a light yellow line separates the navbar from the header. The line does not extend all the way to the edges, so you need to identify an element that has the same properties.

The header extends from edge to edge, but the horizontal menu doesn't. That should give you a good suggestion.

13 Click one of the menu items.

The `div.container` encompasses the entire navbar and looks like a good candidate for a border.

14 Select the `div.container` tag selector.

The Element Display appears. Note that the selection does not extend to the left and right edges.

15 Create the following rule: `nav .container`

Don't forget to add the space after the `nav` element.

16 Add the following properties to the new rule:
```
padding-bottom: 10px
border-bottom: 2px solid #FF3
```

The header is complete and formatted for desktop screens.

17 Choose File > Save All.

In upcoming lessons, you will learn how to adapt and format various page components for desktop screens, smartphones, and tablets.

# Finishing up the layout

There are still a few specifications that need to be applied to the layout. The rest of the work should go pretty quickly.

1   If necessary, open **mylayout.html** in Live view. Make sure the document window is at least 1200 pixels wide.

In the mockup, there are wide borders on the left and right sides of the layout. Since the borders extend to the edges of the screen, the body element is a good target for this styling.

2   In **favorite-styles.css**, create the following rule:

```
body
```

3   Create the following properties in the body rule:

```
border-right: 15px solid #ED5
border-left: 15px solid #ED5
```

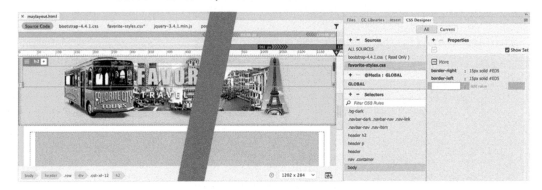

Large borders appear on the left and right sides of the layout.

You will deal with the main content of the page in the next lesson. For this lesson, the last part of the layout you need to address is the footer. First, let's bring over the text from the mockup.

4   Select and copy the footer text in the Extract panel.

5   In **mylayout.html**, select the text in the footer and paste to replace it.

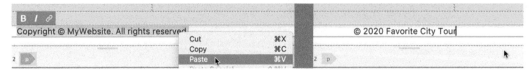

The text in the footer is aligned to the center. By default, text aligns to the left in HTML. So that means something is overriding the default behavior.

6   Select the `footer` tag selector.
Note the class assigned to the `footer` element.

The class `.text-center` applies the styling.

7  Remove the class `.text-center` from the `footer` element.

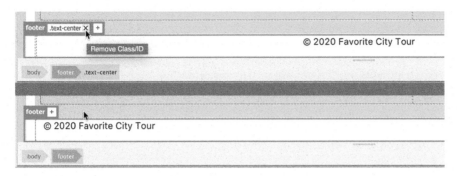

The text now aligns to the left. The last step is to apply the background color.

8  In **favorite-styles.css**, create the following rule:

```
footer
```

9  Create the following properties in the `footer` rule:

```
padding-top: 5px
color: #069
background-color: #ED5
```

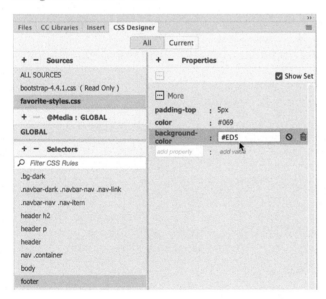

10 Choose File > Save All.

Congratulations! You have learned how to extract styles from a Photoshop mockup and apply them to a predefined Bootstrap template. As you work through the upcoming lessons, you will continue to tweak and format the content and learn a variety of HTML and CSS tricks. In the next lesson, you will turn this Bootstrap starter layout into your Dreamweaver site template.

## Review questions

1 Does Dreamweaver provide any design assistance for beginners?

2 What advantages do you get from using a responsive starter layout?

3 What does the Extract panel enable you to do?

4 Does Extract enable you to download GIF image assets?

5 True or False. All the CSS properties generated by the Extract panel are accurate and are all you need to style a webpage and its content.

6 How many background images can you apply to an element?

## Review answers

1 Dreamweaver CC (2021 release) provides three basic layouts, six Bootstrap templates, four email templates, and three responsive starter layouts.

2 Responsive starter layouts help you jumpstart the design of a site or layout by providing a finished layout complete with predefined CSS and placeholder content.

3 The Extract panel enables you to derive CSS styling, text content, and even image assets from page mockups created in Adobe Photoshop and Adobe Illustrator.

4 No. Extract supports only the PNG and JPEG image formats.

5 False. Although many of the CSS properties are perfectly usable, styling in Photoshop and Illustrator is geared for print output and may not be entirely suitable for web applications.

6 CSS can apply several background images but only one background color.

# 7
# WORKING WITH TEMPLATES

## Lesson overview

In this lesson, you'll learn how to work faster, make updating easier, and be more productive. You'll learn how to do the following:

- Create a Dreamweaver template.
- Insert editable regions.
- Produce child pages.
- Update templates and child pages.

 This lesson will take about 2 hours to complete. To get the lesson files used in this lesson, download them from the webpage for this book at www.adobepress.com/DreamweaverCIB2021. For more information, see "Accessing the lesson files and Web Edition" in the "Getting Started" section at the beginning of this book.

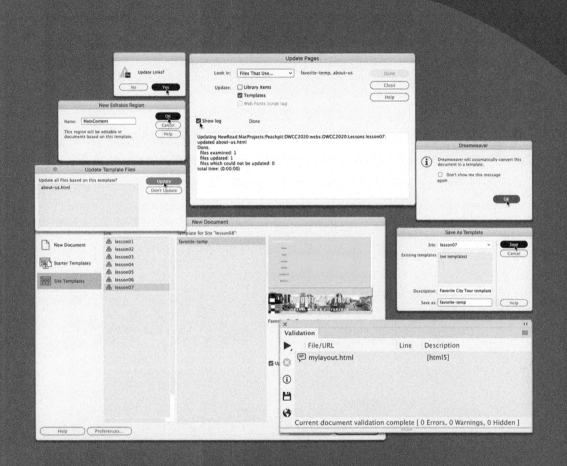

Dreamweaver's site-management capabilities and productivity tools are among its most useful features for a busy designer.

# Creating Dreamweaver templates

A template is a type of master page from which you can create related child pages. Templates are useful for setting up and maintaining the overall look and feel of a website while providing a means for quickly and easily producing site content. A template is different from a regular HTML page in Dreamweaver.

In a normal webpage, Dreamweaver can edit the entire page. In a template, designated areas are locked and cannot be edited. Templates enable a workgroup environment in which page content can be created and edited by several team members, while the web designer controls the page design and the specific elements that must remain unchanged.

Let's take a look at the sample layout and identify the areas that will be locked and the ones that will be editable.

1 Launch Dreamweaver CC (2021 release) or later.

2 Open **mylayout.html** in Live view from the lesson07 folder. Make sure the document window is at least 1200 pixels wide.

3 Examine the layout top to bottom.

The page is divided into areas that focus on different purposes, such as navigation, corporate identity, editorial content, contact information, and copyright notice. These elements are repeated and remain the same on most pages of a website.

Many people call these elements *boilerplate* because they compose the basic structure of each page.

In this template, there are three different types of content models: an image carousel, a card-based section that focuses on images, and a list-based section that focuses on text. These elements will contain the editorial content.

The editorial content is the only thing that will change on each page. The boilerplate areas will be locked and uneditable inside Dreamweaver on pages created from the template.

When the layout is converted into a Dreamweaver template, the section containing the editorial content will be designated an *editable region.* But before we do this, you have some work to do. The current layout is too busy. A template needs to be stripped down to the minimum essential components.

## Removing unneeded components

A template should be pared down to the fewest possible basic elements, or *placeholders.* This will minimize any cleanup work when creating child pages. Let's start with the card-based section.

If your document window is at least 1200 pixels in width, you will see six card elements in two rows. You will use these elements to build tour descriptions in an upcoming lesson. But there's no reason to keep all six elements in the template. One row would be sufficient in the template.

1 Select the 400 x 200 image placeholder in the first element in the second row.

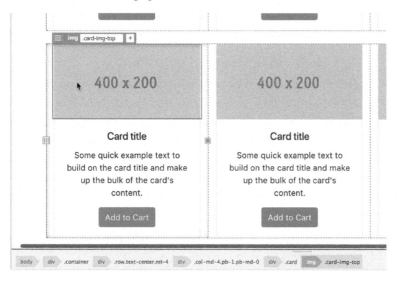

The Element Display appears focused on the `<img>` element.

If you examine the tag selectors, you can see that the image placeholder has four div parents. Using the tag selectors is one of the best ways to divide the structure of your HTML content.

2  Select the first parent of the image placeholder, div.card.

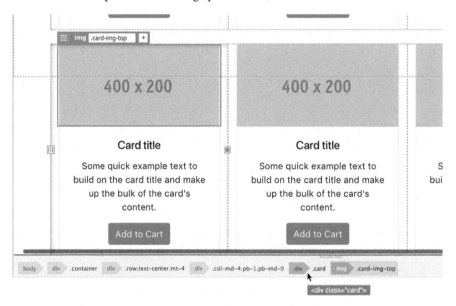

The Element Display changes focus to div.card. You can see by the blue border that most of the first card element is selected. The objective is to select the entire row of elements.

3  Select the div.col-md-4.pb-1.pb-md-0 tag selector.

This tag selector highlights the entire first card.

4  Select the div.row.text-center.mt-4 tag selector.

The entire second row is now selected, but you can see that there is still one more tag selector.

5  Select div.container.

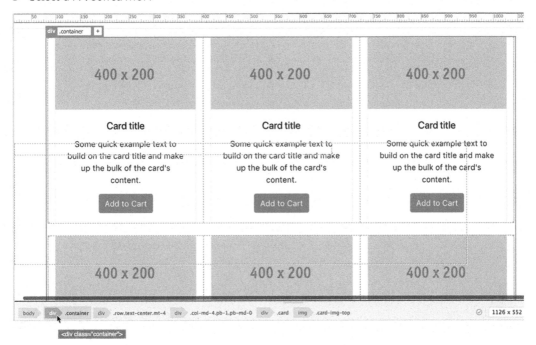

This tag selector highlights the entire card section. We went too far and need to go back to the last selection. In most cases the last tag selector is still visible.

6  Select the div.row.text-center.mt-4 tag selector.
If you don't see the previous tag selector, repeat steps 1–4 to select the proper tag.

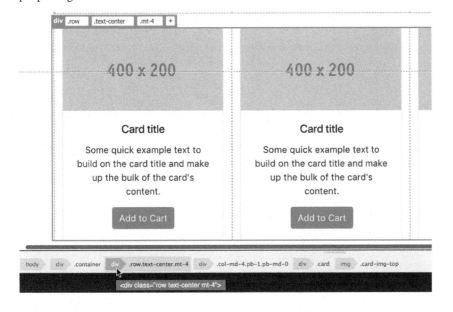

The entire second row is selected again.

7 Press the Delete key.

● **Note:** When deleting elements, be sure the element displays a blue border. An orange border indicates that only the copy within the element is selected and not the element itself.

The row is deleted, leaving only one row of placeholders in the card section. Let's move to the list-based content.

The list-based section is built differently from the card-base one. Deleting the extraneous elements will require a slightly different procedure, but it still starts with the tag selectors. There are three rows of elements in this section. The goal is to have only one row when you're finished.

8 Select the image placeholder on the first element in the third row.

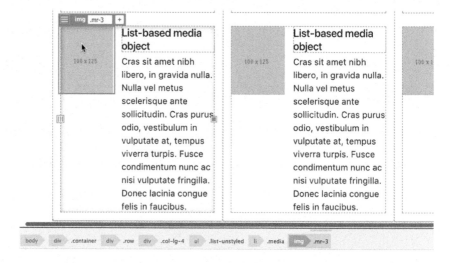

As you can see from the tag selectors, the image placeholder is part of an unordered list. But you can't remove the third row by deleting the list itself.

9  Select the ul tag selector.

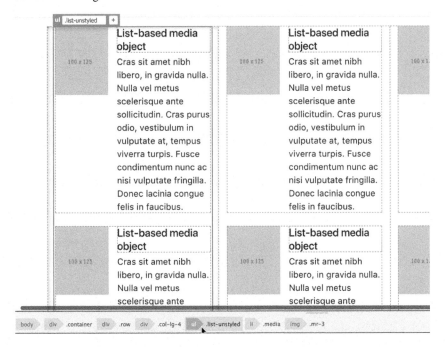

The Element Display highlights the first whole column of the list-based section. The three rows are actually three unordered lists, each with three list items stacked vertically. To delete the second and third rows, you'll have to delete the last two items in each list.

As before, the li tag selector from the third item in the first column should still be visible.

10  Select the li tag selector and press Delete.

▶ **Tip:** If you do not see the li tag selector, you may need to repeat the selection process starting in step 8.

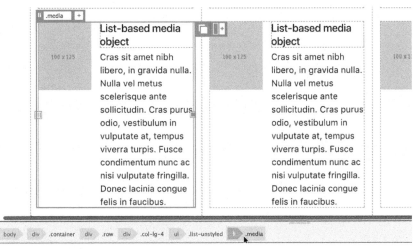

The third item in the first column is deleted.

**11** Repeat step 10 to delete the second and third list items in each column.

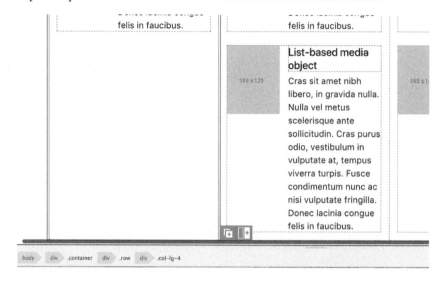

The list-based section now shows one row of elements. Let's turn to the bottom of the layout now.

Above the footer is a section containing three columns of links and an address block.

**12** Click the last link anchor in the first column.
Examine the tag selectors.

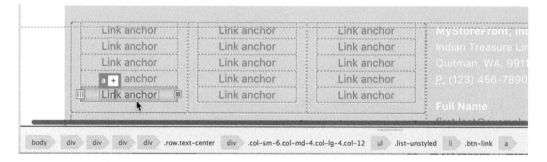

As with the list-based section, the links are contained in three columns of unordered lists.

In Live view, to end up with only one link per column, you'll have to delete the extraneous links one at a time. The DOM panel offers a quicker way.

**13** If necessary, choose Window > DOM to display the DOM panel.

**14** Select the li tag selector.

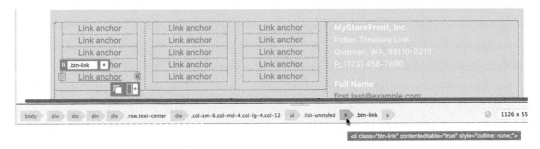

Because you selected the list item in the document window, the DOM panel focuses on that element. You should see the last item selected in the panel.

**15** Hold the Shift key and click the second item in the list.

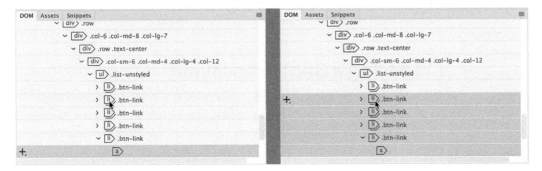

Four of the list items are highlighted.

**16** Press Delete.

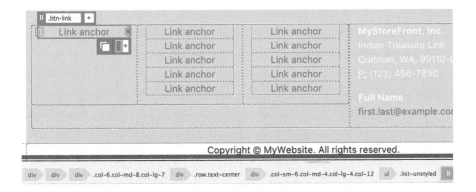

The selected list items are deleted.

**17** Repeat steps 14–16 to delete the unneeded links.

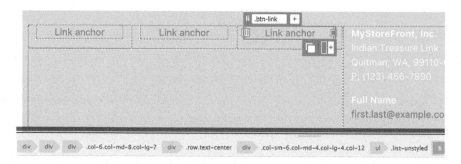

**18** Save the file.

With all the links deleted, there's now a large open space on the side of the page. It would nicer if the three links simply spanned the bottom of the page. In the next exercise, you'll learn how to reformat a Bootstrap layout.

## Modifying a Bootstrap layout

Bootstrap uses a row-and-column metaphor to control the way elements divide up the page. It's based on a 12-column grid in which each element is assigned a specific number of columns. But it doesn't stop there. You can also allocate the columns for each size screen that is viewing the page.

The assignments are made using predefined classes stored in the Bootstrap style sheet. The classes are normally given to div elements that are used to wrap the content. You can see these wrappers sprinkled through the layout you're currently working with. If you look carefully at the structure you were just editing in the DOM panel, you should be able to find the Bootstrap parent element of the three unordered lists.

**1** Select div.col-6.col-md-8.col-lg-7 in the DOM panel.

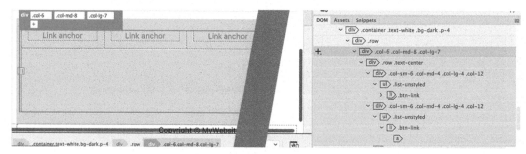

**2** Click the Current button in CSS Designer.
Select Show Set in the Properties pane.

In CSS Designer, you can see the classes assigned in the Selectors pane.

**3** Select the rule `.col-6`.

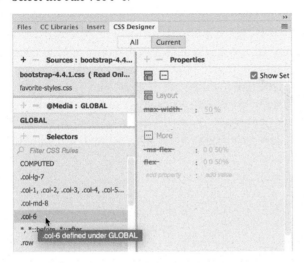

Can you guess what this rule formats? It sets the width of the `div` at six columns. Since Bootstrap uses a 12-column grid, the `div` will assume half the width of its parent element.

In the CSS Designer @Media pane, you can see that the GLOBAL reference is bolded. That means this rule sets the default size of the element. The `div` will be six columns wide no matter what size the screen is unless another rule overrides this style.

**4** Select the rule `.col-md-8`.

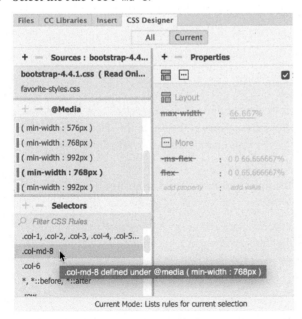

You probably already guessed that this rule sets the width of the div to eight columns. But the rule also has another modifier: md. The letters stand for "medium," or more precisely, medium-sized screens.

Once you know that Bootstrap uses a grid to divide the screen, the next question is: what size screen? Bootstrap answers that question by defining several default screen sizes: extra small (xs), small (sm), medium (md), and large (lg). You can see the sizes displayed in the @Media pane as you click each selector. When you clicked the rule .col-md-8, the media query (min-width:768) was bolded. That means this class is activated whenever the screen is at a minimum width of 768 pixels.

5   Select the rule .col-lg-7.

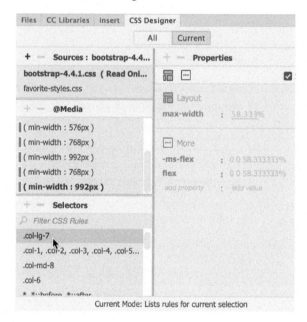

Current Mode: Lists rules for current selection

This rule sets the width to seven columns on *large* screens, or a minimum width of 992 pixels. Note that this rule appears at the top of the selectors list. Since the document window is at 1200 pixels or wider, this rule is being applied, overriding the others.

To change the width of the link section, you need to change the class applied to large screens.

6   In the Element Display, edit the class .col-lg-7.
Update the class as highlighted: .col-lg-12
Press Enter/Return to complete the change.

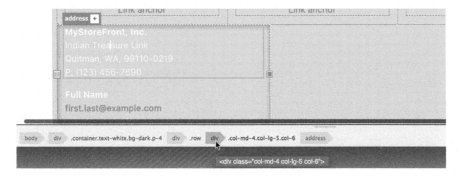

The link section now stretches across the entire bottom. Notice that the address section bumps down because it can't fit on the right side anymore, but it still occupies the same portion of the section as it did before.

That's the way Bootstrap works. Each element is assigned a number of columns and maintains that width regardless of what happens to the other elements. Let's adjust the width of the address block too.

7 Click the `address` element.

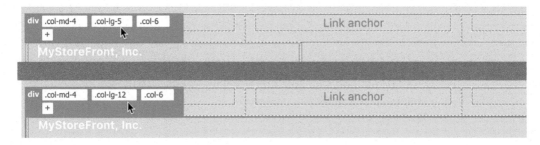

You should be able to see the Bootstrap wrapper in the tag selectors or the DOM panel.

8 Select the `div.col-md-4.col-lg-5.col-6` tag selector.

The address section is assigned five columns on large screens. To fill in the open space to the right, just edit the `lg` class as you did earlier.

9 Edit the class `.col-lg-5` as highlighted: `.col-lg-12`
Press Enter/Return to complete the change.

The change forces the wrapper to extend all the way across the layout. But there's a problem. Although the address section is wider, the line-by-line structure of the address itself still wastes a lot of space.

You may have noticed that the address section has two content elements. The top one is the street address and the bottom is an email address. Using Bootstrap classes, we could make the two elements split the available space side by side.

Although Bootstrap classes are usually assigned to separate div wrappers, there's nothing preventing you from applying the classes directly to an element.

10 Click the company address.
Select the address tag selector.

The Element Display appears focused on the address element.

11 Click the Add Class/ID icon ⊞.
Type .col-lg-6 and press Enter/Return.

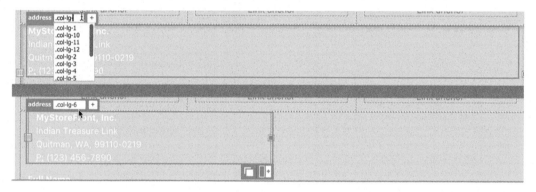

The address element resizes to half the width of the parent. Let's apply the same style to the email address.

12 Click the email address.
Select the address tag selector.

13 Add the class .col-lg-6 to the element.

The element width resizes to half the width of the parent. But there's a problem. The two address elements are still stacked vertically. The class assigned applies the proper width to the elements, but it doesn't control how they align on the page.

If you check the link or the other multicolumn sections, you will see they all have the class `.row` assigned to the wrapper element.

14 Select the `div.col-md-4.col-lg-12.col-6` tag selector.

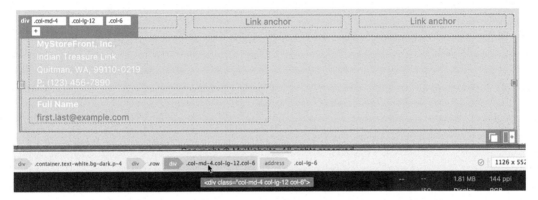

This `div` wraps the two address elements but does not feature the `.row` class.

15 Add the class `.row` to the `div` element.

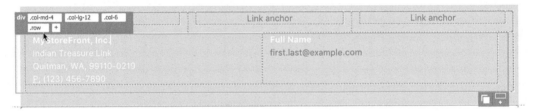

The two `address` elements now display side by side.

That takes care of the layout issues for the moment, but text in the address elements is still formatted for the original black background. A darker color would be more appropriate.

## Modifying text formatting in a Bootstrap element

If you want to change the formatting of content that is already styled, the first step is to identify any rules affecting that element.

1   Select any part of the company address.
    Select the `address` tag selector.

2   Click the Current button, if necessary.

    The Selectors pane displays all the rules styling the `address` element. Inspect the rules, starting at the top of the list and continuing until you find the rule applying the color.

The rule `.text-white` applies the color `#fff`, but that class is not applied to the `address` element. Let's find out where the class is assigned.

3  Examine the tag selectors interface to identify the element displaying the class `.text-white`.

The class appears on `div.container.text-white.bg-dark.p-4`, wrapping the link and address sections.

4  Select the `div.container.text-white.bg-dark.p-4` tag selector.

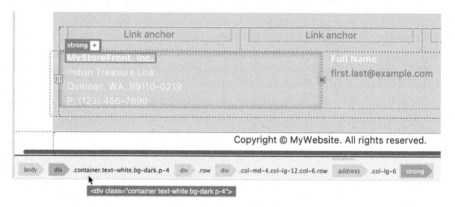

The area highlighted is formatted by the new logo color. There's no longer a need for the white text color, so you can simply delete the class `.text-white` altogether.

5  Click the Remove Class/ID icon ☒.

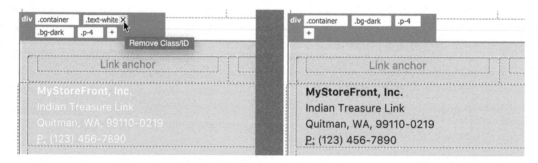

Once the class is removed, the address text displays in black. The site theme shows this text styled in blue. Changing the color will require a new rule.

6  Select the `address` tag selector.

7  In CSS Designer, click the All button.

8  Select **favorite-styles.css**.
   Click the Add Selector icon ✚.

   A custom selector name appears.

9  Create the following selector name: `address`

   This selector will target only the `address` elements.

10 Add the following property to the `address` rule:
   `color: #069`

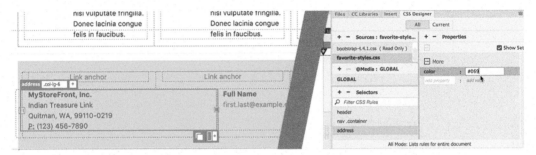

The text in the address elements displays in blue. The formatting of the layout matches the mockup now.

11 Choose File > Save All.

The last task before creating the Dreamweaver template is to complete any boilerplate and placeholder content.

## Adding template boilerplate and placeholders

Boilerplate and placeholder content should always be complete before converting a layout into a Dreamweaver template. Some boilerplate is already in place, as in the top navigation menu. Since the address block is visible now, let's start there.

1  Open **mylayout.html** in Live view from the lesson07 folder. Make sure the document window is at least 1200 pixels wide.

2  Select the text *MyStoreFront, Inc.* and type **Favorite City Tour** to replace it.

3  Select the text *Indian Treasure Link* and type **City Center Plaza** to replace it.

**4** Replace the text *Quitman, WA, 99110-0219* with
**Meredien, CA 95110-2704**

**5** Replace the phone number *(123) 456-7890* with
**(408) 555-1212**

The first `address` element is complete.

**6** Select the text *Full Name* and type
**Contact Us**

**7** Select the text *first.last@example.com* and type
**info@favoritecitytour.com**

The two `address` elements are complete. Let's move back to the top of the layout.

In the navigation menu, the company name is styled in white. You will deal with this styling when you learn more about hyperlinks in Lesson 10, "Working with Navigation." For now, let's leave it as it is. The next boilerplate appears below the image carousel in the phrases *Free Shipping*, *Free Returns*, and *Low Prices*.

Although no similar text appears in the mockup, these links provide an excellent opportunity to improve on the original concept design.

**8** Select the text *Free Shipping* and type
**Get a Quote**

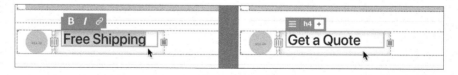

**9** Change *Free Returns* to **Book a Tour**
Change *Low Prices* to **Bargain Deals**

No reason to stop with these links.

**10** Select the headline RECOMMENDED PRODUCTS.
Type **INSERT HEADLINE HERE**

**11** In the first card element, select the text *Card title*.
Type **Product Name** to replace it.

**12** In the card description, select the text *Card title* and change it to **product name** and change *card's content* to **product description**

**13** Select the button text *Add to Cart*.
Type **Get More Info** to replace it.

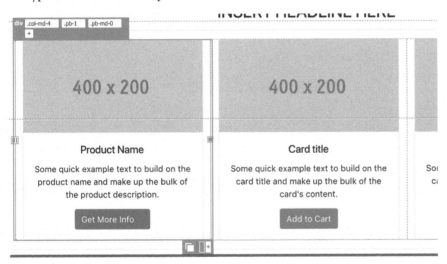

The first card element is complete.

**14** Repeat steps 11–13 on the remaining card elements.

▶ **Tip:** Feel free to copy and paste the entire description from the first item into the other two cards.

The three card elements are all updated.

**15** Select the headline FEATURED PRODUCTS.
Type **INSERT HEADLINE HERE**

**16** Select the text *List-based media object 1*.
Type **Insert Name Here**

**17** Repeat step 16 on the remaining list-based headings.

The text boilerplate is complete.

**18** Save all files.

A few things are still left to finish in the layout; some are visible, some not.

## Fixing semantic errors

With the development of HTML5, a lot of emphasis was placed on developing semantic rules around the code elements and the structures they build. Earlier, you added a semantic element, header, for the company name and logo. Other semantic elements are sprinkled throughout the layout. However, some elements in the current layout violate the spirit of the new rules.

Several horizontal rule <hr> elements in the layout are not used properly. Before HTML5, horizontal rules could be used as graphical elements and as dividers between content. No one really cared.

The new semantic rules define horizontal rules strictly as a content divider. The horizontal rules in this layout are being used incorrectly as graphical elements above and below the main headlines. They may be hard to see in the document window, so we'll use the DOM panel.

1   If necessary, open **mylayout.html** in Live view from the lesson07 folder. Make sure the document window is at least 1200 pixels wide.

2   Select the text INSERT HEADLINE HERE at the top of the layout.

3   Choose Window > DOM.

The h2 element is highlighted in the panel. Note the hr elements above and below the headline. The rule above the headline could meet the sematic criterion, but not the one below. In this instance, we won't keep either one.

4   Select and delete the hr elements in the DOM panel.

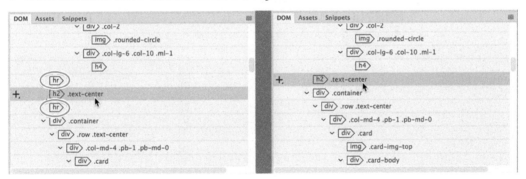

5   Select the headline at the bottom of the layout.
In the DOM panel, select and delete the two hr elements.

If you inspect the DOM panel, you will find one more hr element, near the footer. Let's remove this one too.

6   Select the hr element in the DOM panel and delete it.

All the hr elements have been removed.

When examining the DOM panel, you might have seen another borderline semantic issue. The headings for the content sections are sitting outside the wrapper containing the content that they introduce.

Although no visitor would see or notice this moving, having the headlines inside the wrappers would be more semantically correct. It will also pay dividends if you need to move or delete these sections.

7   Select the headline above the card-based section.

The h2 element is highlighted in the DOM panel. Note the `div.container` element directly below the heading. If the element is collapsed, you can expand it to reveal its structure.

8   If necessary, click the expand icon ❯ for `div.container`.

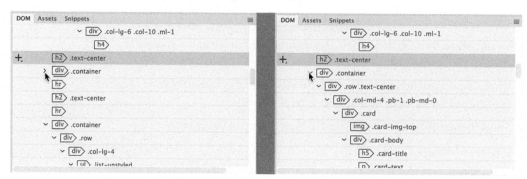

The structure of `div.container` is revealed. The DOM panel enables you to add, edit, delete, or rearrange the HTML elements in the document. Dragging elements can be difficult at first. If you make a mistake, just choose Edit > Undo and try again.

9   Drag the h2 under the `div.container` element.

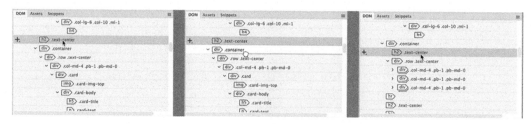

▶ **Tip:** Examine the structure carefully to make sure the h2 is positioned correctly. If you make a mistake, choose Edit > Undo and try again. You may need to drag the element several times before you get it right.

As you move an element, you will see a green line. Make sure the line appears below `div.container` but above `div.row.text-center`. When you're finished, the headline will be under `div.container` but above the content placeholders.

10  Repeat steps 7–9 for the second headline placeholder.

Both headlines are now part of their `.container` elements.

11  Choose Save All.

Up to this point, you've worked on the visible content of the layout. But before you can consider the layout complete, you'll have to create some *invisible* content too. Although few users will ever see it, it could prove very important to the success or failure of your website.

# Inserting metadata

A well-designed webpage includes several important components that users may never see. One such item is the *metadata* that is often added to the <head> section of each page. Metadata is descriptive information about your webpage or its contents that is often used by other applications, such as a browser or a search engine.

Adding metadata—such as the page *title*—is not only a good practice but also vital to your ranking and presence in the various search engines. Each title should reflect the specific content or purpose of the page. But many designers also append the name of the company or organization to help build more corporate or organizational awareness. By adding a title placeholder with the company name in the template, you will save time typing it in each child page later.

1   If necessary, open **mylayout.html** in Live view.

2   Choose Window > Properties, if necessary.
    Dock the panel to the bottom of the document window.

3   In the Document Title field of the Property inspector, select the placeholder text *Bootstrap eCommerce Page Template*.

> **Tip:** The Document Title field is available in the Property inspector in all views.

Many search engines use the page title in their search result. If you don't supply one, the search engine will pick one of its own. Let's replace the generic placeholder with one geared for this website.

4   Type **Insert Title Here - Favorite City Tour** to replace the text. Press Enter/ Return to complete the title.

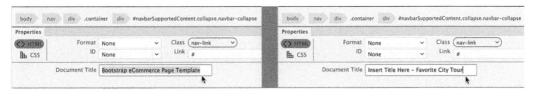

Along with the title, the other piece of metadata that usually appears in these search results is the page *description*. A description is a type of page summary that, in the past, succinctly described the contents in 160 characters or less. At the end of 2017, Google increased the size of the acceptable meta description to 320 characters.

Over the years, web developers have tried to drive more traffic to their sites by writing misleading titles and descriptions or even outright lies. But be forewarned, search engines have become wise to such tactics and will actually demote or even blacklist sites that use these tactics.

To achieve the highest ranking with the search engines, make the description of the page as accurate as possible. Try to avoid using terms and vocabulary that do not appear in the content. In many cases, the contents of the title and the description metadata will appear verbatim in the results page of a search.

5 Choose Insert > HTML > Description.

An empty Description dialog appears.

6 Type **Favorite City Tour - add description here**. Click OK.

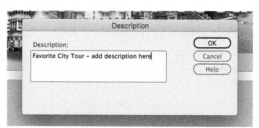

Dreamweaver has added the two metadata elements to the page.

7 If necessary, switch to Code view.

Locate the meta description in the <head> section.

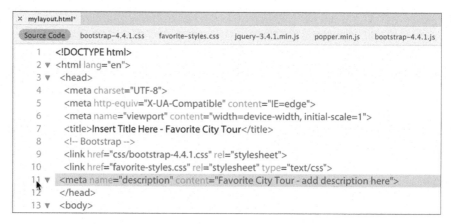

The meta description should be visible, around line 11.

8 Choose File > Save All.

The layout is almost ready to convert to a template. Before you use your template to create new pages, you should validate the code you created.

## Validating HTML code

The goal whenever you create a webpage is to create code that will work flawlessly in all modern browsers. As you made major modifications in the sample layout, there's always a possibility that you may accidentally break an element or create invalid markup. These changes could have ramifications in the quality of the code or on whether it displays in the browser effectively.

Before you use this page as your project template, you should check to make sure the code is correctly structured and that it meets current web standards.

1 If necessary, open **mylayout.html** in Dreamweaver.

2 Choose File > Validate > Current Document (W3C).

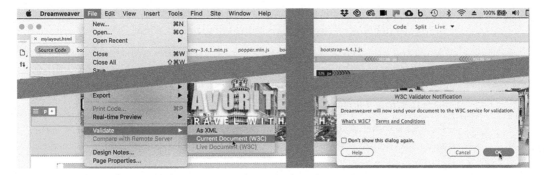

A W3C Validator Notification dialog appears, indicating that your file will be uploaded to an online validator service provided by the W3C. Before clicking OK, make sure you have a live internet connection.

3 Click OK to upload the file for validation.

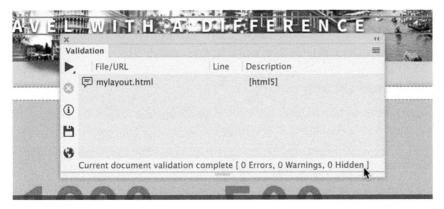

After a few moments, you should receive a report listing any errors in your layout. If you followed the instructions in the lessons correctly, there should be no errors.

4 Close the Validation panel.

Congratulations! You created a workable basic page layout for your project template and learned how to insert additional components, placeholder text, and headings; modified existing CSS formatting; created new rules; and validated the HTML code successfully. Now it's time to learn how to create a Dreamweaver template.

# Working with editable regions

When you create a template, Dreamweaver treats all the existing content as part of the master design. Child pages created from the template would be exact duplicates, and all the content would be locked and uneditable.

This setup is great for repetitive features of the design, such as the navigation components, logos, copyright, contact information, and so on, but the downside is that it stops you from adding unique content to each child page. You get around this barrier by defining *editable regions* in the template.

When you save a file as a template, Dreamweaver creates two editable regions automatically: one for the `<title>` element and another for metadata or scripts that need to be loaded in the `<head>` section of the page; any other editable regions you have to create yourself.

First, give some thought to which areas of the page should be part of the locked template and how they will be used. In this layout, the center portion of the page contains an image carousel and two sample content sections.

## Image carousel

The image carousel shows a series of dynamically rotating images and text. It was not in the original design mockup or page wireframes, but it was a feature of the Bootstrap template selected. The large animated images offer a great way to display travel photos and market various tour products, but you probably don't want to use it on every page of the site. When a template component will be needed only on a few pages, consider making it an *optional* region.

## Card-based section

The card-based section features 400 x 200 pixel placeholder images, headings, descriptive text, and a button. This section will be ideal for listing individual tour products with promotional blurbs. The button can be linked to pages giving more information about the products.

## List-based section

The list-based section features a smaller 100 x 125 image placeholder and larger text blurb. The portrait image orientation is more appropriate for headshots than for travel photos. You can use it for the biographies of the staff and tour guides.

The existing content sections are all geared for selling and marketing products. But there's no place to insert tracks of descriptive or explanatory text. The template is begging for a text-based section.

## Inserting a new Bootstrap element

If you look around the internet, you will see that most product-based sites usually introduce content with one or more paragraphs of text. Let's add a new section under the carousel that can be used for that purpose. The easiest way to insert new HTML structures is using the DOM panel.

1   Switch to Live view.
    In the layout, select the text *Get a Quote*.

    In the DOM panel, the text element is highlighted. When a child element is selected, the entire structure that it belongs to is revealed. The new text-based content section will be a peer to this element's main parent. Can you identify it? When adding a peer element it's a good idea to collapse the child structure completely.

2   In the DOM panel, click the Collapse icon ⌄ on `div.container`.

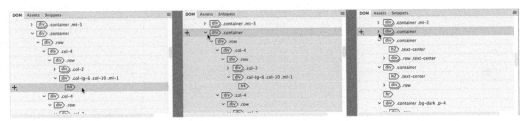

When the selected element is collapsed, you can see the other content sections, which are also based on `div.container`.

3   Click the Add Element icon ✚.
    Select Insert After in the pop-up menu.

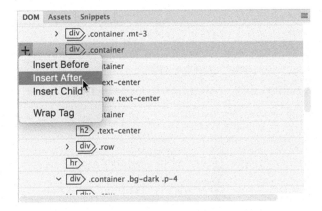

A new `div` element is added to the structure. Let's match the structure of the other content sections.

4  Press Tab to move the cursor into the Class/ID field.

Type `.container` and press Enter/Return to complete the new element.

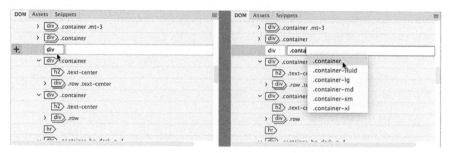

Dreamweaver creates placeholder text with a new `div` element. There's no tag on the text yet. You can use it to create the heading for the new text section.

5  In the layout, select the placeholder text.

Type **INSERT HEADLINE HERE**

Select `Heading 2` from the Format drop-down menu in the Property inspector.

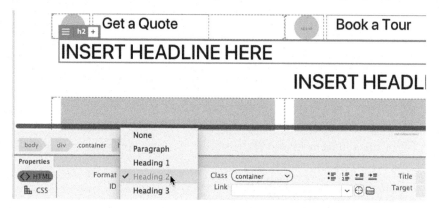

The new placeholder text is now tagged as an h2 element. To center the heading like the others, you can use the same Bootstrap class.

6  In the DOM panel, insert the cursor in the Class/ID field for the h2 element.

7  Type `.text-center` and press Enter/Return.

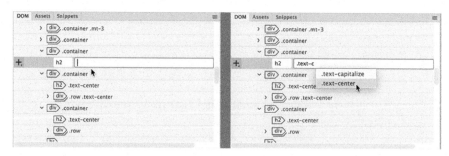

The Bootstrap class centers the heading element and completes it for now; next you need to create the structure to hold the text content. It will consist of two `div` elements and be a sibling of the heading.

8  Click the Add Element icon ✚.
Select Insert After in the pop-up menu.

A new `div` appears below the `h2` element.

9  Press Tab. Type `.row` and press Enter/Return.

The new `div` is the outer wrapper of the new text section. As before, Dreamweaver has populated it with placeholder text. You can use the placeholder text to create the inner Bootstrap content container.

10 Select the placeholder text.
Type **Insert content here.**
Choose Paragraph from the Format menu in the Property inspector.

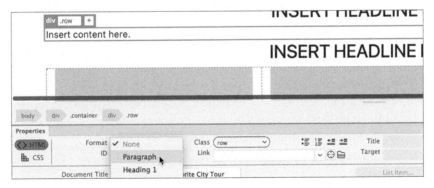

A `p` element appears in the DOM panel.

11 Click the Add Element icon ➕.

Select Wrap Tag in the pop-up menu.

Add the class `.col-lg-12` to the new `div` element.

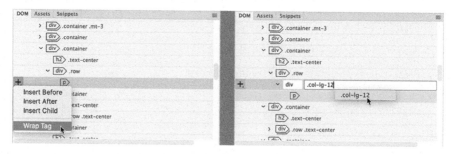

The new text content section is complete.

12 Save all files.

Now you are ready to add the editable regions to the layout.

## Inserting an editable region

As described earlier, most of the editorial content will be inserted in editable regions. Since the image carousel will not appear on every page, you will add it to an editable *optional* region. The other three content sections will be inserted into a single editable region. By putting all three into one region, you can create a child page and simply delete any sections not appropriate for the content on that page.

1 If necessary, open **mylayout.html** from the lesson07 folder in Live view. Make sure the document window is at least 1200 pixels in width.

All three content sections will be added to an editable region, but Dreamweaver can't apply editable regions to more than one selected element at a time. A simple workaround is to wrap the three content sections in a new element first and then apply the editable region to that.

2 Select the heading of the new text section.

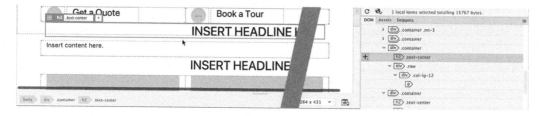

The heading of the text content section is selected in the DOM panel.

3 Select the parent `div.container` of the h2 element.

Hold the Shift key and select the other two `div.container` elements.

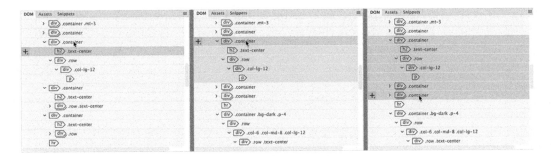

All three sections are now selected.

4  Click the Add Element icon ✚.
   Select Wrap Tag in the pop-up menu.
   Add the class `.wrapper`

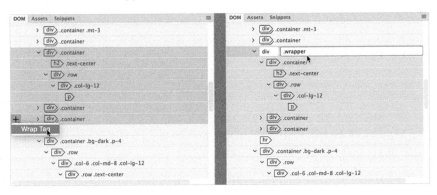

The three content elements are now wrapped by a single `div` element. They are ready to be added to an editable region.

5  Switch to Design view.

6  If necessary, select `div.wrapper` in the DOM panel.
   Choose Insert > Template > Editable Region.

● **Note:** As of this writing, the template workflow works only in Design and Code views. You will not be able to perform any of these tasks in Live view.

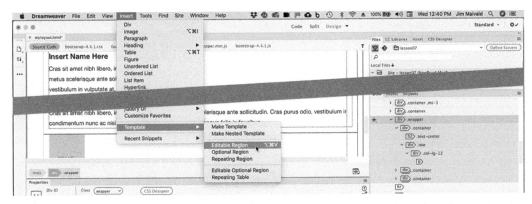

Editable regions can be added only to a Dreamweaver template. A dialog appears, reporting that the program will convert the document to a template when you save the file.

7  Click OK.

The New Editable Region dialog appears, providing a field to name the editable region.

8  Enter **MainContent** in the Name field.

Each editable region must have a unique name, but no other special conventions apply. However, keeping the name short and descriptive is a good practice. The name is used solely within Dreamweaver and has no other bearing on the HTML code.

9  Click OK.

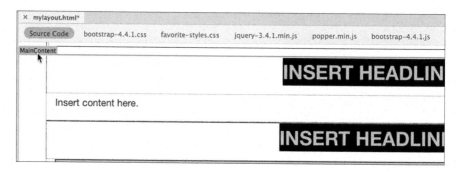

In Design view, you will see the new region name in a blue tab above the designated area identifying it as an editable region. In Live view, the tabs appear orange in child pages. The editable region will encapsulate the `div.wrapper` element and all the content sections within it.

Before you save the file, let's add the editable optional region around the carousel.

## Inserting an editable optional region

Editable optional regions enable you to mark content that you want in some pages but not all pages within the site. The first step is to select the carousel.

1  Click anywhere on the carousel component in the document window.

   The carousel is a complex Bootstrap component composed of several containers and content elements. It's important that you select the entire structure before applying the option editable region.

2  Select the `div.container.mt-3` tag selector.

   If you find the DOM panel easier to use, feel free to use it to select the elements instead.

3  Choose Insert > Template > Editable Optional Region.

   The dialog appears again, indicating that the file will be saved as a template.

4  Click OK.

   The New Optional Region dialog appears. At the time of this writing, a bug in Dreamweaver may prevent you from changing the default name displayed in the dialog. If you experience this bug, you can get around it by first clicking the Advanced tab in the dialog and then switching back to the Basic tab.

5  If necessary, click the Advanced tab.
Click the Basic tab.

The name should be editable now.

6  Type **MainCarousel** and click OK.

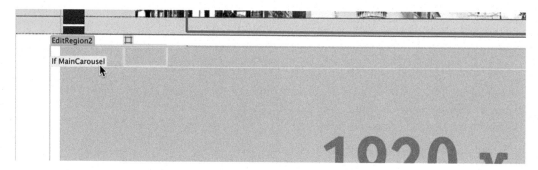

The two editable regions are in place.

7  Choose File > Save.

The Save As Template dialog appears.

8  Enter **Favorite City Tour template** in the Description field.

▶ **Tip:** Adding the suffix "temp" to the file-name is not a require-ment, but it helps to visually distinguish this file from others in the site folder display.

9  Type **favorite-temp** in the Save As field.
Click Save.

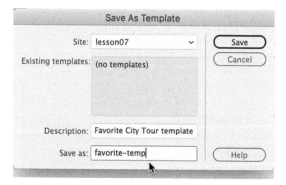

An untitled dialog appears, asking whether you want to update links.

Templates are stored in their own folder, *Templates*, which Dreamweaver automatically creates at the site root level.

10 Click Yes to update the links.

Since the template is saved in a subfolder, updating the links in the code is necessary so that they will continue to work properly when you create child pages later. Dreamweaver automatically resolves and rewrites links as necessary when you save files anywhere in the site.

Although the page still looks exactly the same, you can identify that it's a template by the file extension displayed in the document tab: .dwt, which stands for Dreamweaver template.

Before we finish the template, there's a small error we need to deal with in the `<head>` section. When you saved the layout as a template, the title and meta description should have been inserted into their own editable regions. As of this writing, Dreamweaver has a bug that causes it to miss the meta description.

11 Switch to Code view and locate the meta description placeholder, around line 13.

If the meta description is outside the editable region, you won't be able to change it on any child pages made from the template.

12 Select the entire `<meta>` element and drag it between the tags
`<!-- InstanceBeginEditable name="head" -->` and
`<!-- InstanceEndEditable -->`.

```
12    <link href="../favorite-styles.css" rel="stylesheet" type="text/css">
13 ▼  <meta name="description" content="Favorite City Tour - add description here">
14    <!-- TemplateParam name="MainCarousel" type="boolean" value="true" -->
15    <!-- TemplateBeginEditable name="head" -->
16    <!-- TemplateEndEditable -->
17    </head>
```

```
12    <link href="../favorite-styles.css" rel="stylesheet" type="text/css">
13
14    <!-- TemplateParam name="MainCarousel" type="boolean" value="true" -->
15    <!-- TemplateBeginEditable name="head" -->
16    <meta name="description" content="Favorite City Tour - add description here">:<!-- TemplateEndEditable -->
17    </head>
```

Now the template is complete and you're ready to create some child pages.

13 Save and close all files.

A Dreamweaver template is *dynamic*, meaning that the program maintains a connection to all pages within the site that are derived from the template. Whenever you add or change content within the dynamic regions of the template and save it, Dreamweaver passes those changes to all the child pages automatically, keeping them up to date.

● **Note:** A dialog may appear asking you to update all pages based on this template. You may dismiss the dialog.

# Working with child pages

Child pages are the *raison d'être* for Dreamweaver templates. Once a child page has been created from a template, only the content within the editable regions can be modified in the child page. The rest of the page remains locked within Dreamweaver. It's important to remember that this behavior is supported only within Dreamweaver and a few other HTML editors. Be aware that if you open the page in a text editor, such as Notepad or TextEdit, the code is fully editable.

## Creating a new page

The decision to use Dreamweaver templates for a site should be made at the beginning of the design process so that all the pages in the site can be made as child pages of the template. In fact, that is the purpose of the layout you've built up to this point: to create the basic structure of your site template.

1 Launch Dreamweaver CC (2021 release) or later, if necessary.

One way to access site templates is using the New Document dialog.

2 Choose File > New, or press Ctrl+N/Cmd+N.

The New Document dialog appears.

3 In the New Document dialog, select the Site Templates option.

4 Select lesson07 in the Site list, if necessary.

5 Select **favorite-temp** in the Template For Site "lesson07" list.

6 Select the Update Page When Template Changes option, if necessary.

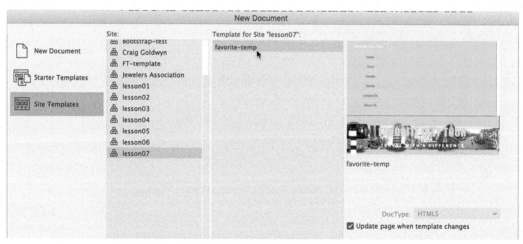

7 Click Create.

Dreamweaver creates a new page based on the template.

**8**   If necessary, switch to Design view.

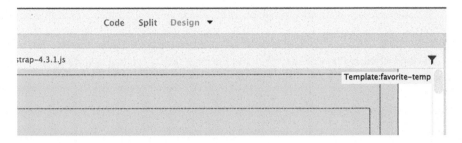

Typically, Dreamweaver defaults to the last document view (Code, Design, or Live) that you were using for the new document. In Design view, you will see the name of the template file displayed in the upper-right corner of the document window. Before modifying the page, you should save it.

● **Note:** Some users report not seeing the template label in the upper-right corner.

**9**   Choose File > Save.

The Save As dialog appears.

▶ **Tip:** The Save As dialog provides a handy button, Site Root, that takes you to the site root with a single click. Feel free to use it in any exercise, as needed.

**10** In the Save As dialog, navigate to the site root folder.

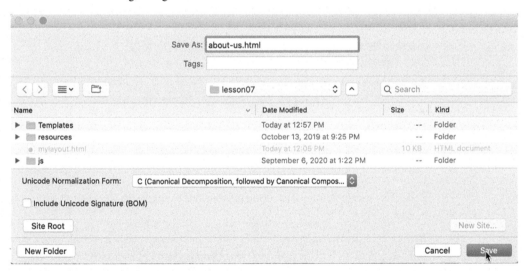

Name the file **about-us.html** and click Save.

The child page has been created. When you save the document in the site root folder, Dreamweaver updates all links and references to external files. The template makes it easy to add new content.

## Adding content to child pages

◆ **Warning:** If you open a template in a text editor, all the code is editable, including the code for the non-editable regions of the page.

When you create a page from a template, only the editable regions can be modified.

1   Open **about-us.html** in Design view, if necessary.

You'll find that many of the features and functionality of templates work properly only in Design or Code view, although you should be able to add or edit content in the editable regions from Live view.

2   Position the cursor over each area of the page. Observe the cursor icon.

When the cursor moves over certain areas of the page, such as the horizontal menu, header, and footer, the Locked icon ⃠ appears. These areas are uneditable regions that are locked and cannot be modified within the child page inside Dreamweaver. Other areas, such as `MainCarousel` and `MainContent`, can be changed.

3   Select the first placeholder text, *INSERT HEADLINE HERE.*
Type **ABOUT FAVORITE CITY TOUR** to replace the text.

---

**ABOUT FAVORITE CITY TOUR**

re.

**INSERT HEADLINE HERE**

---

4   In the Files panel, double-click **aboutus-text.rtf** in the lesson07 resources folder to open the file.

Dreamweaver opens only simple, text-based file formats, such as .html, .css, .txt, .xml, .xslt, and a few others. When Dreamweaver can't open a file, it passes it to a compatible program, such as Microsoft Word, Excel, WordPad, TextEdit, and so on. The file contains content for the text-based content section.

● **Note:** Although you should be able to use any word processor, I recommend using a simple editor like TextEdit or Notepad.

5  Press Ctrl+A/Cmd+A to select all the text.

Press Ctrl+C/Cmd+C or choose Edit > Copy to copy the text.

● **Note:** Feel free to use any method you know to select and copy the content.

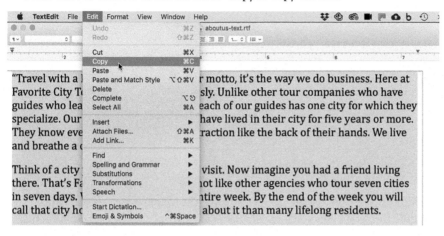

6  Switch back to Dreamweaver.

7  Click anywhere in the placeholder text *Insert content here*.

Select the p tag selector.

8  Press Ctrl+V/Cmd+V, or choose Edit > Paste, to paste the text.

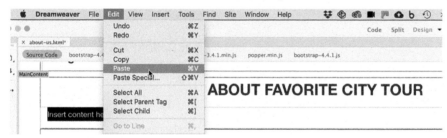

The placeholder text is replaced by the new content.

9  Save the file.

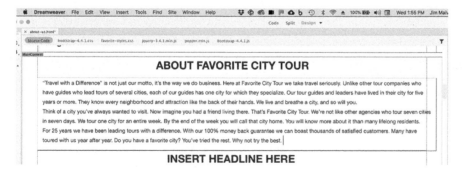

Once the visible content has been added to a page, you can deal with the invisible content or metadata.

## Adding metadata to a child page

Earlier, you added metadata placeholders in the template. This metadata should be updated before any page can be considered complete.

1 Open the Property inspector, if necessary.

2 In the Title field, select the placeholder text *Insert title here*.

3 Type **About Favorite City Tour** and press Enter/Return.

Although you can't see the title anywhere in the layout, it has been updated within the code. Next you'll update the meta description placeholder. Although you can always edit it in Code view, the DOM panel offers another method.

4 In the DOM panel, expand the `head` section.
Expand the `mmtinstance editable` element.

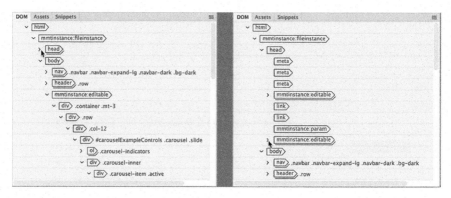

You should see the several meta elements in the `head` section, including the description inside the expanded element. The content of the meta elements will display in the Property inspector when you select each element in the DOM panel.

● **Note:** You may have to click the meta element more than once to get the content to display in the Property inspector.

5 Click the meta element in the DOM panel.

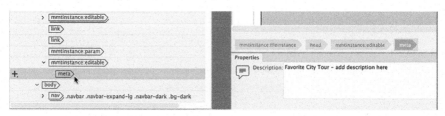

The Property inspector displays the content of the meta description.

**6** Select the text *add description here* and type

**For 25 years Favorite City Tour has been showing people how to travel with a difference. It's not just a motto, it's a way of life.**

**7** Save the file.

In the next exercise you will update various aspects of the template and learn how to update child pages. This will give you a better idea how templates work.

## Updating a template

Templates can automatically update any child page made from that template. But only areas outside the editable regions will be updated. Let's make some changes to editable and noneditable sections to demonstrate how Dreamweaver templates work.

**1** In the Files panel, double-click **favorite-temp.dwt** to open it. Make sure the document window is at least 1200 pixels wide.

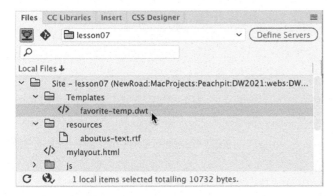

**2** Switch to Design view.

**3** In the navigation menu, select the text *Home*.
Type **Home Page** to replace the text.

4 Select the text *Events*.
Type **Calendar** to replace the text.

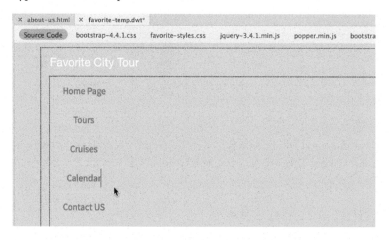

5 Select and replace the text *Insert* with the word **Add** wherever it appears in the
`MainContent` editable region.

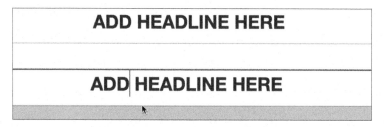

6 Switch to Live view.

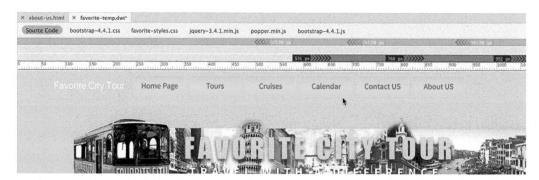

You can now clearly see the changes to the menu and content areas.

7  Save the file.

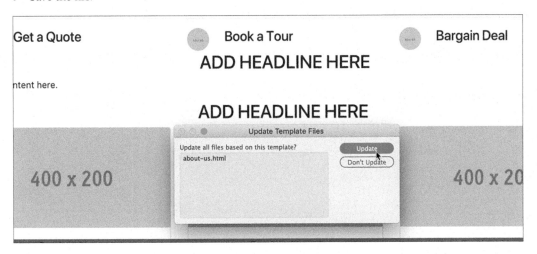

The Update Template Files dialog appears. The filename **about-us.html** appears in the update list. This dialog will list all files based on the template.

8  Click Update. The Update Pages dialog appears.

9  If necessary, select the Show Log option.

● **Note:** The Update Pages function can sometimes take a long time to complete. If your update freezes, the dialog provides a Stop button with which you can exit the process before it finishes.

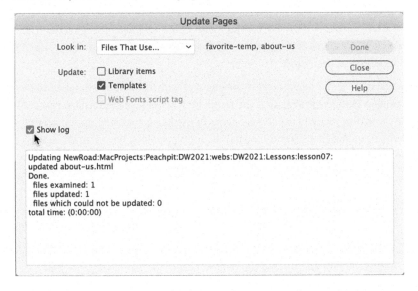

A window displays a report that lists which pages were successfully updated and which ones were not. It should report that **about-us.html** was updated successfully.

10  Close the Update Pages dialog.

**11** Switch to **about-us.html** by clicking the document tab.

Observe the page and note any changes.

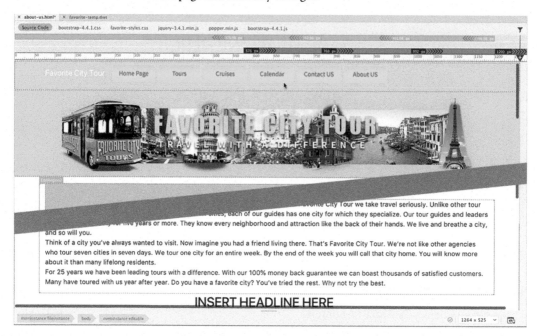

The changes made to the horizontal menu in the template are reflected in this file, but the changes to the main content sections were ignored. The content you added remains unaltered.

As you can see, you can safely make changes and add content to the editable regions without worrying that the template will delete all your hard work. At the same time, the boilerplate elements of the header, footer, and horizontal menu all remain consistently formatted and up to date, based on the status of the template.

**12** Switch to **favorite-temp.dwt**.

**13** Switch to Design view.

**14** Delete the word *Page* from the *Home Page* link in the navigation menu. Change the word *Calendar* back to **Events**.

**15** Save the template and update the related files.

**16** Click the document tab for **about-us.html**.

Observe the page and note any changes.

> **Tip:** If an open page has been changed during the update, it will be updated but not saved by Dreamweaver and show an asterisk by its name in the document tab.

The horizontal menu has been restored to its previous content. As you can see, Dreamweaver even updates linked documents that are open at the time. The only concern is that some changes have not been saved. Note that the document tab shows an asterisk, which means the file has been changed but not saved.

If Dreamweaver or your computer were to crash at this moment, all the changes you made would be lost; you would have to update the page manually or wait until the next time you make changes to the template to take advantage of the automatic update feature.

17 Select File > Save.

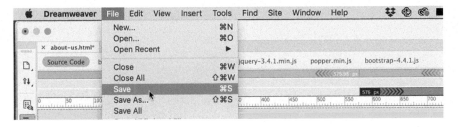

▶ **Tip:** Always use the Save All command whenever you have multiple files open that may have been updated by a template. In most cases, it's better to update a template when all the child pages are closed. That way, the pages are saved automatically.

● **Note:** Dreamweaver added a limited auto-backup feature in a previous version. If the program crashes, some or all of the changes you have made may be preserved.

18 Close **favorite-temp.dwt**.

Once the content has been added to the new page, you can delete the content sections you no longer need. Let's first address the editable optional region.

## Removing an optional region from a child page

Optional regions and editable optional regions are removed and added to a child page in the same way. There is a conditional reference in the <head> section that controls the display and removal of the region.

1 Switch to Code view in **about-us.html**.

```
13
14 ▼  <!-- InstanceParam name="MainCarousel" type="boolean" value="true" -->
15     <!-- InstanceBeginEditable name="head" -->
```

Around line 14, you should find a reference to MainCarousel. Note the value="true" attribute. When the value is *true*, the carousel will be added to the document. When the value is *false*, the carousel will be removed.

2 Select the value true and type false to replace it.

```
13
14     <!-- InstanceParam name="MainCarousel" type="boolean" value="false" -->
15     <!-- InstanceBeginEditable name="head" -->
```

To remove the carousel from the page, you need to use the template update command.

3 Switch to Design view.

● **Note:** The template commands are enabled only in Design and Code views.

Keep an eye on the carousel at the top of the page.

4   Choose Tools > Templates > Update Current Page.

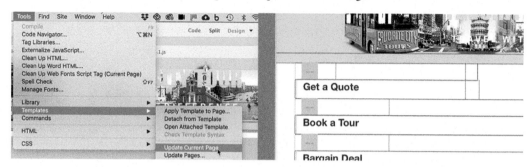

The carousel disappears after the page is updated. Later, if you want to insert the carousel back into the layout, just change the value back to `true`.

5   Save the page.

Next we'll remove the card-based and list-based sections that were not used.

## Removing unused sections from a child page

There are several ways to delete components from a page. The easiest ones rely on the tag selector interface or the DOM panel.

1   Switch to Live view.

2   Select any of the 400 x 200 image placeholders in the card-based section.

Identify the parent element for the entire card-based section.

3   Select the `div.container` tag selector.

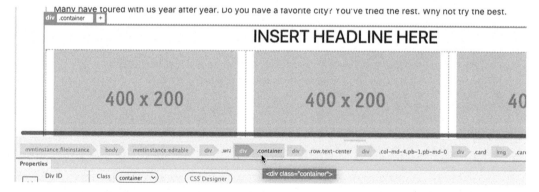

4   Press Delete.

The entire card-based section is deleted. Let's use the DOM panel to delete the list-based section.

5   Click the headline placeholder in the list-based section.

In the DOM panel, `h2.text-center` is highlighted.

**6** Select the parent element `div.container`.
Press Delete.

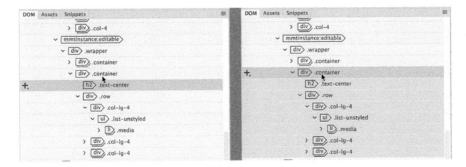

The list-based section is deleted.

**7** If necessary, scroll up and down and review the page.

The empty content sections are removed, and all content elements for this page are complete.

**8** Save the file.

Dreamweaver's templates help you build and automatically update pages quickly and easily. In the upcoming lessons, you will use the newly completed template to create all the files for the project site. Although choosing to use templates is a decision you should make when first creating a new site, it's never too late to use them to speed up your workflow and make site maintenance faster and easier.

## Review questions

1 What is the purpose of a Dreamweaver template.

2 How do you create a template from an existing page?

3 Why is a template dynamic?

4 What must you add to a template to make it useful in a workflow?

5 How do you create a child page from a template?

6 Can templates update pages that are open?

## Review answers

1 A template is a predefined HTML page layout, with image and text placeholders, that allows you to create derivative child pages quickly and easily.

2 To create a .dwt file, choose File > Save As Template, and enter the name of the template in the dialog.

3 A template is dynamic because Dreamweaver maintains a connection to all pages created from it within a site. When the template is updated, it passes any changes to the locked areas of the child pages and leaves the editable regions unaltered.

4 You must add editable regions to the template; otherwise, unique content can't be added to the child pages.

5 Choose File > New, and in the New Document dialog, select Site Templates. Locate the desired template and click Create. Or right-click the template name in the Assets > Template category and choose New From Template.

6 Yes. Open pages based on the template are updated along with files that are closed. The only difference is that files that are open are not automatically saved after being updated.

# 8 WORKING WITH TEXT, LISTS, AND TABLES

## Lesson overview

In this lesson, you'll create several webpages from your new template and work with headings, paragraphs, and other text elements to do the following:

- Enter heading and paragraph text.
- Insert text from another source.
- Create bulleted lists.
- Insert and modify tables.
- Spell-check your website.
- Search and replace text.

 This lesson will take about 3 hours to complete. To get the lesson files used in this lesson, download them from the webpage for this book at www.adobepress.com/DreamweaverCIB2021. For more information, see "Accessing the lesson files and Web Edition" in the "Getting Started" section at the beginning of this book.

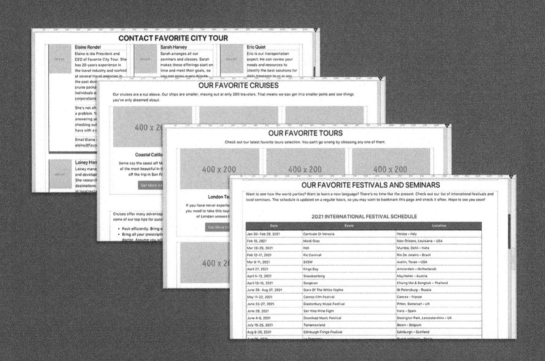

Dreamweaver provides numerous tools for creating, editing, and formatting web content, whether it's created within the program or imported from other applications.

# Previewing the completed file

To get a sense of the files you will work on in this lesson, let's preview the completed pages in Dreamweaver.

1 Launch Adobe Dreamweaver CC (2021 release) or later, if necessary. If Dreamweaver is already running, close any open files.

2 Define a new site for the lesson08 folder, as described in the "Getting Started" section at the beginning of the book. Name the new site **lesson08**.

● **Note:** To open consecutive files, hold the Shift key before selecting. If the files are not listed consecutively, Ctrl/Cmd-click to select the files.

3 If necessary, press F8 to open the Files panel. Select lesson08 from the site drop-down list.

Dreamweaver allows you to open one or more files at the same time.

4 Open the lesson08/finished folder.

5 Select **tours-finished.html**.

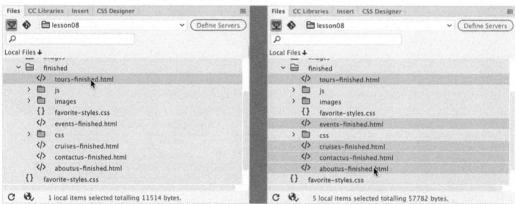

Hold Ctrl/Cmd, and then select **events-finished.html, cruises-finished.html, contactus-finished.html**, and **aboutus-finished.html**.

By holding Ctrl/Cmd before you click, you can select multiple nonconsecutive files.

● **Note:** Files may be displayed differently than shown.

6 Right-click any of the selected files. Choose Open from the context menu.

All four files open. Tabs at the top of the document window identify each file.

● **Note:** Be sure to use Live view to preview each of the pages.

**7** Click the **tours-finished.html** tab to bring that file to the top, and switch to Live view if necessary.

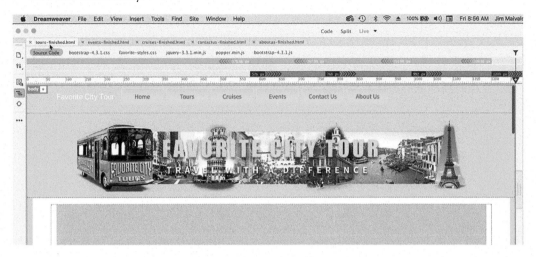

Note the headings and text elements used.

**8** Click the **cruises-finished.html** document tab to bring that file to the top.

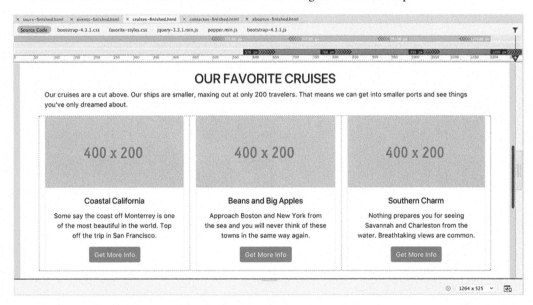

Note the bulleted list elements used.

**9** Click the **events-finished.html** tab to bring that file to the top.

Note the two HTML-based tables used.

**10** Click the **contactus-finished.html** tab to bring that file to the top.

Note that the text elements are formatted with custom borders.

**11** Choose File > Close All.

In each of the pages, a variety of elements are used, including headings, paragraphs, lists, bullets, indented text, and tables. In the following exercises, you will create these pages and learn how to format each of these elements.

## Creating and styling text

Most websites are composed of large blocks of text with a few images sprinkled in for visual interest. Dreamweaver provides a variety of means for creating, importing, and styling text to meet any need.

### Importing text

In this exercise, you'll create a new page from the site template and then insert heading and paragraph text from a text document.

1 Choose Window > Assets to display the Assets panel.

Click the Templates category icon.

Right-click **favorite-temp** and choose New From Template from the context menu.

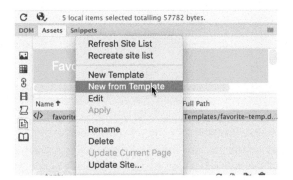

▶ **Tip:** The Assets panel may open as a separate, floating panel. To save screen space, feel free to dock the panel on the right side of the screen, as shown in Lesson 1, "Customizing Your Workspace."

● **Note:** The Templates tab of the Assets panel appears only in Design and Code views when documents are open or when no documents are open at all.

A new page is created based on the site template.

2 Save the file as **tours.html** in the site root folder.

Make sure the document window is at least 1200 pixels wide.

When you create a file, it's a good idea to immediately update or replace the various metadata placeholder text elements in the new page. These items are often overlooked or forgotten in all the hubbub around creating the text and images for the main content. First, you'll update the page title.

▶ **Tip:** The Property inspector may not be visible in the default workspace. You can access it in the Window menu and dock it to the bottom of the document window.

3 If necessary, choose Window > Properties to display the Property inspector.

The Document Title field is featured in the Property inspector most of the time you are working in a document and when no page elements are selected.

4 In the Document Title field, select the placeholder text *Insert Title Here*.

Type **Our Favorite Tours** and press Enter/Return to complete the title.

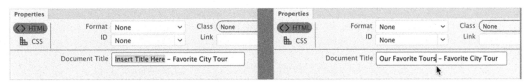

Each page also has a meta description element, which provides valuable information about your page content to search engines. You can edit it in Code view or using the Property inspector with help from the DOM panel.

5 Choose Window > DOM to display the DOM panel, if necessary.

The meta description is located in the <head> section of the page.

6 Expand the head element in the DOM display.

When the head section expands, you should see the various elements contained within it. There are three meta elements, two links, and two editable regions. One editable region contains the title, which may be visible. The other contains the meta description.

7 Expand the second editable region.

You should see a meta element within the editable region.

8 Click to highlight the meta element in the DOM panel.

The content of the meta element appears in the Property inspector.

9 Select the text *add description here* and type the following:
**We worked hard to develop these tours for you. They are guaranteed to be your favorite, too!**

Once the metadata is updated, you can start working on the main content.

10 In the Files panel, double-click **favorite-tours.rtf** in the lesson08/resources folder.

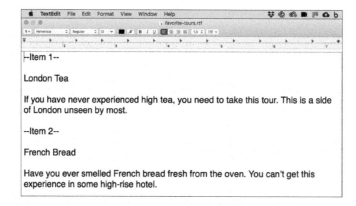

Dreamweaver automatically launches a program that is compatible with the file type selected. The text is unformatted and features extra lines between each paragraph. These extra lines are intentional. For some reason, Dreamweaver swaps out single paragraph returns for `<br>` tags when you copy and paste them from another program. Adding a second paragraph return in your source text forces Dreamweaver to use paragraph tags instead of the break tag.

▶ **Tip:** When you use the clipboard to bring text into Dreamweaver from other programs, you can then use Live or Design view if you want to honor the paragraph returns.

This file contains nine tour descriptions that you will use to populate the card-based content section.

11 In the text editor or word-processing program, position the cursor before the text *London Tea*.

12 Drag to select the heading.

13 Press Ctrl+X/Cmd+X to cut the text.

14 Switch back to Dreamweaver.

15 Switch to Live view, if necessary.

The sample page has three card-based placeholders in the middle content section, each titled *Product Name*. The content you cut from **favorite-tours.rtf** will be inserted into the first placeholder.

16 In the card-based section, select the text *ADD HEADLINE HERE*. Type **OUR FAVORITE TOURS** to replace it and press Enter/Return to create a new line.

▶ **Tip:** Starting in this version of Dream-weaver, you can directly edit text in Live view.

When you press Enter/Return in Live view, Dreamweaver automatically creates a new `<p>` element.

17 Type **Check out our latest favorite tours selection. You can't go wrong by choosing any one of them.**

The introductory text would look nicer centered under the heading. You may remember applying the Bootstrap class `.text-center` to center the place-holder heading in the previous lesson.

18 In the Element Display on the new paragraph, click the Add Class/ID icon ⊞.

19 Type `.text-center` and press Enter/Return to apply the class to the `<p>` element.

20 Select the text *Product Name* in the first card-based element.

21 Press Ctrl+V/Cmd+V to paste the text from **favorite-tours.rtf** that you cut in step 13.

The heading *London Tea* replaces the placeholder text.

22 Switch to **favorite-tours.rtf**.
Select the tour description for Item 1.

23 Press Ctrl+X/Cmd+X to cut the description.

▶ **Tip:** When selecting the text, be sure you don't grab the paragraph return. This will add an extra blank line to the card.

24 Switch to Dreamweaver and select the placeholder description in the first card-based element.

25 Press Ctrl+V/Cmd+V to paste.

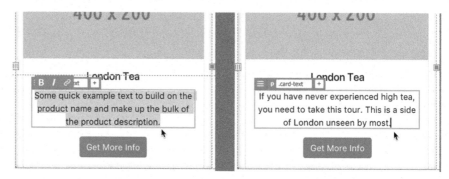

The description is replaced by the text from **favorite-tours.rtf**.

The text in the first card-based element has been replaced.

26 Switch to **favorite-tours.rtf**.
Repeat steps 22–25 to move items 2 and 3 to **tours.html**.

27 Save **tours.html**.

The three card-based elements are populated by the tour titles and descriptions. Next, you'll create two additional rows of tour descriptions that you can then fill with the remaining text in **favorite-tours.rtf**.

## Duplicating Bootstrap rows

The row-and-column scheme that Bootstrap uses to support various screen sizes can be very tedious to build by hand. Fortunately, Dreamweaver provides a built-in interface that makes this a simple point-and-click task. In this exercise, you will learn how to create additional rows in your Bootstrap structure.

1   Select any of the image placeholders in the card-based section.

2   Select the `div.row.text-center` tag selector.

When the element is selected, the Element Display shows two additional icons on the lower- or upper-right corner of the element. The icons enable you to create a new Bootstrap row or to duplicate it. If you were to click the Add A New Row icon 🖽, you'd have to re-create all the elements used in the card-based elements. Since the first row already has all the elements we need, let's just duplicate it to save a lot of time and effort.

3   Click the Duplicate Row icon 🗖.

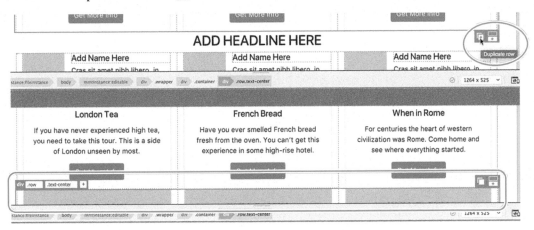

A new row appears below the selection, with duplicate content and structure. Notice that the new row is butting up to the first row. It could use a little spacing. You may have noticed the Bootstrap class `.mt-4` applied to various elements in the layout. This class adds a `margin-top` property to an element.

4   Select any of the image placeholders in the second row of the card-based section.

5   Select the `div.row.text-center` tag selector.

6   In the Element Display on the new paragraph, click the Add Class/ID icon ⊞.

7   Type `.mt-4` and press Enter/Return to apply the class.

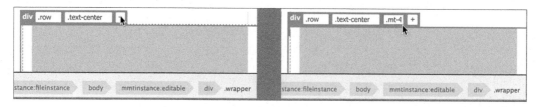

The entire row moves down. Once you have created and formatted the second row, you might as well add the third row. Depending on where the new row displays in the document window, the Duplicate Row icon may appear at the top or bottom of the selection.

● **Note:** If the selected element displays an orange border, the duplicate command will not work. Click the Element Display to display the blue border.

8   Click the Duplicate Row icon 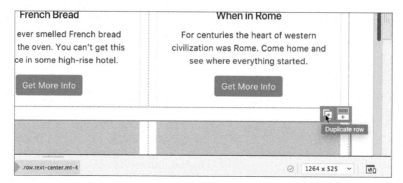.

A duplicate row appears below the second row. Now you can bring over the remaining content.

9   Move the remaining tour titles and descriptions from **favorite-tours.rtf**.

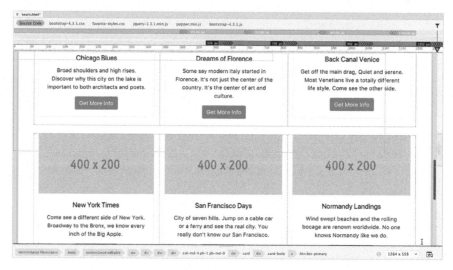

**10** Close but do not save **favorite-tours.rtf**.

By not saving the file you will be able to access the content later if you want to redo this lesson.

**11** Save **tours.html**.

Once the text has been moved over and the content is complete, you can delete the content elements you do not need.

## Deleting unused Bootstrap components

The template was set up with an image carousel and three content sections. For **tours.html** you used the card-based content section. In Lesson 9, "Working with Images," you'll learn how to add images to the carousel, so we'll leave the carousel in the template. The text-based section under the carousel and the list-based section are unused and unneeded, so let's delete them.

**1** Select the text ADD HEADLINE HERE in the text-based section.

**2** Select the div.container tag selector and press Delete.

▶ **Tip:** Look for the blue border when deleting selected elements. The orange border indicates that the content is selected. Click the tag selector again or the Element Display itself to activate the blue border. You can also use the DOM panel to easily delete elements.

The text-based section is deleted. The card-based section moves up, butting up against the link section under the carousel. It could use a bit of spacing above it. You can use the .mt-4 class again.

**3** Select the headline OUR FAVORITE TOURS.

**4** Select the div.container tag selector.

**5** Using the Element Display, add the class .mt-4.

The element moves down.

6   Select the text ADD HEADLINE HERE in the list-based section.

7   Select the `div.container` tag selector and press Delete.

Notice the blue border around the element before pressing Delete. The entire list-based section is deleted, and the layout is complete for now.

8   Save the file and close it.

Next you'll learn how to create HTML lists.

# Creating lists

Formatting should add meaning, organization, and clarity to your content. One method of doing this is to use the HTML list elements. Lists are the workhorses of the web because they are easier to read than blocks of dense text; they also help users find information quickly.

In this exercise, you will learn how to make an HTML list.

1   Open the Assets panel.
    In the Templates category, right-click **favorite-temp**.
    From the context menu, choose New From Template.

    A new page is created based on the template.

● **Note:** The Template category is not visible in Live view when a document is open. To create, edit, or use Dreamweaver templates, you must switch to Design view or Code view or close all open HTML documents.

2   Save the file as **cruises.html** in the site root folder. Switch to Live view, if necessary.
    Make sure the document window is at least 1200 pixels wide.

3   In the Property inspector, select the placeholder text *Insert Title Here* in the Document Title field. Type **Our Favorite Cruises** to replace the text, and press Enter/Return.

4   Switch to Code view.
    Locate the `meta description` element.

    Select the text *add description here.*

5   Type **Our cruises can show you a different side of your favorite cities** and save the file.

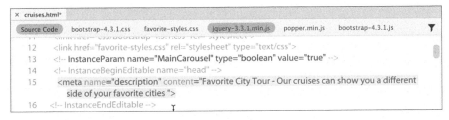

The new description replaces the placeholder.

6   In the Files panel, double-click **cruise-tips.rtf** in the resources folder of lesson08.

The file opens outside Dreamweaver. The content consists of a list of tips on how to make your cruise experience better.

7   In **favorite-tips.rtf**, press Ctrl+A/Cmd+A.
Press Ctrl+X/Cmd+X to cut the text.
Close, but do not save changes to, **cruise-tips.rtf**.

You have selected and cut all the text.

8   Switch back to Dreamweaver. Switch to Live view.

9   Select *ADD HEADLINE HERE* in the text-based content section under the image carousel.
Type **TOP TIPS FOR CRUISERS** to replace it.

10  Click the text *Add content here*.

The Element Display appears focused on the p placeholder element, but the border around the text may be orange.

11  If necessary, press the Esc key to obtain the blue element border. Otherwise, skip to step 12.

When the blue border is visible, you have the HTML element selected.

12  Press Ctrl+V/Cmd+V.

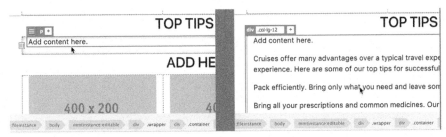

The text from **cruise-tips.rtf** appears below the placeholder element. Before we deal with the new text, let's delete the placeholder.

13  Select and delete the entire placeholder element *Add content here*.

The text from **cruise-tips.rtf** is currently formatted entirely as HTML paragraphs. Dreamweaver makes it easy to convert this text into an HTML list. Lists come in two flavors: *ordered* and *unordered*.

### Creating an ordered list

In this exercise, you will convert some of the paragraph text into an HTML ordered list.

1 Select all the text, starting with *Cruises offer many advantages.*
In the Property inspector, click the Ordered List icon .

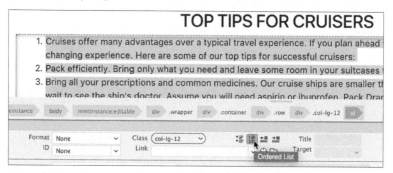

An ordered list adds numbers automatically to the entire selection. Semantically, it prioritizes each item, giving them intrinsic values relative to one another. However, this list doesn't seem to be in any particular order. Each item is more or less equal to the next one, so it's a good candidate for an unordered list—used when the items are in no particular order. Before you change the formatting, let's take a look at the markup.

2 Switch to Split view.

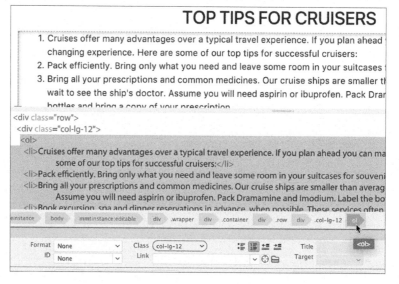

Observe the list markup in the Code section of the document window.

The markup consists of two elements: `<ol>` and `<li>`. Note that each line is formatted as an `<li>` (list item). The `<ol>` parent element begins and ends the list and designates it as an ordered list. Changing the formatting from numbers to bullets is simple and can be done in Code view or Design view.

Before changing the format, ensure that the formatted list is still entirely selected. You can use the `<ol>` tag selector, if necessary.

### Creating an unordered list

In this exercise, you will convert the ordered list into an unordered list.

1  In the Properties panel, click the Unordered List icon ▦.

> ▶ **Tip:** You could also change the formatting by editing the markup manually in the Code view window. But don't forget to change both the opening and closing tags.

> ▶ **Tip:** The easiest way to select the entire list is to use the `<ol>` tag selector.

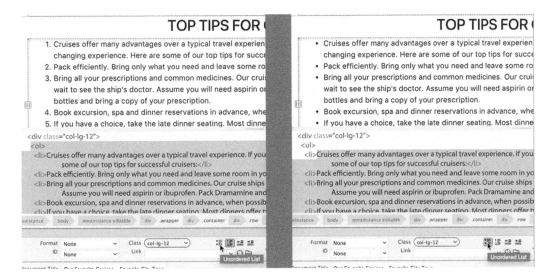

All the items are now formatted as bullets.

If you observe the list markup, you'll notice that the only thing that has changed is the parent element. It now says `<ul>`, for *un*ordered list.

Before you close this file, let's complete the rest of the page.

2  In the card-based content section, select the placeholder heading ADD HEADLINE HERE.

3  Type **OUR FAVORITE CRUISES** to replace the selection.

4 In the Files panel, double-click **favorite-cruises.rtf** in the lesson08/resources folder.

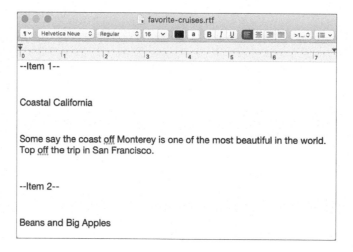

The **favorite-cruises.rtf** file opens. The text should be inserted in the card-based content section.

5 Copy and paste the text into the appropriate placeholders in the card-based content section.

The three card-based elements are now populated with cruise descriptions. Once the content is in place, it's time to delete the unneeded placeholder elements. The carousel will be updated with cruise photos in Lesson 9, but you can delete the list-based content section.

6 Select and delete the list-based content section.

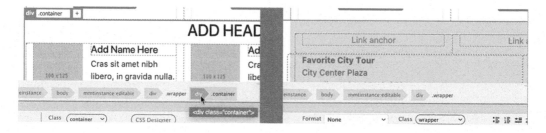

The layout is nearly complete. Since the page is focused on selling cruises, it makes sense to put the cruise descriptions above the tips content. The DOM panel makes it easy to move elements around in the layout.

7 Select Window > DOM, if necessary, to display the DOM panel.

8 In the document window, select the headline TOP TIPS FOR CRUISERS.

The h2 element in the DOM panel is highlighted. You can see the structure of the text-based content section. The parent element for the entire section is div.container.

9 Select the headline OUR FAVORITE CRUISES.

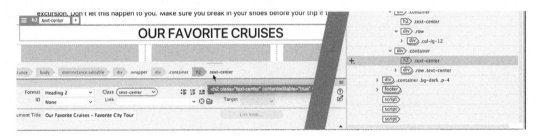

The h2 in the card-based content section is highlighted. Like the text-based section, the card-based section is also based on div.container. By dragging one of these elements, you can swap the two sections in the layout.

At the moment, the two HTML structures are expanded. Collapsing the parent elements can help make moving the elements a bit easier.

10 Collapse the structure display for the two div.container elements.

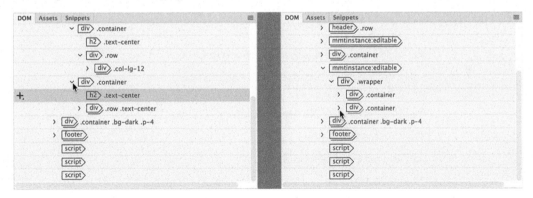

When collapsed, the elements are stacked one above the other at the same level of the structure. Seeing the two elements this way simplifies the change.

**11** Drag the card-based section above the text-based section.

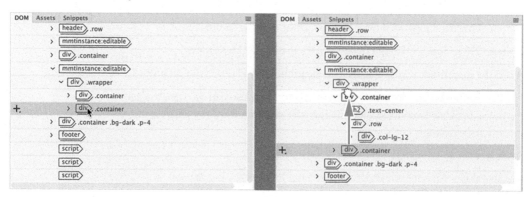

● **Note:** When you're dragging the element, Dreamweaver might expand the structure.

▶ **Tip:** If the element appears in the wrong position, choose Edit > Undo and try again.

A green line indicates where the element will appear. The cruise descriptions now appear above the cruise tips section. As before, the card-based OUR FAVORITE CRUISES section butts up against the links and needs a bit of spacing.

**12** Select the headline OUR FAVORITE CRUISES.
Select the `div.container` tag selector.
Add the class `.mt-4` to `div.container`.

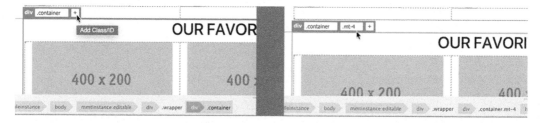

The tips section could also use some extra space.

**13** Select the headline TOP TIPS FOR CRUISERS.
Select the `div.container` tag selector.
Add the class `.mt-4` to `div.container`.

The layout is complete.

**14** Save and close **cruises.html**.

**15** Close **favorite-cruises.rtf** without saving any changes.

You've learned how to use lists in the traditional way. But lists can also be used to build elaborate content structures. The template features such a content section.

# Basing content structures on lists

Semantically, lists sequentially display a series of words or phrases of a related topic, usually one over the other. But in HTML, lists can feature much more complex content, including multiple paragraphs of text, images, and more. To the search engines this is a totally valid structure.

In this exercise, you will use the list-based content section in the template to create the company's employee contact list. The list will be composed of six individual bios, stacked two high in three columns.

1. Create a new page from the **favorite-temp.dwt**.
   Save the page as **contact-us.html**.

2. Select the `title` placeholder in the Property inspector.
   Type `Meet our favorite people`

   The new page has three content sections. You will use the list-based section at the bottom. Before we get to that, you will remove all the components that are unneeded. Let's start with the image carousel.

3. Switch to Code view.

   The carousel is part of the optional editable region. You control its display by changing a value in an HTML comment in the `<head>` section.

4. Locate the comment in the `<head>` section (around line 13).

   The comment currently says `value="true"`.

5. Select the value `true` and type `false` to replace it.

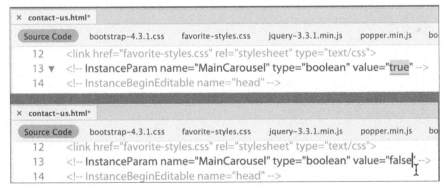

6. Choose Tools > Templates > Update Current Page.

   The carousel is removed from the layout. While you are in Code view, you should edit the meta description.

7. In the meta description, select and replace the text `add description here` with `Meet the staff of Favorite City Tour`

   Let's remove the text-based content section next.

8  Switch to Live view.

Since the carousel was removed, the text-based section is now at the top of the layout.

9  Select the `div.container` tag selector for the text-based section.

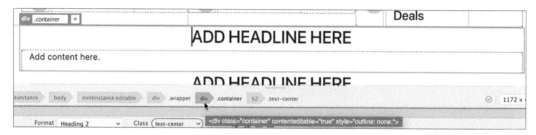

▶ **Tip:** It may be difficult to get the blue border in Live view at times. Use the DOM panel if you have any trouble deleting elements.

The Element Display appears around the selection. If the border is blue, you can skip to step 11.

10  Click the Element Display.

The border displays in blue.

11  Press Delete.

The text-based section is deleted.

12  Repeat steps 9–11 to select and delete the card-based section.

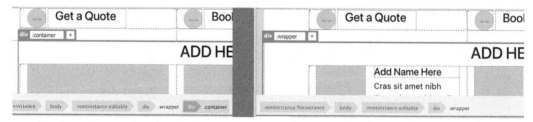

Only the list-based section is still part of the layout.

13  Select the placeholder text ADD HEADLINE HERE.
Type **CONTACT FAVORITE CITY TOUR** to replace the selection.

**14** Click an image placeholder in one of the list-based items. Examine the tag selectors at the bottom of the document window.

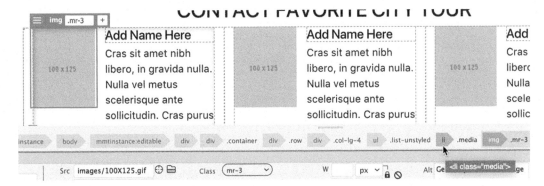

Note that the `<img>` element is a child of an `<li>` element.

**15** Select the `li.media` tag selector.

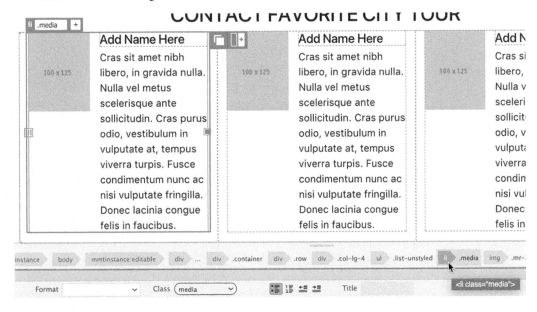

The `<li>` element is composed of a heading, an image placeholder, and a paragraph of text.

**16** Select the `ul` tag selector.

The `<ul>` element comprises one column in the section. You will populate these elements with content in a text file.

**17** Open **contactus-text.txt** from the lesson08/resources folder.

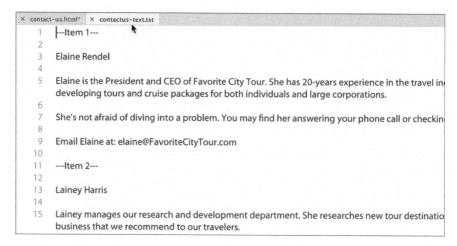

The text file opens in Dreamweaver itself. It contains the bios for the Favorite City Tour staff.

**18** Select the name *Elaine Rendel* and copy it.

**19** Switch to **contact-us.html**.
Select the text *Add Name Here* in the first item and paste to replace it.

Elaine's name appears in the <h5> element. Next you'll move the three paragraphs of Elaine's bio into the element. But you'll have to learn a new trick for pasting multiple elements in Live view.

## Pasting multiple elements in Live view

Dreamweaver presents some challenges to pasting multiple elements when using Live view. If you are used to working in Design view, you'll have to learn a few tricks and have a keen eye before you can successfully paste two or more elements.

**1** Switch to **contactus-text.txt** and copy the three paragraphs under the name *Elaine Rendel*.

**2** Switch to **contact-us.html** in Dreamweaver.
Select the placeholder text under Elaine's heading.

Note the orange box around the selection. This indicates you are in text-editing mode. This mode does not support pasting multiple paragraphs. If you paste the text copied in step 1, it will come in as one continuous block. There's a simple trick to pasting multiple paragraphs in Live view.

3   Press Delete.

The placeholder text is deleted. The Element Display may appear on the `<h5>` element or on `<div.media-body>`. If the border is blue, skip to step 5.

4   Click the Element Display on the `<h5>` element.

The border displays in blue. When an element is selected this way in Live view, you can paste one or more elements and preserve the HTML structure.

5   Press Ctrl+V/Cmd+V to paste.

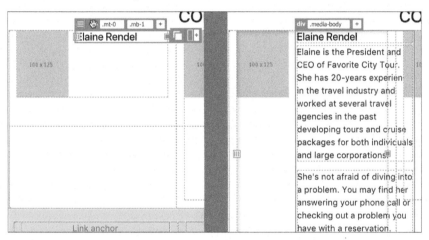

The three paragraphs copied in step 1 appear below the heading within the `<li>` structure, as desired. In Live view the paragraphs seem to extend beyond the borders of the `<div>`. Don't worry—they will display properly in the browser. The first staff bio is complete. Next, you'll create a second row to add another bio.

## Creating new list-based items

If you were to look at the structure of the list-based bio, you would quickly see how complex it is. Since it uses a Bootstrap structure, Dreamweaver provides a simple way to create a second row in the first column.

1   Select the `li.media` tag selector for Elaine's bio.

When it's selected in Live view, you should see the Bootstrap element interface you used to build the tour descriptions earlier. It sounds counterintuitive, but to add a second row you will click the icon labeled Duplicate Column.

**Note:** The Bootstrap controls may appear at the top right or bottom right of a selected element, depending on the space available in the document window.

2   Position the cursor over the Bootstrap controls at the bottom of the selected element.
Click the Duplicate Column icon ⊡.

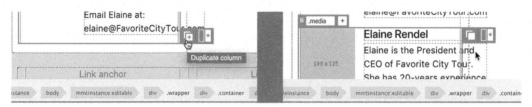

An exact duplicate `<li>` element appears below the first. Note that the new element butts up against the first. Let's use the `.mt-4` class to put a little space between them.

3   Select the `li.media` tag selector for the duplicate bio.
Apply the class `.mt-4` to the element.

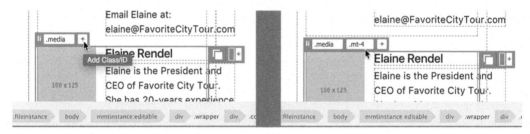

The two bios are now separated nicely.

4   Copy the content from item 2 in **contactus-text.txt** and replace the text in the duplicate bio.

5   Use the text for items 3 and 4 for the second column.
Use the text for items 5 and 6 for the third column.
Create duplicate `<li>` elements as needed.

The six bios are now in place. Note that the list-based section butts up against the row of links at the top. Let's add the `.mt-4` class to it.

6   Select the `div.container` tag selector.
Apply the `.mt-4` class to the element.

Finally, we'll add a bit of style to the layout by adding some borders to the individual bios. To make sure the styling is applied only to these employee profiles, you'll need to create a custom class that you can assign to them.

7   Select the li.media tag selector containing Elaine's bio. Click the Add Class/ID icon.

8   Type .profile as the new class name.

   ● **Note:** Don't forget to type the period at the beginning of the class name.

   As you type, the hinting list appears and displays the names of existing rules. The class .profile doesn't exist yet, but the Element Display enables you to create it on the fly.

9   Press Enter/Return once.

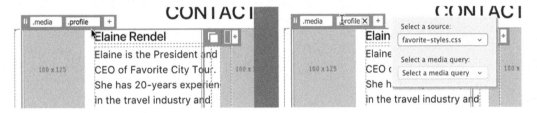

The CSS Source pop-up window appears.

Whenever you enter a new class or id in the Element Display that does not exist in a linked or embedded style sheet, the CSS Source pop-up window will appear. This pop-up enables you to create a new matching selector in any style sheet embedded in the file or linked to it. You can even use it to start a new style sheet, if necessary.

Since the site template is already linked to an external style sheet, **favorite-styles.css** appears in the Select A Source drop-down menu.

10  Press Enter/Return a second time.

   Because you pressed Enter/Return again, the selector .profile is created in the selected style sheet. If you do not want to create a selector for the class or id entered, press the Esc key instead. Once the selector is created, you can use it to style the content.

11  Display the CSS Designer. Click the Current button.

   ▶ **Tip:** When creating specifications manually, enter the property name in the field and press Tab. A value field will appear to the right. When Show Set is enabled, hinting may not appear in the value field.

   The class .profile appears at the top of the list of selectors. If you look at the Properties pane, you can see that no styles are set.

**12** Enter the following properties for the rule `.profile`:

```
border-left: 3px solid #069
border-bottom: 10px solid #069
```

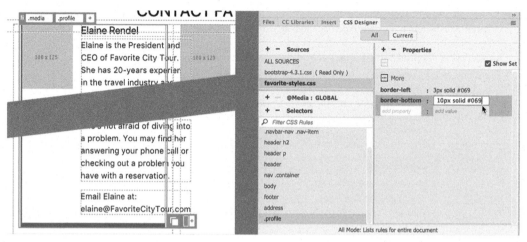

Borders appear on the left and bottom of Elaine's bio. The borders help to visually group the bio text under its heading. You can now style the other bios in the same way.

**13** Apply the class `.profile` to the other staff bios.

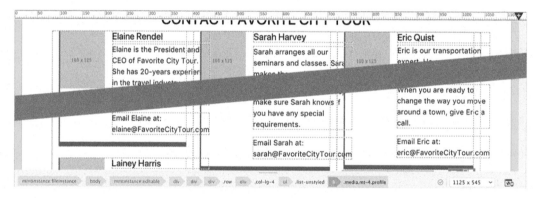

The list-based content section is complete for now.

**14** Save and close all files.

Next, you'll learn how to create and work with HTML tables.

# Creating and styling tables

Before the advent of CSS, HTML tables were often used to create page layouts. At that time, it was the only way to create multicolumn layouts and maintain some control over the content elements. But tables proved to be inflexible and hard to adapt to the changing internet, as well as just being a bad design choice. CSS styling provides so many more options for designing and laying out a webpage that tables were quickly dropped from the designer's toolkit.

That doesn't mean tables are no longer used on the web at all. Although tables are not good for page layout, they are good, and necessary, for displaying many types of data, such as product lists, personnel directories, and timetables, to name a few.

Dreamweaver enables you to create tables from scratch, to copy and paste them from other applications, and to create them instantly from data supplied from other sources, including database and spreadsheet programs such as Microsoft Access or Microsoft Excel.

## Creating tables from scratch

In this exercise, you will learn how to create an HTML table.

1 Create a new page from **favorite-temp**.
Save the file as **events.html** in the site root folder.

2 Enter **Fun Festivals and Seminars** to replace the *Title* placeholder text in the Property inspector.

3 Select the meta description placeholder and type **Favorite City Tour supports a variety of festivals and seminars for anyone interested in learning more about the world around them** to replace it.

4 Switch to Live view, select the *ADD HEADLINE HERE* placeholder heading in the text-based section, and type **OUR FAVORITE FESTIVALS AND SEMINARS** to replace it.

Although the festivals and seminars lists will be displayed in tables, it's always nice to introduce such information with a paragraph of text or two.

5 Select the placeholder text *Add content here.*

6 Type the following text: **Want to see how the world parties? Want to learn a new language? There's no time like the present. Check out our list of international festivals and local seminars. The schedule is updated on a regular basis, so you may want to bookmark this page and check it often. Hope to see you soon!**

### OUR FAVORITE FESTIVALS AND SEMINARS

Want to see how the world parties? Want to learn a new language? There's no time like the present. Check out our list of international festivals and local seminars. The schedule is updated on a regular basis, so you may want to bookmark this page and check it often. Hope to see you soon!

You are now ready to add a table.

7  Choose Insert > Table.

The Position Assist dialog appears.

8  Select After.

The Table dialog appears.

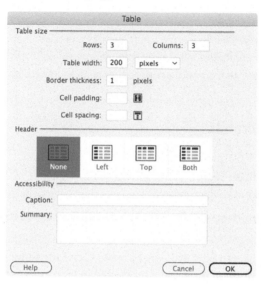

Although CSS has taken over most of the design tasks formerly done by HTML attributes, some aspects of the table may still be controlled and formatted by those attributes. The only advantage HTML has is that its attributes continue to be well supported by all popular browsers, both old and new. When you enter values in this dialog, Dreamweaver still applies them via HTML attributes. But whenever you have a choice, avoid using HTML to format tables.

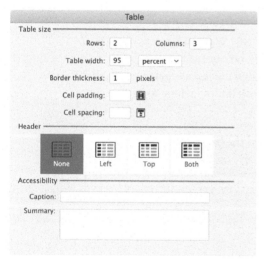

9  Enter the following specifications for the table:
Rows: **2**
Columns: **3**
Table Width: **95%**
Border Thickness: **1**

You would normally set the border thickness to 0 (zero), but that setting makes the table structure basically invisible in Live view. You will change the border thickness later, after the table is complete.

▶ **Tip:** When first creating tables, set the border thickness to 1 to make it easier to work with. You can change it to 0 (zero) after entering data.

**10** Click OK to create the table.

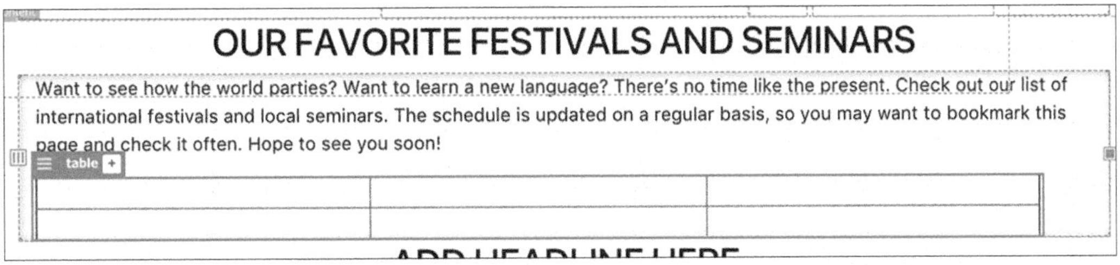

A three-column, two-row table appears below the main heading. The table is ready to accept input. You could enter the data right now, but Live view is not optimized for data entry. If you have large amounts of data to enter, you're better off using Design view.

### Adding data to a table

In this exercise, you'll learn how to add data to a table manually.

**1** Switch to Design view.

**2** Insert the cursor in the first cell of the table.
Type **Date** and press the Tab key.

The cursor moves into the next cell of the same row.

> ▶ **Tip:** When your cursor is in a table cell in Design view, pressing the Tab key moves the cursor to the next cell on the right. Hold the Shift key before pressing the Tab key to move to the left, or backward, through the table.

**3** In the second cell, type **Event** and press Tab.

> ● **Note:** Design view does not display complex CSS styling properly. The sidebars may overlap the tables. If the preview is too hard to work with, try adjusting the width of the document window.

The text appears and the cursor moves to the next cell, but you may find it hard to see it. In some cases, you may need to adjust the size of the document window.

**4** Type **Location** and press Tab.

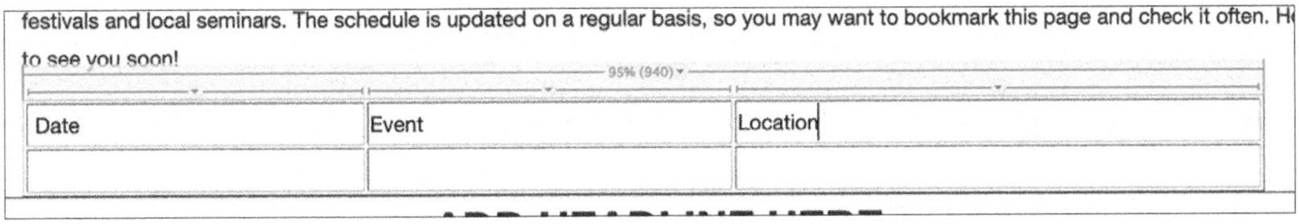

The cursor moves to the first cell of the second row.

5  In the second row, type **May 1, 2021** (in cell 1),
   **May Day Parade** (in cell 2), and
   **Meredien City Hall** (in cell 3).

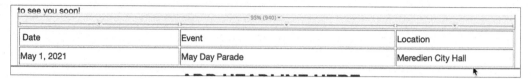

When the cursor is in the last cell, inserting additional rows in the table is easy.

### Adding rows to a table

Dreamweaver provides several ways to add rows and columns to an existing table. In this exercise, you will learn how to add rows to a table.

1  If necessary, insert your cursor in the last cell of the second row. Press Tab.

   A new blank row appears at the bottom of the table. Dreamweaver also allows you to insert multiple new rows at once.

2  Select the `<table>` tag selector.

   ▶ **Tip:** If the Property inspector is not visible, choose Window > Properties. Dock the panel to the bottom of the document window.

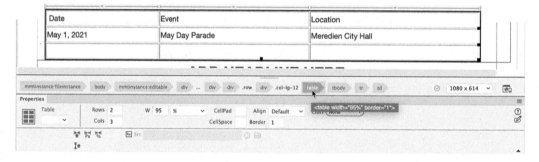

The Property inspector fields create HTML attributes to control various aspects of the table, including table width, cell width and height, text alignment, and so on. It also displays the current number of rows and columns and even allows you to change the number.

**3** Select the number 3 in the Rows field.

Type **5** and press Enter/Return.

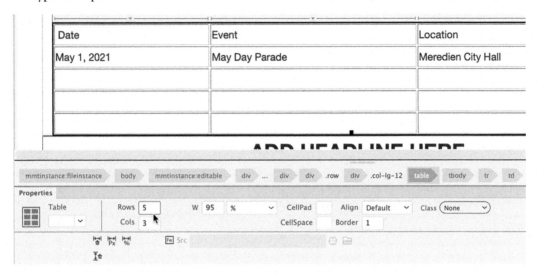

Dreamweaver adds two new rows to the table. You can also add rows and columns to the table interactively using the mouse.

**4** Right-click the last row of the table.

Choose Table > Insert Row from the context menu.

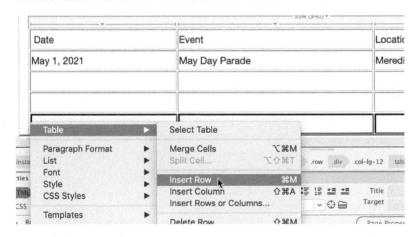

Another row is added to the table. The context menu can also insert multiple rows or columns at once.

**5** Right-click the last row of the table.

Choose Table > Insert Rows Or Columns from the context menu.

The Insert Rows Or Columns dialog appears.

6  Insert four rows below the selection and click OK.

   Four more rows are added to the table, for a total of 10 rows.

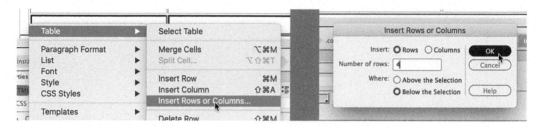

7  Save all files.

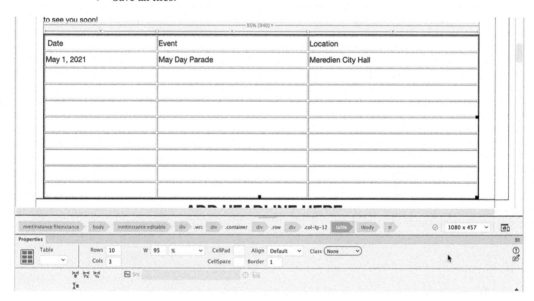

Creating tables from scratch is a handy feature in Dreamweaver, but in many cases the data you need already exists in digital form—say, in a spreadsheet or even another webpage. Luckily, Dreamweaver provides support for moving such data from one page to another or even for creating tables directly from it.

## Copying and pasting tables

Although Dreamweaver allows you to create tables manually inside the program, you can also move tables from other HTML files, or even from other programs, by using copy and paste.

1  Open the Files panel and double-click **festivals.html** in the lesson08/resources folder to open it.

   This HTML file opens in its own tab in Dreamweaver. Note the table structure—it has three columns and numerous rows.

When moving content from one file to another, it's important to match views in both documents. Since you were working in Design view in **events.html**, you should use Design view in this file too.

2 Switch to Design view, if necessary.

3 Insert the cursor in the table.
Click the `<table>` tag selector.
Choose Edit > Copy or press Ctrl+C/Cmd+C.

● **Note:** Dreamweaver allows you to copy and paste tables from some other programs, such as Microsoft Word. Unfortunately, copy and paste doesn't work with every program.

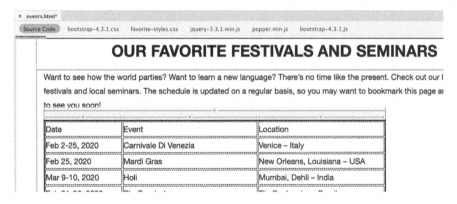

4 Close **festivals.html**.

5 In **events.html**, insert the cursor in the table.
Select the `<table>` tag selector.
Press Ctrl+V/Cmd+V to paste the table.

The new *Festivals* table completely replaces the existing table elements. This workflow will work in Design and Code views. But you must match views in both documents before you copy and paste.

6 Save the file.

If you look carefully at the text in the table, you can see that it appears larger than the text in other parts of the page. This usually indicates that the default Bootstrap styling has its own set of CSS properties. In cases like this, you'll want to override the defaults and set your own properties.

## Styling tables with CSS

In this exercise, you will create CSS styling for the content of the table.

1   Switch to Live view. Click the table.
    Select the `table` tag selector.

2   In the CSS Designer, click the All button.
    Select **favorite-styles.css** in the Sources pane.
    Create a new selector: `table`

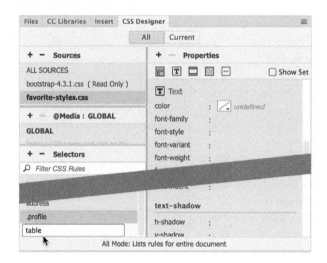

The text in the table is larger than the other text on the page. You can use the new rule to control the size of the text.

3   If necessary, deselect the Show Set option.

4   Click the Text category icon 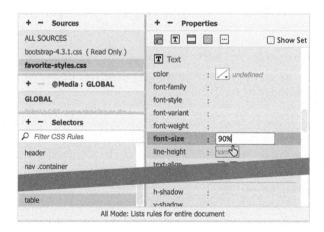.

5   Create the following property for the rule `table`:
    `font-size: 90%`

The text in the table reduces in size. When you set the width property as a percentage, the browser allocates the space based on the size of the parent element—in this case, the containing `<div>` element. This means the table will adapt automatically as the parent structure changes too.

CSS can control all aspects of the table formatting. When creating properties, you can use the extended interface in CSS Designer or you can enter properties manually. Once you get comfortable with the CSS specifications, this method can be much faster and more efficient.

6 If necessary, select the Show Set option.

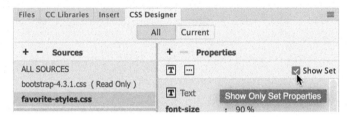

The Property pane now filters the properties showing only options that are set within the rule. At the bottom of the Properties pane is a field labeled *More*. New properties have to be entered manually into this field.

7 Type `width: 95%` into the field and press Enter/Return to create the property.

The table resizes, assuming 95% of the width of its parent element.

8 Create the following properties in the rule `table`:

```
margin-bottom: 2em
border-bottom: 3px solid #069
border-collapse: collapse
```

A blue border and an extra space are added to the bottom of the table.

9 Choose File > Save All.

The rule you just created formats only the overall structure of the table, but it can't control or format the individual rows and columns. In the next exercise, you will turn your attention to a table's inner workings.

## Styling table cells

Just as with tables, column styling can be applied by HTML attributes or CSS rules. Formatting for columns can be applied via two elements that create the individual cells: `<th>`, for *table header*, and `<td>`, for *table data*.

It's a good idea to create a generic rule to reset the default formats of the `<th>` and `<td>` elements. Later, you will create custom rules to apply more specific settings.

1 Create a new selector in **favorite-styles.css**:

```
td, th
```

● **Note:** Remember that the order of the rules can affect the style cascade, as well as how and what styling is inherited.

By adding a comma, the selector targets both tags. Since `td` and `th` elements have to be in tables anyway, there's really no need to put `table` in the selector name.

2. Create the following properties for the new rule:

```
padding: 4px
text-align: left
border-top: 1px solid #069
```

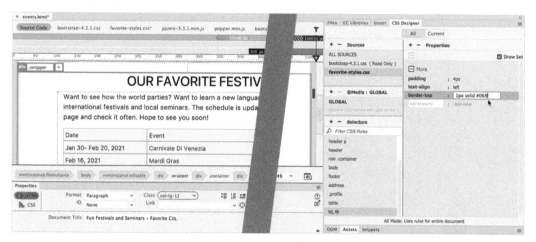

Once you've added a border to the rows, the HTML border attribute is no longer needed.

▶ **Tip:** If you have any problems editing the table properties, try switching to Design view.

3. Select the `table` tag selector.

The Properties panel should display the table properties. If you do not see the table properties, click the tag selector until you see them.

4. Change the Border value to 0 (zero).

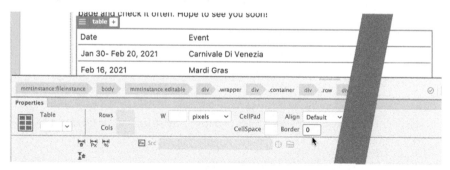

● **Note:** The display of HTML table attributes is a holdover feature in Dreamweaver. CSS styling will override these settings in most modern browsers, but it doesn't hurt to set these to zero and prepare the tables for older browsers or devices.

Once the border attribute is set to zero, the residual HTML styling of the table is removed in the document window. A thin blue horizontal border displays above each row of the table, making the data easier to read. The vertical borders are gone. As you format the table, the goal is to make the data easier to find and read.

## Adding header rows to tables

Long columns and rows of undifferentiated data can be tedious to read and hard to decipher. Headers are often used to help the reader identify data. In some browsers, the text in header cells is formatted in bold and centered by default to help it stand out from the normal cells. But this default styling is not universally honored, so don't count on it. You can make the headers stand out by giving them a touch of color of their own.

● **Note:** The stand-alone th rule for the `<th>` element must appear after the rule styling th and td elements in the CSS or some of its formatting will be reset.

1  Create a new rule: `th`

2  Create the following properties in the rule `th`:
   ```
   color: #FFC
   text-align: center
   border-bottom: 6px solid #046
   background-color: #069
   ```

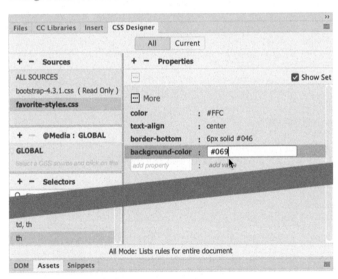

The rule is created, but it still needs to be applied. There are no headers in the table yet. Dreamweaver makes it easy to convert existing `<td>` elements into `<th>` elements.

3  Click the first cell of the first row of the table.
   In the Property inspector, select the Header option.
   Note the tag selector and Element Display.

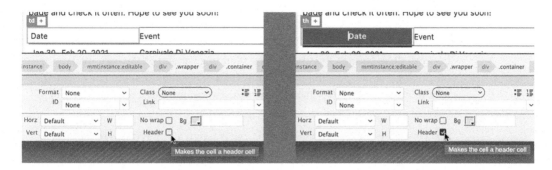

The cell background is filled with blue. The Element Display changes from the td element to th.

When you click the Header checkbox, Dreamweaver automatically rewrites the markup, converting the existing <td> tags to <th> and thereby applying the CSS formatting. This functionality will save you lots of time over editing the code manually. In Live view, to select more than one cell, you have to use the enhanced table-editing function.

4 Select the table tag selector.

The Element Display appears focused on the table element. To enable the special editing mode for tables, you must first click the sandwich icon in the Element Display.

5 Click the sandwich icon ▤.

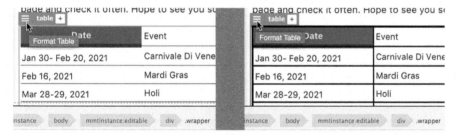

When you click the icon, Dreamweaver enables an enhanced table-editing mode. Now you can select two or more cells, entire rows, or columns.

6 Click the second cell of the first row and drag to select the first row.

7 In the Property inspector, select the Header option to convert the table cells to header cells.

The whole first row is filled with blue as the table cells are converted to header cells.

8 Save all files.

## Controlling table display

Unless you specify otherwise, empty table columns will divide the available space between them equally. But once you start adding content to the cells, all bets are off. Tables seem to get a mind of their own and divvy up the space in a different way. In most cases, they'll award more space to columns that contain more data, but that's not guaranteed to happen.

To provide the highest level of control, you'll assign unique classes to the cells in each column. Creating them first makes it easier to assign them to the various elements later.

1   Choose **favorite-styles.css**.
    Create the following new selectors:
    `.date`
    `.event`
    `.location`

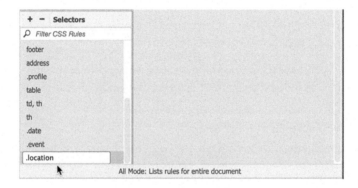

Three new rules appear in the Selectors window but contain no styling information. Even without styling, the classes can be assigned to each column. Dreamweaver makes it easy to apply classes to an entire column.

● **Note:** If you have difficulty working with tables in Live view, you can perform all these actions in Design view.

2   Using the enhanced table-editing mode, position the cursor at the top of the first column of the table.
    Click to select the entire column.

The column borders turn blue, indicating that the column is selected.

**3** Click to open the Class menu in the Property inspector.

A list of classes appears in alphabetical order. Since the Bootstrap style sheet is linked to this page, the list of selectors and classes will be very long.

**4** Choose *date* from the list.

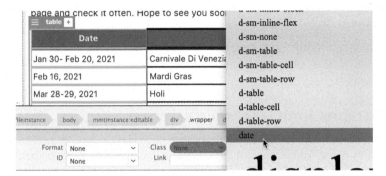

The cells in the first column should now have the class .date applied to them. But after applying the class to the first column, you may notice that Dreamweaver has returned the table to normal mode again.

**5** Select the table tag selector.
Click the sandwich icon in the Element Display.
Apply the .event class to the second column.

**6** Repeat step 5 to apply the .location class to the remaining column.

Controlling the width of a column is quite simple. Since the entire column must be the same width, you can apply a width specification to only one cell. If cells in a column have conflicting specifications, typically the largest width wins. Since you just applied a class to each column, any settings added to the class will affect every cell in that column.

● **Note:** Even if you apply a width that's too narrow for the existing content, by default a cell can't be any smaller than the largest single word or graphic element contained within it.

**7** Add this property to the rule .date:
width: 25%

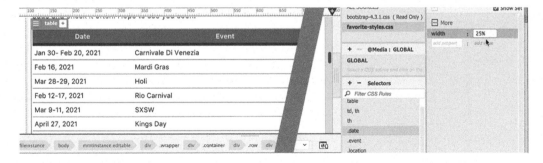

The Date column resizes. In this case, the parent of the Date column is the `<table>` element itself. It will occupy 20 percent of the overall table width. In turn, the remaining columns automatically divvy up the space left over.

8  Add the following property to the rule .location:
   `width: 30%`

   The Location column resizes to a width of 30 percent of the entire table. Since the outer two columns have specific widths set, there's no need to set the width of the Event column.

9  Save all files.

Now, if you want to control the styling of the columns individually, you have the ability to do so. Note that the tag selectors and the Element Display show the class names for each cell, such as th.location or td.location.

## Inserting tables from other sources

In addition to creating tables by hand, you can also create them from data exported from databases and spreadsheets. In this exercise, you will create a table from data that was exported from Microsoft Excel to a comma-separated values (CSV) file. The import feature does not work in Live view.

1  Switch to Design view.
   Insert the cursor in the existing *Events* table.
   Select the table tag selector.

2  Press the right arrow key.

   In Design view, this technique moves the cursor after the closing </table> tag within the code.

3  Choose File > Import > Tabular Data.

   The Import Tabular Data dialog appears.

4  Click the Browse button and select **seminars.csv** from the lesson08/resources folder. Click Open.
   Select Comma in the Delimiter menu, if necessary.

5  Enter the following values in the Import Tabular Data dialog:
   Table Width: 95% Border: 0

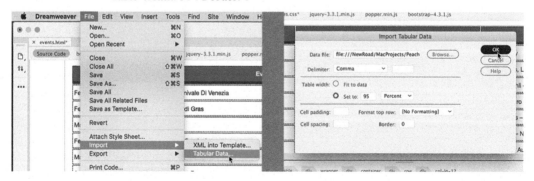

   Although you set the width in the dialog, as you did for the *Events* table, remember that the table width will actually be controlled by the table rule created earlier. HTML attributes will be honored in browsers or devices that do not support CSS, although this is rare. Because this is the case, make sure that the HTML attributes you use don't break the layout.

6 Click OK.

A new table—containing a seminar schedule—appears below the first. Note that the first row of the table is a header row. In Design view you can select table rows and columns directly.

7 In the *Seminars* table, position the cursor near the left edge of the first row.

A black arrow should appear at the edge of the row. Depending on whether you are in Windows or macOS, the arrow may point right or down. It works the same way regardless of which direction it points. Note that the first row is highlighted with red borders.

8 Click to select the first row.

9 Click the Header option in the Property inspector.

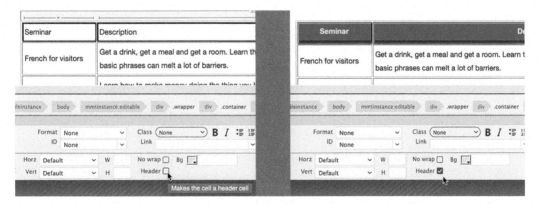

The header cells now display in blue with white text. The new table is complete.

Semantically, the two tables do not relate to each other. Although human visitors may be able to distinguish where one table ends and another begins, adding a semantic structure to your content makes it easier for search engines and assistive devices to derive sense from the content. The tables should each be placed in their own separate HTML structures.

## Creating semantic text structures

Adding semantic structures should be your goal whenever possible. This is encouraged not only to support accessibility standards but also to improve your SEO ranking. In this exercise, you will insert each table into its own `<section>` element.

1  In Design view, select the `table` tag selector for the *Festivals* table.

2  Choose Insert > Section.
Select **Wrap Around Selection** from the Insert menu.
Click OK to insert the `<section>` element.

The *Festivals* table is inserted into a `<section>` element. You should be able to see the new element in the tag selector interface. Now, let's take care of the *Seminars* table.

3  Select the `table` tag selector for the *Seminars* table.

4  Choose Insert > Section.
Select **Wrap Around Selection** from the Insert menu.
Click OK to insert the `<section>` element.

Both tables are now in their own `<section>` elements.

The *Seminars* table has two more columns than the *Festivals* table. The text is wrapping awkwardly in the last three columns. You will fix this display issue by creating some additional CSS classes.

5 In the CSS Designer, create a new selector: `.cost`
Add the following properties:
`width 10%`
`text-align: center`

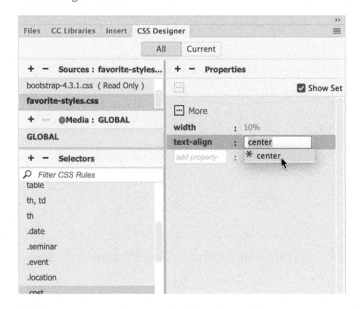

6 In the *Seminars* table, select the Cost column.
Apply the class `.cost` to the selection.

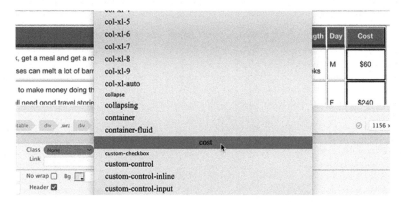

The Cost column widens noticeably. We can use the same specifications on the other two columns, but you'll make custom rules for each one.

7 In CSS Designer, right-click the rule `.cost`.
Choose Copy All Styles from the context menu.

8   Create a new selector: `.length`
    Right-click the new selector.
    Select Paste Styles from the context menu.

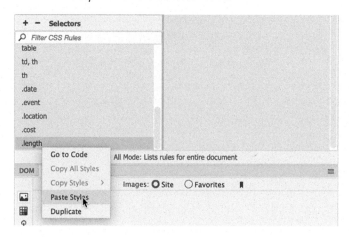

    The new rule now has the same styling as the `.cost` rule.

9   Repeat step 6 to apply the `length` class to the Length column in the *Seminars* table.

    Dreamweaver also provides an option for duplicating rules.

10  Right-click the rule `.length`.
    Choose Duplicate from the context menu.
    Enter `.day` as the new selector.

11  Apply the `.day` class to the Day column in the *Seminars* table, as in step 9.

    By creating and applying custom classes to each column, you have the means to modify each column individually in the future. You need to make two more rules: one to format the Seminar column and the other to format the Description column.

12  Duplicate the rule `.date`.
    Enter `.seminar` as the new rule name.

13 Duplicate the rule `.event`.

Enter `.description` as the new name.

At the moment, these rules have no styling properties assigned to them. But you can use them in the future to control all aspects of these columns.

14 Apply the `.seminar` class to the Seminar column.

Apply the `.description` class to the Description column.

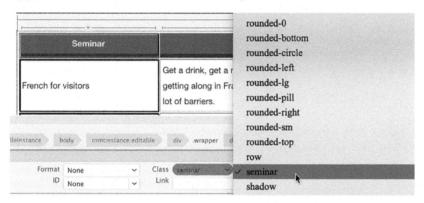

All columns in both tables now have custom CSS classes assigned to them.

15 Save all files.

Tables should have descriptive titles or captions that help visitors and search engines differentiate between them.

## Adding and formatting caption elements

The two tables you inserted on the page contain different information but don't feature any labels or titles. Let's add a title to each. The `<caption>` element was designed to identify the content of HTML tables. This element is inserted as a child of the `<table>` element itself.

1 Open **events.html** in Live view, if necessary.

Make sure the document window is at least 1200 pixels wide.

2 Insert the cursor in the *Festivals* table.

Select the `table` tag selector.

Note the color of the element display. If the border is blue, you can skip to step 4.

3 Click the Element Display.

The border of the Element Display changes to blue.

4 Switch to Code view.

By selecting the table first in Live view, Dreamweaver automatically highlights the code in Code view, making it easier to find.

5 Locate the opening `<table>` tag.

Insert the cursor directly after this tag.

Press Enter/Return to insert a new line.

6 Type `<caption>` or select it from the code-hinting menu when it appears.

7 Type `2021 INTERNATIONAL FESTIVAL SCHEDULE` and then type `</` to close the element, if necessary.

```
111 ▼        <section>
112 ▼         <table border="0">
113 ▼          <caption>2021 INTERNATIONAL FESTIVAL SCHEDULE </caption>
114            <tr>
11             th  l    "d t il" D t    /th
```

| mmtinstance:fileinstance | body | mmtinstance:editable | div | div | .container | div | .row | div | .col-lg-12 | section |

8 Repeat steps 2 through 6 for the *Seminars* table.

Type `2021 SEMINAR SCHEDULE` and then type `</` to close the element, if necessary.

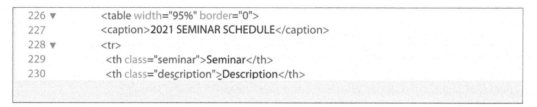

```
226 ▼        <table width="95%" border="0">
227           <caption>2021 SEMINAR SCHEDULE</caption>
228 ▼         <tr>
229            <th class="seminar">Seminar</th>
230            <th class="description">Description</th>
```

9 Switch to Live view.

The default captions appear at the bottom of the tables and are relatively small and understated. The captions are lost amid the color and formatting of the table. Let's beef them up a bit with their own custom CSS rule and move them up to the top of the tables.

10 Create a new selector: `table caption`

**11** Create these properties for the rule `table caption`:

```
margin-top: 20px
padding-bottom: 10px
color: #069
font-size: 160%
font-weight: bold
line-height: 1.2em
text-align: center
caption-side: top
```

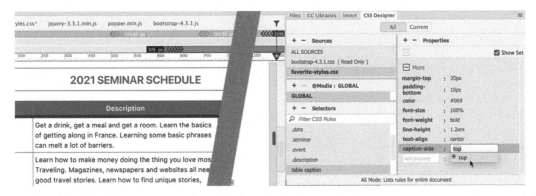

The captions now appear at the top of the tables, sufficiently large and impressive.

**12** Save all files.

Formatting the tables and the captions with CSS has made them much easier to read and understand. Feel free to experiment with the size and placement of the captions and with the other specifications affecting the tables.

# Spell-checking webpages

It's important to ensure that the content you post to the web is error-free. Dreamweaver includes a robust spell-checker capable of identifying commonly misspelled words and of creating a custom dictionary for nonstandard terms that you might use on a regular basis.

**1** Open **contact-us.html**, if necessary.

**2** Switch to Design view. Insert the cursor at the beginning of the heading *CONTACT FAVORITE CITY TOUR*. Choose Tools > Spell Check.

The spell-checker starts wherever the cursor has been inserted. If the cursor is located lower on the page, you will have to restart the spell-checker at least once to examine the entire page. It also does not check content locked in noneditable template regions.

**Note:** The spell-checker runs only in Design view. If you are in Code view or Live view, the command will be grayed out.

The Check Spelling dialog highlights the word *Rendel*, which is the CEO's last name. You could click the option Add To Personal to insert the word into your custom dictionary, but for now you will skip over other occurrences of the name during this check.

3  Click Ignore All.

Dreamweaver's spell-checker highlights Elaine's name in her email address.

4  Click Ignore All again.

Dreamweaver highlights the domain for the email address elaine@FavoriteCityTour.com.

5  Click Ignore All.

Dreamweaver highlights Lainey's name. For real names in your own company or website, you may want to click the Add button to insert the names permanently into the dictionary.

6  Click Ignore All for Lainey and any other proper names.

Dreamweaver highlights the word *busines*, which is missing an *s*.

7  To correct the spelling, locate the correctly spelled word (*business*) in the Suggestions list and click Change.

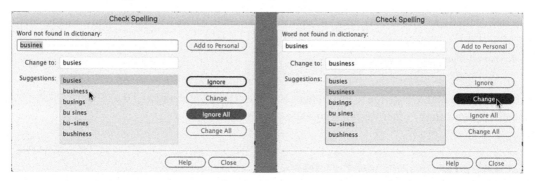

8  Continue the spell-check to the end.
Correct any misspelled words and ignore proper names, as necessary. If a dialog prompts you to start the check from the beginning, click Yes.

Dreamweaver will start spell-checking from the top of the file to catch any words it may have missed.

9  Click OK when the spell-check is complete.
Save the file.

It's important to point out that the spell-checker is designed to find only words that are *spelled* incorrectly. It will not find words that are *used* incorrectly. In those instances, nothing takes the place of a careful reading of the content.

# Finding and replacing text

The ability to find and replace text is one of Dreamweaver's most powerful features. Unlike other programs, Dreamweaver can find almost anything, anywhere in your site, including text, code, and any type of whitespace that can be created in the program. You can search the entire markup, or you can limit the search to the rendered text or to the underlying tags.

Advanced users can enlist powerful pattern-matching algorithms known as *regular expressions* to perform sophisticated find-and-replace operations. And then Dreamweaver takes it one step further by allowing you to replace the targeted text or code with similar amounts of text, code, and whitespace.

If you are a user of older versions of Dreamweaver, you will see some significant changes in the Find And Replace function.

In this exercise, you'll learn some important techniques for using the Find And Replace feature.

1   Open **events.html**, if necessary.

    There are several ways to identify the text or code you want to find. One way is to simply type it in the Find field. In the *Events* table, the word *visitor* was used. The word *traveler* was a better choice. Since *visitor* is an actual word, the spell-checker won't flag it as an error and give you the opportunity to correct it. So you'll use Find And Replace to make the change instead.

2   Switch to Code view, if necessary.
    Choose Find > Replace In Current Document.

    The Find And Replace panel appears at the bottom of the document window. If you have not used the feature before, the Find field should be empty.

3   Type **visitor** in the Find field.

    As you type, Dreamweaver finds the first occurrence of *visitor* and indicates how many matches it has found in the document.

4   Type **traveler** in the Replace field.

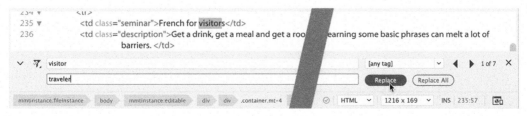

5 Click Replace.

Dreamweaver replaces the first instance of *visitor* and immediately searches for the next instance. You can continue to replace the words one at a time, or you can choose to replace all occurrences.

6 Click Replace All.

When you click Replace All, the Search Report panel expands to list all the changes made.

7 Right-click the Search Report tab and select Close Tab Group from the context menu. Click the Close icon ✖ on the Find panel to recover the screen space.

Another method for targeting text and code is to select it *before* activating the command. This method can be used in either Design or Code view.

8 In Code view, locate and select the code
`<div class="wrapper">`, around line 105.

## Superpowerfindelicious!

Find And Replace is one of the most powerful features in the program. It allows you to target, or limit, the search to the source code, to text only, to be based on case, and to whole words, and it gives you the ability to use *regular expressions* and to *ignore whitespace*. I could write an entire book on all the ways you could use this feature.

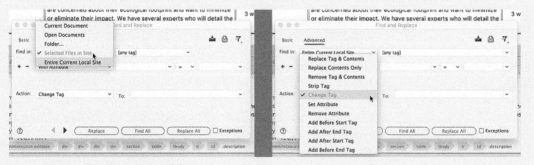

**9** Press Ctrl+F/Cmd+F.

The Find And Replace panel appears. The selected text is automatically entered into the Find field by Dreamweaver. This technique will work with small snippets of text or code. With the text selected like this, Dreamweaver will find the occurrence of this code element in the current file. But we want to find it throughout the entire site.

● **Note:** The Find And Replace panel typically appears with the Replace function hidden.

**10** Choose Find > Find And Replace In Files.

▶ **Tip:** In the Find And Replace dialog, the Basic tab should be displayed by default; if not, go ahead and click it.

The Find And Replace dialog appears. The selected code is automatically added to the search field. Note that the Find In field should be targeting Entire Current Local Site.

**11** Click Find All.

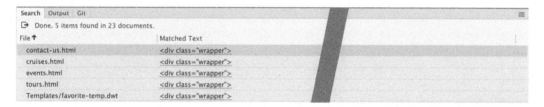

The Search panel appears, displaying all instances of the selected code within the site. The selected `<div>` element contains all the primary content of the site. Semantically, the page structure should use the `<main>` element instead. But we cannot just change the opening tag. We need to change both the opening and closing tags.

**12** Choose Find > Find And Replace In Files again.

The Find And Replace dialog appears. The code `<div class="wrapper">` appears in the search field. Dreamweaver has identified all instances of the tag we need to change, but if you tried to replace the tag now it would simply swap out the opening tag. Instead, we need to use the advanced features of the dialog.

**13** Click the Advanced tab in the Find And Replace dialog.

Dreamweaver may automatically populate the attribute field with the wrapper class name. It's a good idea to target the exact tag whenever possible.

**14** In the Find In field, select div from the drop-down menu on the right. If necessary, select With Attribute and class from the appropriate drop-down menus.
Enter wrapper in the class drop-down menu.

Next you can target the tag you want to end up with.

**15** In the Action field, choose Change Tag, if necessary.
Choose main from the To drop-down menu.

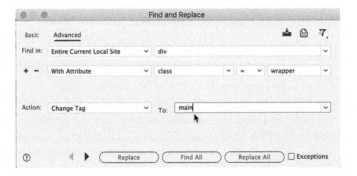

**16** Click Replace All.

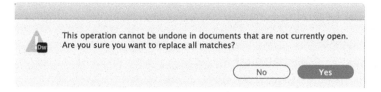

An unnamed dialog appears, reporting that the replace operation cannot be undone in any closed documents.

**17** Click Yes.

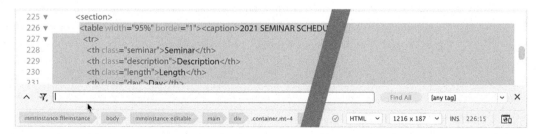

The Search Results panel displays the list of elements replaced in the site. It should show five pages in the list. The `<div class="wrapper">` element is replaced, in all the documents where it was found, with `<main class="wrapper">`.

**18** Right-click the Search Results tab and select Close Tab Group from the context menu.

When searching for text and code, you have seen that you can enter text into the search field and select text prior to activating the Find command. Unfortunately, there's a limit to the amount of text Dreamweaver will add to the field automatically. For larger blocks of text and code, Dreamweaver also allows you to copy and paste into the search field.

**19** In Code view, insert the cursor in the *Seminars* table. Select the `table` tag selector.

The entire `<table>` element is selected, which represents nearly 100 lines of code.

**20** Press Ctrl+C/Cmd+C to copy the selected code.

The Search panel appears, but notice that the Find field is empty. The selected code is just too much for the automatic feature. This is where copy and paste comes in handy.

**21** Press Ctrl+F/Cmd+F.

**22** Insert the cursor in the Find field.
Press Ctrl+V/Cmd+V to paste the selected code.

The entire markup of the table appears in the Find field. But this power is not limited to the Find field.

**23** Click to expand the Find panel to show the Replace field.

**24** Insert the cursor in the Replace field.
Press Ctrl+V/Cmd+V, or right-click in the field and choose Paste from the context menu, to paste the code.

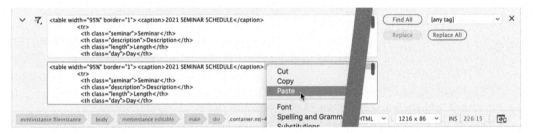

The entire table markup appears in the Replace field. As you can see, Find And Replace enables you to search for almost any type of markup or content and replace it wherever it appears in the site.

**25** If necessary, close the Find And Replace panel.
Save all files.

In this lesson, you created four new pages and learned how to import text and data from multiple sources. You formatted text as headings and lists, and then styled it using CSS. You inserted and formatted two tables and added captions to both. And you reviewed and corrected text and code elements using Dreamweaver's spell-checker and Find And Replace tools.

# Review questions

1  Explain how to turn paragraph text into an ordered or unordered list.

2  Describe two methods for inserting HTML tables into a webpage.

3  What element controls the width of a table column?

4  What items will not be found by Dreamweaver's spell-checker?

5  Describe three different ways to insert content in the Find field.

# Review answers

1  To create an ordered or unordered list, highlight the text with the cursor and click the Ordered List or Unordered List button, respectively, in the Property inspector.

2  You can copy and paste a table from another HTML file or from a compatible program. Or you can insert a table by importing the data from a delimited file.

3  The width of a table column is controlled by the widest `<th>` or `<td>` element that creates the individual table cell within the specific column.

4  The spell-checker finds only words that are *spelled* incorrectly, not those that are *used* incorrectly.

5  You can type text into the Find field, you can select text before you open the panel and then allow Dreamweaver to insert the selected text, or you can copy the text or code and then paste it into the field.

# **9** WORKING WITH IMAGES

## Lesson overview

In this lesson, you'll learn how to work with images and include them in your webpages. You'll learn how to do the following:

- Insert an image into a webpage.
- Use Photoshop Smart Objects.
- Copy and paste an image from Photoshop.
- Make images responsive to different devices and screen sizes.
- Use tools in Dreamweaver to resize, crop, and resample web-compatible images.

 This lesson will take about 90 minutes to complete. To get the lesson files used in this lesson, download them from the webpage for this book at www.adobepress.com/DreamweaverCIB2021. For more information, see "Accessing the lesson files and Web Edition" in the "Getting Started" section at the beginning of this book.

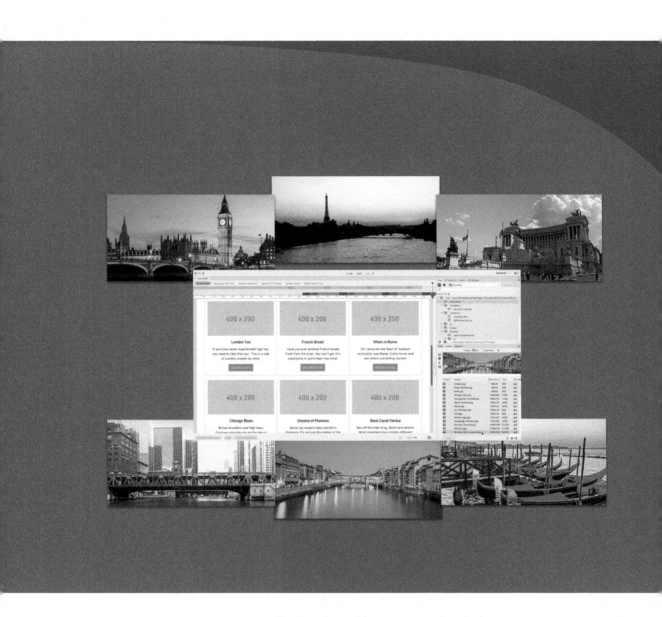

Dreamweaver provides many ways to insert and adjust graphics, both within the program and in tandem with other Creative Cloud tools, such as Adobe Photoshop.

# Web image basics

The web is not so much a place as it is an experience. Essential to that experience are the images and graphics—both still and animated—that populate most websites. In the computer world, graphics fall into two main categories: vector and raster.

Vector graphic formats excel in line art, drawings, and logo art. Raster technology works better for storing photographic images.

**Vector**                                         **Raster**

## Vector graphics

Vector graphics are created by math. They act as discrete objects that you can reposition and resize as many times as you want without affecting or diminishing their output quality. The best application of vector art is wherever geometric shapes and text are used to create artistic effects. For example, most company logos are built from vector shapes.

Vector graphics are typically stored in the AI, EPS, PICT, or WMF file formats. Unfortunately, most web browsers don't support these formats. The vector format that is supported is SVG (Scalable Vector Graphic). The simplest way to get started with SVG is to create a graphic in your favorite vector-drawing program—such as Adobe Illustrator or CorelDRAW—and then export it to this format. If you are a good programmer, you may want to try creating SVG graphics using XML (Extensible Markup Language). Visit www.w3schools.com/html/html5_svg.asp to find out more about creating SVG graphics.

## Raster graphics

Although SVG has definite advantages, web designers primarily use raster-based images in their webpages. Raster images are built from *pixels*, which stands for *picture elements*. Pixels have three basic characteristics:

- They are perfectly square in shape.
- They are all the same size.
- They display only one color at a time.

Raster-based images are composed of thousands, even millions, of pixels arranged in rows and columns, in patterns that create the illusion of an actual photo, painting, or drawing. It's an illusion, because there is no real photo on the screen, just a bunch of pixels that fool your eyes into seeing an image. And as the quality of the image increases, the illusion becomes more realistic. Raster image quality is based on three factors: resolution, size, and color.

The inset image shows an enlargement of the flowers, revealing the pixels that compose the image itself.

## Resolution

Resolution is the best known of the factors affecting raster image quality. It is the expression of image quality measured in the number of pixels that fit in 1 inch (ppi). The more pixels you can fit in 1 inch, the more detail you can depict in the image. But better quality comes at a price. An unfortunate byproduct of higher resolution is larger file size. That's because each pixel must be stored as bytes of information within the image file—information that has real overhead in computer terms. More pixels means more information, which means larger files.

**Note:** Printers and printing presses use round "dots" to create photographic images. Quality on a printer is measured in dots per inch, or dpi. The process of converting the square pixels used in your computer into the round dots used on the printer is called screening.

**72 ppi**

**300 ppi**

Resolution has a dramatic effect on image output. The web image on the left looks fine in the browser but doesn't have enough quality for printing.

Luckily, web images have to appear and look their best only on computer screens, which are based mostly on a resolution of 72 ppi. This is low compared to other applications or types of output—such as professional four-color printing—where 300 dpi is considered the lowest acceptable quality. The lower resolution of the computer screen is an important factor in keeping most web image files at a reasonable size for downloading from the internet.

### Size

*Size* refers to the vertical and horizontal dimensions of the image. As image size increases, more pixels are required to create it, and therefore the file becomes larger. Since graphics take more time to download than HTML code, many designers in recent years have replaced graphical components with CSS formatting to speed up the web experience for their visitors. But if you need or want to use images, one method to ensure snappy downloads is to keep image size small. Even today, with the proliferation of high-speed internet service, many websites still avoid using full-screen graphics, although that too has changed.

Although these two images have identical resolution and color depth, you can see how image dimensions can affect file size.

**500KB**

**1.6MB**

### Color

*Color* refers to the color space, or *palette*, that describes each image. Most computer screens display only a fraction of the colors that the human eye can see. And different computers and applications display varying levels of color, expressed by the term *bit depth*. Monochrome, or 1-bit color, is the smallest color space, displaying only black and white, with no shades of gray. Monochrome is used mostly for line-art illustrations, for blueprints, and to reproduce handwriting or signatures.

The 4-bit color space describes up to 16 colors. Additional colors can be simulated by a process known as *dithering*, where the available colors are interspersed and juxtaposed to create an illusion of more colors. This color space was created for the first color computer systems and game consoles. Because of its limitations, this palette is seldom used today.

The 8-bit palette offers up to 256 colors or 256 shades of gray. This was the basic color system of all computers, mobile phones, game systems, and handheld devices. This color space also includes what is known as the *web-safe* color palette. Web-safe refers to a subset of 8-bit colors that are supported on both Mac and Windows computers. Most computers, game consoles, handheld devices, and even phones now support higher color palettes, so 8-bit is not as important anymore. Unless you need to support non-computer devices, you can probably disregard the web-safe palette altogether.

Today, only a rare cellphone or handheld game supports the 16-bit color space. This palette is named *high color* and sports a grand total of 65,000 colors. Although this sounds like a lot, 16-bit color is not considered good enough for most graphic design purposes or professional printing.

The highest color space is 24-bit color, which is named *true color*. This system generates up to 16.7 million colors. It is the gold standard for graphic design and professional printing. Several years ago, a new color space was added to the mix: 32-bit color. It doesn't offer any additional colors, but it provides an additional 8 bits of data for an attribute known as *alpha transparency*.

Alpha transparency enables you to designate parts of an image or graphic as fully or partially transparent. This trick allows you to create graphics that seem to have rounded corners or curves and can even eliminate the white bounding box typical of raster graphics.

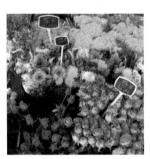

**24-bit color**       **8-bit color**       **4-bit color**

Here you can see a dramatic comparison of three color spaces and what the total number of available colors means to image quality.

As with size and resolution, color depth can dramatically affect image file size. With all other aspects being equal, an 8-bit image is more than seven times larger than a monochrome image. And the 24-bit version is more than three times larger than the 8-bit image. The key to the effective use of images on a website is finding the balance of resolution, size, and color to achieve the desired optimal quality.

Optimizing your images is essential, even as more people get smartphones and tablets, because there are still millions of people all across the United States, and around the world, who don't have high-speed wired access to the internet. The FCC released a report 2020 describing the state of broadband access and adoption in the

United States. This report indicates that 19 million American do not have access to broadband and that, more importantly, 100 million who do have access have not subscribed to a service. That means almost one-third of America does not have high-speed internet. Check out https://tinyurl.com/broadband-coverage to see the specific details. While using large, colorful images on the web is very popular, it could also cause severe problems for your target audience, depending on where they live.

## Raster image file formats

Raster images can be stored in a multitude of file formats, but web designers have to be concerned with only three: GIF, JPEG, and PNG. These three formats are optimized for use on the internet and are compatible with virtually every browser. However, they are not equal in capability.

### GIF

GIF (Graphics Interchange Format) was one of the first raster image file formats designed specifically for the web. It has changed only a little in the last 30 years. GIF supports a maximum of 256 colors (8-bit palette) and 72 ppi, so it's used mainly for web interfaces—buttons and graphical borders and such. But it does have two interesting features that keep it pertinent for today's web designers: index transparency and support for simple animation.

### JPEG

JPEG, also written JPG, is named for the Joint Photographic Experts Group that created the image standard back in 1992 as a direct reaction to the limitations of the GIF file format. JPEG is a powerful format that supports unlimited resolution, image dimensions, and color depth. Because of this, most digital cameras use JPEG as their default file type for image storage. It's also the reason most designers use JPEG on their websites for images that must be displayed in high quality.

This may sound odd to you, since "high quality" (as described earlier) usually means large file size. Large files take longer to download to your browser. So why is this format so popular on the web? The JPEG format's claim to fame comes from its patented user-selectable image compression algorithm, which can reduce file size as much as 95 percent. JPEG images are compressed each time they are saved and then decompressed as they are opened and displayed.

Unfortunately, all this compression has a downside. Too much compression damages image quality. This type of compression is called *lossy*, because it loses quality. In fact, the loss in quality is great enough that it can potentially render an image totally useless. Each time designers save a JPEG image, they face a trade-off between image quality and file size.

| **Low quality**<br>**High compression**<br>**130K** | **Medium quality**<br>**Medium compression**<br>**150K** | **High quality**<br>**Low compression**<br>**260K** |

## PNG

PNG (Portable Network Graphics) was developed in 1995 because of a looming patent dispute involving the GIF format. At the time, it looked as if designers and developers would have to pay a royalty for using the .gif file extension. Although that issue blew over, PNG has found many adherents and a home on the internet because of its capabilities.

PNG combines many of the features of GIF and JPEG and adds a few of its own. For example, it offers support for unlimited resolution, 32-bit color, and full alpha transparency. It also provides lossless compression, which means you can save an image in PNG format and not worry about losing any quality when you save the file.

The only downside to PNG is that its most important feature—alpha transparency—may not be fully supported in older browsers. Luckily, these browsers are retired year after year, so this issue is becoming less of a concern to most web designers.

But as with everything on the web, your own needs may vary from the general trends. Before using any specific technology, it's always a good idea to check your site analytics and confirm which browsers your visitors are actually using.

# Previewing the completed files

To get a sense of the files you will work on in this lesson, let's preview the completed pages in a browser.

1   Launch Adobe Dreamweaver CC (2021 release) or later.

2   Define a new site for the lesson09 folder, as described in the "Getting Started" section at the beginning of the book. Name the new site **lesson09**.

**Note:** If you have not already downloaded the project files for this lesson to your computer from your Account page, make sure to do so now. See "Getting Started" at the beginning of the book.

3 Open **contactus-finished.html** in Live view from the lesson09/finished folder.

The page includes several images.

4 Open **aboutus-finished.html** in Live view from the lesson09/finished folder.

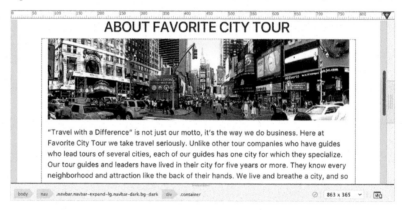

The *About Us* page contains an image that adapts automatically to the size of the screen.

5 Drag the scrubber to the left to change the width of the document window. Notice that the image in the text area scales with the layout.

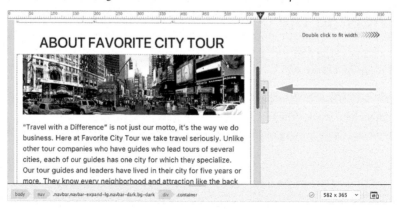

6   Open **tours-finished.html** and observe the image carousel.

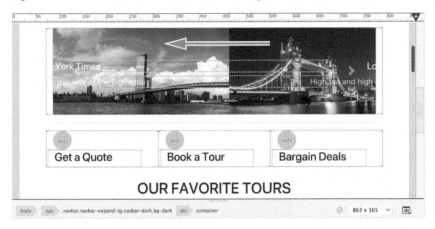

The image carousel displays a large image that animates by moving from right to left. It pauses for a moment and then another image slides onto the screen. Note the headings and text that accompany each image.

7   Close all sample files.

In the following exercises, you will insert these images into these pages using a variety of techniques and format them to work on any screen.

# Inserting an image

Images are key components of any webpage, both for developing visual interest and for telling stories. Dreamweaver provides numerous ways to populate your pages with images, using built-in commands and even using copy and paste from other Adobe apps.

1   In the Files panel, open **contact-us.html** in Live view. Make sure the document window is at least 1200 pixels wide.

The layout contains six profiles of the Favorite City Tour staff. Each profile contains an image placeholder. You may have noticed the numbers 100 x 125 that appear in the placeholder. These indicate the dimensions of the placeholder and the replacement images. In most cases, you will want to resize and resample images before you place them in the layout.

When a layout uses placeholder images, the easiest way to replace them is by using the Property inspector.

2   If necessary, choose Window > Properties to display the Property inspector. Dock it to the bottom of the document window.

● **Note:** When working with images in Dreamweaver, you should be sure that your site's default images folder is set up according to the directions in the "Getting Started" section at the beginning of the book.

3   Select the image placeholder in the profile for Elaine.

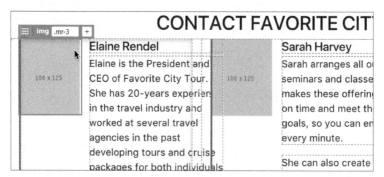

The Element Display appears focused on the img element. Note the class .mr-3 applied to it. The Property inspector displays the properties for image elements.

In HTML, images do not actually appear in the code. Instead, the <img> element references an image file somewhere on the web server or elsewhere on the internet. Then, the browser locates that file and renders it in the page. The Property inspector enables you to identify the assigned image source file and specify a new one.

4   Examine the Src field in the Property inspector.

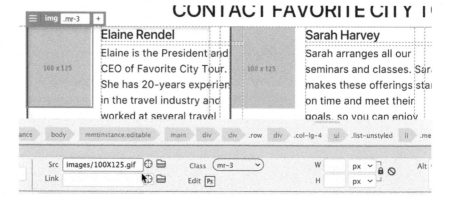

The Src field says images/100X125.gif, which is the name and location of the image placeholder. You can use this field to load the image for Elaine.

**5** Click the Browse For File icon 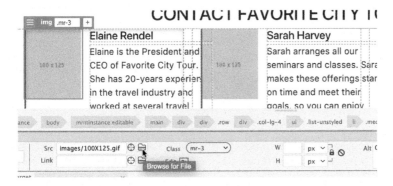 on the Src field.

A file window opens.

**6** Select **elaine.jpg** and click OK/Open.

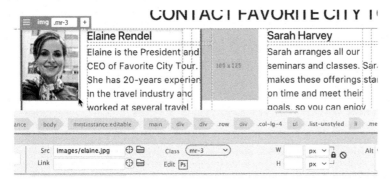

Elaine's picture appears in the `<img>` element.

Alt text provides descriptive metadata about images. In some browsers, alt text may be seen if the image doesn't load properly, or it may be accessed by individuals with visual disabilities. You should always add alt text to your images.

**7** In the Alt field in the Property inspector, enter **Elaine, Favorite City Tour President and CEO** as the alternate text to replace the existing content.

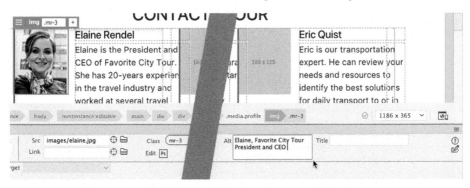

The image title attribute is similar to alt text. It provides additional information about the image. Search engines don't use it for result rankings, but it's a good idea to fill it in as well.

**Note:** The content of the Title field will show as a tool tip in most browsers when you position the cursor over the image.

8   In the Title field in the Property inspector, enter **Elaine, Favorite City Tour President and CEO** as the title text.

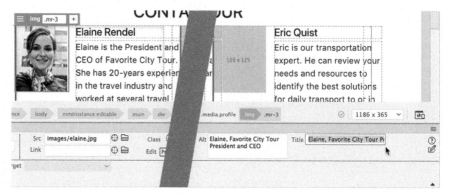

9   Choose File > Save.

Design view provides an easier way to deal with placeholder images.

# Inserting images in Design view

Dreamweaver provides several ways to insert images. When the layout has place-holders or existing images, Design view provides a simple way to replace them.

1   Switch to Design view.

The Bootstrap styling is not supported in Design view, so the layout will look totally different. The first thing you will notice is that card elements appear in a different order than they do in Live view.

2   Scroll down to find the image placeholder for Sarah.

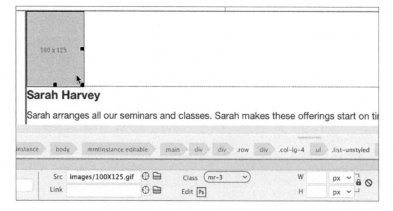

Sarah will be the third item in the section.

You could use the Property inspector to replace this placeholder, as you did before, but Design view has a few advantages over Live view.

3   Double-click the placeholder.

A file window opens.

4   Select **sarah.jpg** from the lesson09/images folder.
Click OK/Open.

Sarah's image appears in the `<img>` element.

5   In the Property inspector, enter **Sarah Harvey, Favorite City Tour Events Coordinator** in the Alt field and in the Title field.

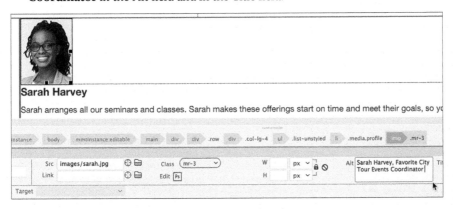

Sarah's image is complete.

6   Double-click the placeholder for Eric.

7   Select **eric.jpg** from the lesson09/images folder.
Click OK/Open.

Eric's photo replaces the placeholder.

8   In the Property inspector, enter **Eric Quist, Favorite City Tour Transportation Research Coordinator** in the Alt field and in the Title field.

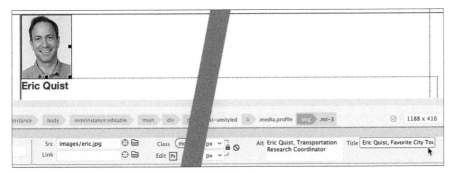

Eric's image is complete.

9   Save the file.

Sometimes you'll get images that have not been prepared in advance for a particular layout. In those cases, you can transfer the image to Photoshop for corrections or resampling.

## Resizing images

At certain times you may receive an image that is the wrong size. Sometimes you may need to resize graphics that have already been placed on the page.

1  If necessary, open **contact-us.html** in Design view or switch to it. Scroll to the placeholder for Lainey.

2  Double-click the placeholder.

3  Select **lainey.jpg** and click Open.

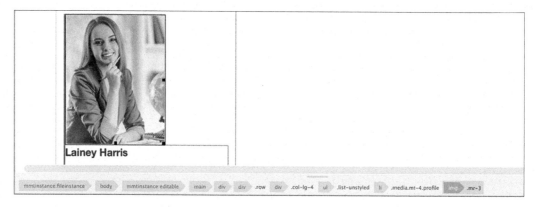

The image is too large, and there's barely any room for it in the column. It could use some resizing. You can resize images in Design or Live view.

4  Observe the Property inspector. Click the Reset ⊘ icon.

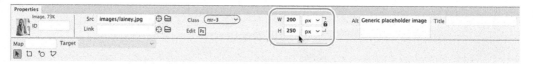

The image is twice as large as the other images. You can reduce the dimensions of an image in Dreamweaver in two ways. You can manually resize the image using the handles visible on the image itself, or you can enter the desired dimensions in the Property inspector. First, you will use the Property inspector.

5  If necessary, click the Toggle Size Constraint icon 🔒 to select the locked icon.

This icon locks the width and height so that any changes to one automatically affects the other proportionally.

6   In the Height field enter **125 px** and press Enter/Return.

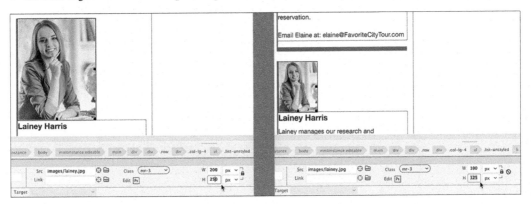

The height of the image is now 125 pixels. The image should scale smaller proportionally. If not, make sure the Toggle Size Constraint icon 🔒 shows the locked icon.

The change is temporary; nothing has actually been done to the image. You could leave the new size applied to the image and upload everything to your web server, and the image will display at the new size as long as the settings remain the same. But this forces the visitor to download an image larger than they need to. A better solution is to resize the image permanently.

7   Right-click Lainey's image.
Choose Edit With > Adobe Photoshop 2021.

● **Note:** The programs and versions appearing in your menu may differ. Photoshop may be downloaded and installed with a full Creative Cloud subscription.

Photoshop launches and loads the image from the local site.

8   Choose Image > Image Size.

The Image Size dialog appears. You can resize and resample an image using this dialog.

9  Change the dimensions to 100 x 125 pixels and click OK.

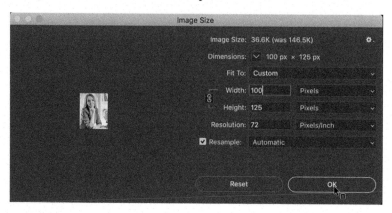

The image is actually resized. Now you just have to save it.

10  Close and save the image.

11  Switch back to Dreamweaver.
Select and observe Lainey's image.

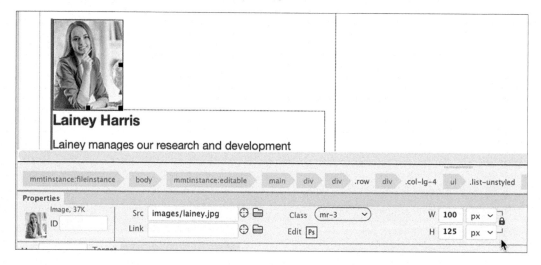

When you select the image, the Property inspector shows final dimensions without the Commit and Reset icons.

● **Note:**  Although you made the size change permanent, the file is still not changed permanently. You can undo the change up until you save the file. At that point the change is final and applied to the file.

Lainey's image is now the proper size. Let's add the Alt and Title text.

**12** Enter **Lainey Harris, Research and Development Coordinator** in the Alt and Title fields in the Property inspector.

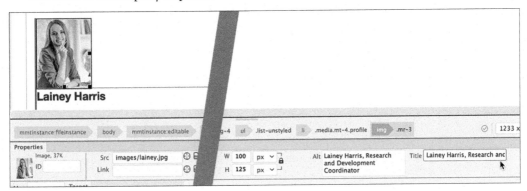

Lainey's image is complete.

**13** Save the file.

So far, you have inserted only web-compatible image formats. But Dreamweaver is not limited to the file types GIF, JPEG, and PNG; it can work with other file types too. In the next exercise, you will learn how to insert a Photoshop document (PSD) into a webpage.

# Inserting Photoshop Images

Dreamweaver has had a special affinity with Photoshop images for years. Unfortunately, in Dreamweaver (2021 release) you can no longer insert Photoshop images directly into the layout or use Photoshop Smart Objects. But that doesn't mean you have to avoid them altogether. In this exercise, you will learn how to work with Photoshop images and insert them in your layout.

**1** If necessary, open **contact-us.html** in Design view.

**2** Double-click the image placeholder for Margaret. Navigate to **the resources folder in lesson09**. Observe the file **margaret.psd**.

> ● **Note:** In Windows, you may need to select the option to show all files before you can see the PSD.

The Photoshop document is grayed out, indicating that Dreamweaver cannot insert the file directly. Luckily, all is not lost.

● **Note:** You may need to click the Creative Cloud icon to access the Upload PSD button.

3 Close the file window.
Choose Window > Extract.

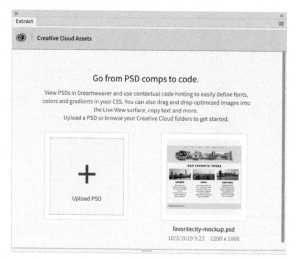

The Extract panel opens. The Favorite City Tour mockup, which you uploaded in Lesson 5, appears in the panel along with the option for uploading a PSD. Although you can no longer use a Photoshop image directly in Dreamweaver, you can use Extract to convert the file and its contents to web-compatible file formats.

4 Click the Upload PSD button.

5 Navigate to the resources folder in lesson09.
Select **margaret.psd** and click OK/Open.

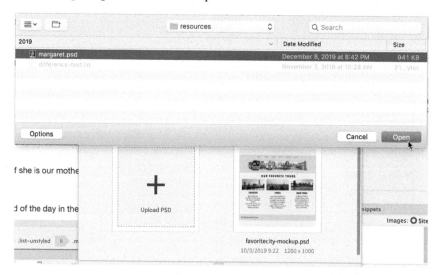

Margaret's image is uploaded and appears in the panel.

6 Click Margaret's preview image to select it.

The Photoshop file is loaded into the Extract panel. You could simply click the image to download it as an asset in your site, but there's another trick up our sleeve.

7 Click the Layers button.

The Layers pane opens in the Extract panel, showing two available layers in the image. The layer *New Background* shows that it is hidden.

8 Click the eye icon 👁 for the *New Background* layer to display its contents.

The background of the image changes to show a harbor scene. Now the image is ready to download to your site. However, if you download the image as is, you will download only the selected layer. You need to select both layers to download the composite image.

9  Hold the Shift key and select both layers.

Click the Extract Asset icon ↓ that appears over Margaret's image.

The Save As dialog appears, enabling you to specify the file type and properties you want to create. You can choose from three options: JPG, PNG 8, and PNG 32.

● **Note:** When an image has to be converted this way, Dreamweaver usually saves the converted image into the site's default images folder.

10  Choose JPG.

Note the Optimize slider.

11  If necessary, move the slider to 80.

This setting produces a high-quality image with a moderate amount of compression. If you lower the Optimize setting, you automatically increase the compression level and reduce the file size; increase the Optimize setting for the opposite effect. The secret to effective design is to select a good balance between quality and compression. The default setting of 80 is sufficient for your purposes.

When you selected the *New Background* layer, the name appearing in the dialog may have changed to match the selected layer. The downloaded image should display Margaret's name.

12  If necessary, enter **margaret** in the filename field.

Enter 1x in the Scale At field.

13  Click the Save button to download the JPEG image to the site's default images folder.

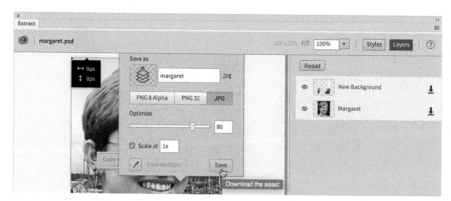

The image should be downloaded to the images folder. Let's insert it into the layout.

14  Close the Extract panel.

15  Double-click the image placeholder for Margaret.

16  Navigate to the images folder in lesson09.

17  Select **margaret.jpg** and click OK/Open.

The new image appears in the layout, but it's much too large.

**18** Right-click Margaret's image.
Choose Edit With > Adobe Photoshop 2021

Photoshop launches and loads the image from the local site.

**19** Choose Image > Image Size.

**20** Change the image size to 100 x 125 pixels and click OK.

**21** Close and save the image.

For JPEG files, you will see an optimization dialog when saving.

**22** Choose 8 in the Quality field and click OK.

The image is now permanently resized. Margaret's image is almost complete.

▶ **Tip:** The Element Display and the Property inspector can be used interchangeably to enter alt text.

**23** Enter **Margaret Julian, Office Manager** in the Alt and Title fields in the Property inspector.

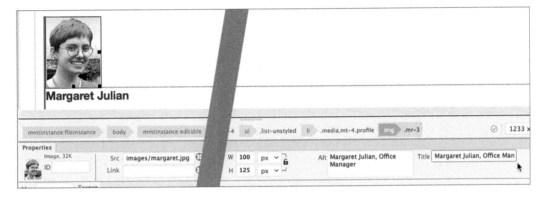

Margaret's image is now complete. There's only one image missing.

**24** Double-click the image placeholder for Matthew.
Select **matthew.jpg** and click OK/Open.

Matthew's image appears above his description.

**25** Enter **Matthew, Information Systems Manager** in the Alt and Title fields in the Property inspector.

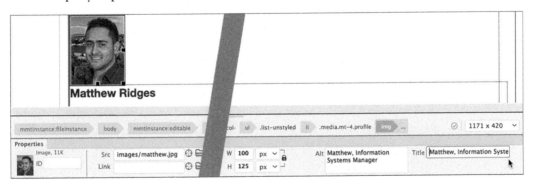

26 Save the file.

All the staff images are now complete. In the next exercise, you will insert an image using the Assets panel.

## Right size, wrong size

Until the latest mobile devices appeared on the scene, deciding what size and resolution to use for web images was pretty simple. You picked a specific width and height and saved the image at 72 pixels per inch (ppi). That's all you needed to do.

But today, web designers want their sites to work well for all visitors, no matter what type or size of device they want to use. Many new phones and tablets have resolutions exceeding 300 ppi. So the days of picking one size and one resolution may be gone forever. But what's the answer? At the moment, there isn't one perfect solution.

One trend simply inserts an image that is larger or one that has higher resolution and then resizes it using CSS. This allows the image to display more clearly on high-resolution screens, such as Apple's Retina display. The downside is that lower-resolution devices are stuck downloading an image that's larger than they need. This not only slows the loading of the page for no visual benefit but can incur higher data charges for smartphone users.

Another idea is to provide multiple images optimized for different devices and resolutions and use JavaScript to load the proper image as needed. But many developers object to using scripts for such basic resources as images. Others want a standardized solution.

W3C is working on a technique that uses a new element, named `<picture>`, that will not require JavaScript at all. Using this new element, you would select several images and declare how they should be used, and then the browser would load the appropriate image. Unfortunately, this element is so new that Dreamweaver doesn't support it yet, and few browsers even know what it is.

Implementing a responsive workflow for images is outside the scope of this course. But you should keep an eye on this trend and be prepared to implement the new solutions that evolve.

# Inserting images using the Assets panel

In many instances you will not have placeholder images marking the spots for your images. You will have to insert them manually using one of several tools in Dreamweaver. In this exercise, you will learn how to use some of these tools.

1   If necessary, open **contact-us.html** in Design view.
    Scroll down to the heading CONTACT FAVORITE CITY TOUR.

    This is one of the three pages you've created that don't have an image carousel.
    You will enhance the layouts on these pages by adding an attractive travel-
    related image and some marketing text promoting the quality of the staff,
    products, and services.

2   Open **difference-text.txt** from the lesson09/resources folder.

3   Select and copy all the text.
    Close the file.

4   In **contact-us.html**, insert the cursor at the end of the headline. Press Enter/
    Return to insert a new line.

5   Paste the text copied in step 3.

6   Choose Window > Assets to display the Assets panel, if necessary. Click the
    Images category icon to display a list of all images stored within the site.

7   Locate and select **travel.jpg** in the list.

    A preview of **travel.jpg** appears in the Assets panel. The panel lists the image's
    name, dimensions in pixels, size in kilo- or megabytes, and file type, as well as
    its full directory path.

8   Note the dimensions of the image.

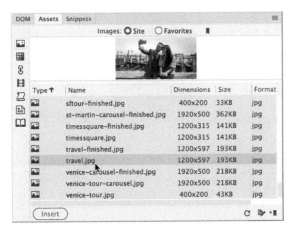

▶ **Tip:** The Assets
panel should be
populated as soon as
you define a site and
Dreamweaver creates
the cache.

● **Note:** You may
need to drag the edge
of the panel to widen
it to see all the asset
information.

● **Note:** The Images
window shows all
images stored any-
where in the defined
site—even ones outside
the site's default images
folder—so you may see
images stored in the
lesson subfolders too.

The image is 1200 by 597 pixels in size. You will insert the image at the beginning of the paragraph.

9  Insert the cursor at the beginning of the paragraph.

10 At the bottom of the Assets panel, click the Insert button.

The selected image appears below the heading and fills the layout from edge to edge.

Before mobile devices were introduced, a web designer had to determine only the maximum dimensions of an image and then resize it to fit the space. Each image had to be only one size.

Today, images have to fit a variety of screen sizes interactively. Each image that doesn't do this threatens to destroy the carefully constructed layout. Fortunately, Bootstrap provides built-in features that can control and adapt the display of images automatically, but to see how these features work you have to use Live view.

## Adapting images to mobile design

The advantages of using a web framework like Bootstrap is that it does most of the hard work for you. And one of the most difficult functions is adapting web images to mobile design. Dreamweaver taps into much of this power right in the interface.

1  Switch to Live view. Make sure the document window is at least 1200 pixels in width.

The image **travel.jpg** stretches past the edge of the layout. To make the image honor the Bootstrap layout, you simply have to make it a Bootstrap component.

**2** Select the image **travel.jpg**.

The Element Display appears on the `img` element. Note that the image has no special classes applied to it.

**3** Click the hamburger icon ▤.

The Quick Property inspector appears.

**4** Select the Make Image Responsive checkbox.

The image resizes to conform to the width of the column. It no longer extends beyond the edge of the screen. This is not a Dreamweaver trick. Note the new class `.img-fluid` applied to the `img` element. The image is now a Bootstrap component and will conform to any structure that it is inserted into. But what happens when the screen gets smaller?

**5** Drag the scrubber to the left to make the document window narrower.

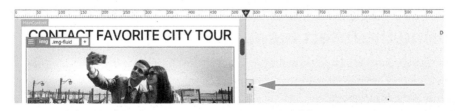

As you drag the scrubber, the layout changes and adapts to the smaller screen. The multicolumn design converts eventually to a single column. The **travel.jpg** image scales down seamlessly with the layout.

6 Drag the scrubber all the way back to the right.

The layout changes again and returns to its original multicolumn design. The image looks nice, but it is butting up tightly against the text. It could use some extra spacing.

You have used the `.mt-4` class several times to add margin spacing at the top of various elements. In this case, you need extra margin spacing at the bottom of the element. If you had to guess what Bootstrap class name would add a bottom margin, what would it be?

7 Click the Add Class/ID icon ⊞.

8 Add the class `.mb-4` to the `img` element.

The class name stands for `margin-bottom`. This Bootstrap class adds extra margin space at the bottom of the image. By adding two Bootstrap classes, you have adapted the image to the layout and added additional spacing below it.

9 Save the file.

Let's add similar images to the other pages that do not have image carousels.

## Using the Insert menu

The Assets panel is a handy visual way to find and insert images stored within the site. Another tool for inserting images, other HTML elements, and other components is the Insert menu.

1 Open **about-us.html** in Live view.

Make sure the document window is at least 1200 pixels wide.

The *About Us* page has a text block describing the history and mission of Favorite City Tour. Like the *Contact Us* page, it does not have an image carousel. Let's add an image above the text block.

2 Insert the cursor in the text that starts *"Travel with a Difference" is not just our motto.*

The Element Display appears with an orange box around the first paragraph.

3 Choose Insert > Image.

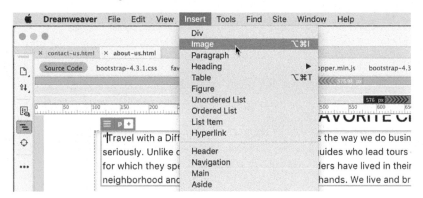

The Position Assist dialog appears.

4 Click Before.

A file window opens.

5   Select **timessquare.jpg** from the lesson09/images folder and click OK/Open.

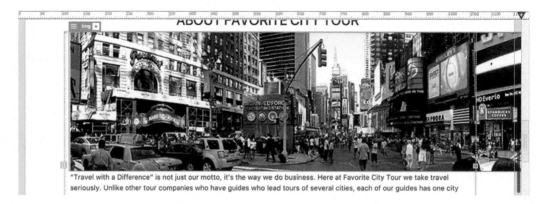

The image **timessquare.jpg** appears above the paragraph. Like the previous image, it stretches across and off the layout.

6   Click the hamburger icon ☰.
Select the option Make Image Responsive.

The image **timessquare.jpg** resizes to fit the column.

7   Add the class `.mb-4` to the img element.

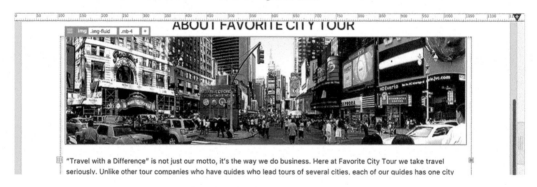

The class adds margin spacing below the image.

8   Save the file.

The Insert panel duplicates key menu commands and makes inserting images and other code elements quick and easy. You can even dock it to the top of the document window to have it available all the time.

## Working with the Insert panel

Some users find the Insert menu fast and easy to use. Others prefer the ready nature of the panel, which allows you to focus on one element and quickly insert multiple copies of it at once. Feel free to alternate between the two methods, as desired, or even use the keyboard shortcut.

In this exercise, you will use the Insert panel to add an image to one of the pages.

1  Open **events.html** in Live view.

   Make sure the document window is at least 1200 pixels wide.

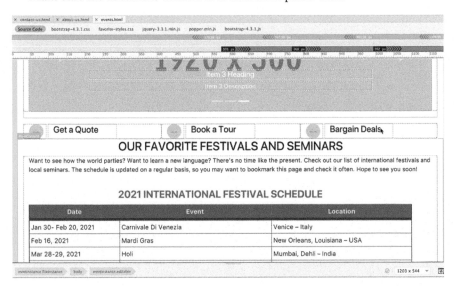

The *Events* page features two tables, one listing international festivals and the other seminars given by Favorite City Tour. The text block provides a quick overview of the information on the page. Let's add an image above the text block.

2  Insert the cursor into the text that starts *Want to see how the world parties?*

3  Choose Window > Insert.

   The Insert panel appears. The panel is part of the Standard workspace, so it should be docked to the right side of the document window.

4  In the Insert panel, choose the HTML category from the drop-down menu.

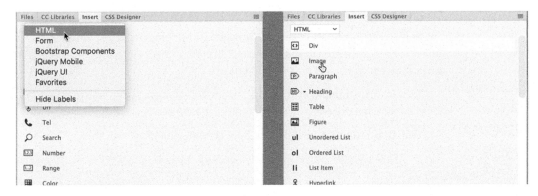

5 Click the Image button in the Insert panel.

The Position Assist dialog appears.

6 Click Before.

A file dialog appears.

7 Select **festivals.jpg** from the site images folder.
Click OK/Open.

The image **festivals.jpg** appears in the layout. You can add the Bootstrap classes using the Element Display.

8 Add the class `.img-fluid` to the `img` element.
Add the class `.mb-4` to the `img` element.

The image **festivals.jpg** resizes and repositions itself properly in the layout now.

9 Save the file.

On each of the pages, you can see three small image placeholders in the links under the header or image carousel. If you try to select these placeholders, you'll discover that they are not part of the editable page. To update them, you'll have to open the template.

## Inserting images into the site template

The only image that's part of the site template is the company logo, but that was added to the page before it was converted. Inserting images into the template is not much different from working in a child page.

1 Open **favorite-temp.dwt** from the lesson09/Templates folder in Live view.
Make sure the document window is at least 1200 pixels wide.

2 Scroll down to the three links that appear below the image carousel.

3   Select the first placeholder.

In Live view, a bug in Dreamweaver prevents you from interacting with any part of the layout. Until this bug is fixed, any work in the template will have to be done in Design or Code view.

4   Switch to Design view.

When you switch, you may need to scroll back to the links.

5   Select the first placeholder for the link *Get a Quote*.

Notice that the placeholders are not round in Design view. The round shapes are created by the CSS property border-radius. Since this is an advanced CSS property, it is not supported in Design view.

In Design view, you can replace images by double-clicking them.

6   Double-click the placeholder.

A file window appears.

7   Select **quote.jpg** and click OK/Open.

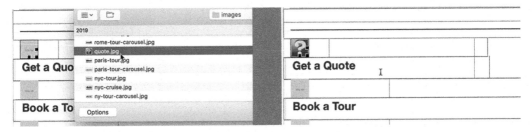

The image **quote.jpg** replaces the placeholder. You can also use the Property inspector to select the replacement images.

8   Select the second placeholder.
In the Property inspector, click the Browse icon in the Src field.

9   Select **book.jpg** and click OK/Open.

The image **book.jpg** replaces the placeholder. You can also insert images using Code view.

10  Select the third placeholder.

**11** Switch to Split view.

The placeholder code is highlighted in Code view. Note the `src` attribute. It's pointing to `../images/40X40.gif`. In Lesson 4, "Working with Code," you learned that Code view can help you preview assets and write the code itself.

**12** Position the cursor over the image reference `40X40.gif`.

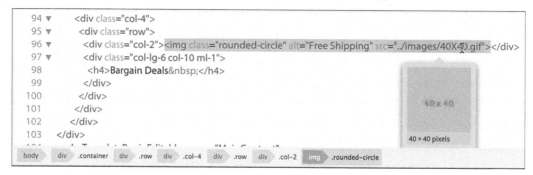

A preview image of the placeholder pops up next to the cursor.

**13** Select and delete only the image reference `40X40.gif`.

**14** Type `bar`

As you type, code hinting appears displaying the name of an image file that matches the text being entered. You can continue typing the rest of the name (`bargain`) if you want, or simply press Enter/Return to complete the image source.

**15** Press Enter/Return to complete the image name as suggested.

The image reference `bargain.jpg` appears in the code.

**16** Position the cursor over the reference `bargain.jpg`.

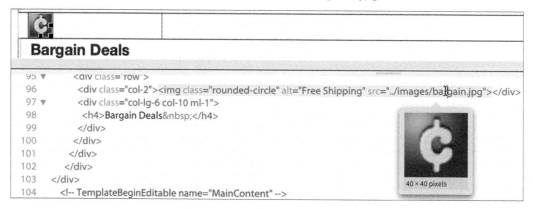

A preview of the image appears beside the cursor. The three placeholders are now replaced. Note that the images are square in shape.

17 Switch to Live view.

The new images appear in the link section. The advanced CSS properties are supported in Live view, and the buttons are now round in shape. The last step to the process is to update all the child pages. Remember that template commands work only in Design or Code view or when no files are open.

18 Switch back to Design view.
Choose File > Save.

The Update Template Files dialog appears, listing all the child pages that will be updated.

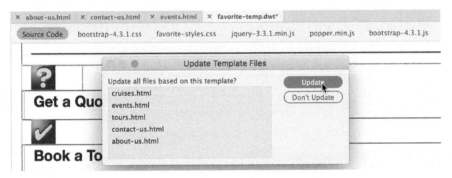

19 Click Update.

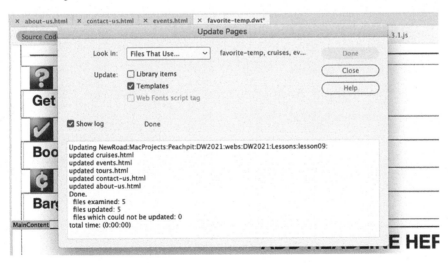

The Update Pages dialog appears. If necessary, click the Show Log option to observe the progress of the update. If successful, all five child pages should be updated. You may notice that the three pages you had open display asterisks on their document tabs. This tells you that the pages were updated but not saved. Let's see if the linked images were added to these pages successfully.

20 Close the Update Pages dialog.
Click the document tab for **contact-us.html**.
Examine the link section.

The button images were added to the link section on this page.

21 Switch to and check **about-us.html** and **events.html**.

All three pages were updated successfully. But you may have noticed that the link section butts up against the header when there is no carousel. To add extra spacing above it, you can use the Bootstrap class .mt-4 again, but since the link section is not in an editable region, you have to add it in the template.

## Adding CSS classes to template structures

You can see how the link section butts up against the header when the image carousel is removed from the page. In fact, you have added the class .mt-4 to content sections on several of the pages to address this issue. Since this will be a problem every time you create a new page, it's best to address it in the template.

In this exercise, you will add the class to the link and content sections as needed.

1 Switch to **favorite-temp.dwt**.
If necessary, scroll to the image carousel.

You should still be in Live view. There is a bug in Dreamweaver that sometimes makes it difficult or impossible to select elements in the document window in a template. If you cannot directly select elements in the window, you can use the DOM panel.

2 Click the image carousel.

The Element Display should appear focused on one of the image placeholders.

3 Choose Window > DOM.

The DOM panel appears. If you were able to select the image carousel in step 2, one of the image placeholders should be highlighted. If not, you can use the panel to locate the component. It should appear within the element mmtemplate:if.

4   If necessary, expand the structure of the element `mmtemplate:if` in the DOM panel.

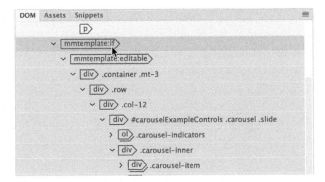

Inside the element, you should see `mmtemplate:editable`.

5   If necessary, expand the structure of the element `mmtemplate:editable`.

Note that the first child of the editable region is `div.container.mt-3`.

6   Click `div.container.mt-3` in the DOM panel.

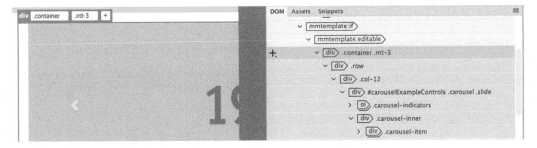

The Element Display should appear on the image carousel focused on `div.container.mt-3`. This element already has the class `.mt-3`, so we can move on to the next content section.

7   Collapse `mmtemplate:if`.

The next element after `mmtemplate:if` is `div.container`.

8   Click `div.container` in the DOM panel.

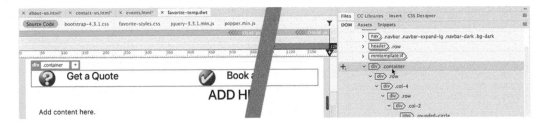

The Element Display appears in the document window focused on div.container. This is the link section, and you can see that it doesn't have the Bootstrap class applied to it.

9 In the DOM panel, double-click the class .container.

10 Insert the cursor after the existing class.
Press the spacebar to insert a space, and enter .mt-4

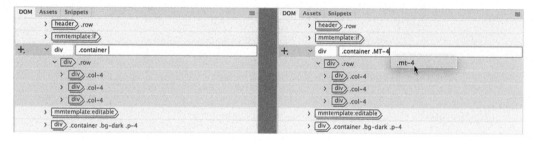

11 Press Enter/Return to complete the change.

The DOM and tag inspector display now show div.container.mt-4.

The next three sections are part of the MainContent editable region.

12 Expand the structure of the element mmtemplate:if in the DOM panel.

13 If necessary, expand the elements mmtemplate:editable and main.wrapper.

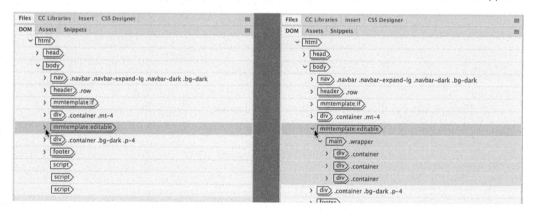

Once the editable region is expanded, you will see the three content sections. The change is pretty straightforward from here.

**14** Add the `.mt-4` class to all three `div.container` elements.

All the content sections now have the `.mt-4` class.

**15** Choose File > Save.

The Update Template Files dialog appears, listing all the child pages that will be updated.

**16** Click Update.

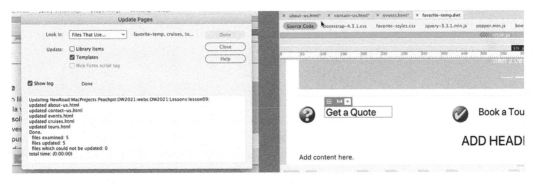

All five child pages should be updated. Asterisks appear in all the document tabs except the template **favorite-temp.dwt**.

As you learned in Lesson 7, "Working with Templates," when a template is saved, only the locked portions of the page are updated. If one of the editable content sections did not have the `.mt-3` class before the update, it still won't have it now. But by adding the class to the template, any child pages created from this point forward will have the class assigned to them.

**17** Choose File > Save All.

The asterisks on the document tabs disappear.

**18** Choose File > Close All.

Next you'll learn how to add images to the image carousels.

# Adding images to a Bootstrap carousel

At the moment, two of your site pages contain image carousels. In this exercise, you will learn how to insert images into the Bootstrap carousel.

1. Open **tours.html** in Live view. Make sure the document window is at least 1200 pixels wide.

   The page contains an image carousel and six tour descriptions. In Live view, you can see the carousel animation as one image placeholder slides across the screen replacing another. Note that each slide also contains some text elements.

2. Click the image carousel.

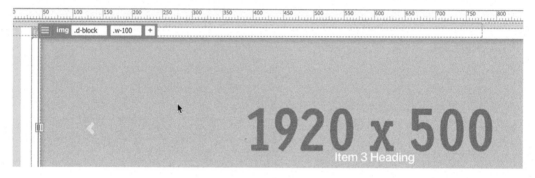

   The carousel is in the editable optional region and should be selectable. Depending on where you click, the Element Display appears focused on one of the image placeholders or on part of the carousel structure.

   Although you learned how to insert images in Live view, the carousel offers a unique challenge. How do you select and replace a moving object? Although it's possible to do so in Live view, using Code view will be much easier.

3. Switch to Code view.

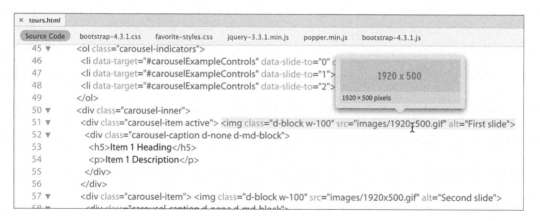

Dreamweaver highlights the code of the selected element. The carousel contains three placeholder images. Since the carousel rotates, you could have selected any of the three placeholders. Locate the first `<img>` element in the element `<div class="carousel-inner">`, around line 51. Notice the filename. All the placeholders use the same placeholder image, `1920x500.gif`. You will replace each one with a different image.

4  Select the code `1920x500.gif` and enter `london`

As you type, the hinting menu appears and displays any filenames that match what you are typing. A preview image of the highlighted file appears above or below its name.

▶ **Tip:** When more than one filename appears in the hinting list, press the up or down arrow key to view the preview of the other images.

5  Select `london-tour-carousel.jpg` in the hinting menu.

The London image reference has replaced the placeholder image. Note that there are heading and description placeholders within the same structure.

6  Select the heading `Item 1 Heading`.
   Type `London Tea` to replace it.

```
50 ▼        <div class="carousel-inner">
51 ▼            <div class="carousel-item active"> <im
52 ▼                <div class="carousel-caption d-none d
53 ▼                    <h5>Item 1 Heading</h5>
54                      <p>Item 1 Description</p>
55                  </div>
```

```
50 ▼        <div class="carousel-inner">
51 ▼            <div class="carousel-item active"> <im
52 ▼                <div class="carousel-caption d-none
53                      <h5>London Tea</h5>
54                      <p>Item 1 Description</p>
55                  </div>
```

7  Select the text `Item 1 Description`.
   Type `High tea and high adventure in London towne` to replace it.

```
50 ▼        <div class="carousel-inner">
51 ▼            <div class="carousel-item active"> <img class="d-block
52 ▼                <div class="carousel-caption d-none d-md-block">
53                      <h5>London Tea</h5>
54                      <p>Item 1 Description</p>
55                  </div>
```

```
50 ▼        <div class="carousel-inner">
51 ▼            <div class="carousel-item active"> <img class="d-block w-
52 ▼                <div class="carousel-caption d-none d-md-block">
53                      <h5>London Tea</h5>
54                      <p>High tea and high adventure in London towne </p>
55                  </div>
```

The first carousel element is complete.

8  Locate the second carousel placeholder image, around line 57.

9  Replace `1920x500.gif` with `venice-tour-carousel.jpg`.

**10** Replace Item 2 Heading with `Back Canal Venice`

Replace Item 2 Description with `Come see a different side of Venice`

```
57 ▼    <div class="carousel-item"> <img class="d-block w-100" src="images/venice-tour-carousel.jpg"
58 ▼    <div class="carousel-caption d-none d-md-block">
59        <h5>Back Canal Venice</h5>
60        <p>Come see a different side of Venice</p>
61      </div>
```

The second carousel element is complete.

**11** Locate the next image placeholder element, around line 63.

**12** Change `1920x500.gif` to `ny-tour-carousel.jpg`

Change Item 3 Heading to `New York Times`

Replace Item 3 Description with `You've never seen this side of the Big Apple`

You've replaced all the carousel placeholders. Let's review the changes.

**13** Save the file.

**14** Switch to Live view. Make sure the document window is at least 1200 pixels wide. Observe the image carousel.

The three images slide from right to left, pause for a moment, and then slide off as they are replaced by the next image. The images look great, but the headings and descriptions are muted and kind of lost in the details of the images. They need to be given a little more emphasis.

## Styling headings and text in a Bootstrap carousel

The text headings and descriptions are hard to read on top of the images in the carousel. Let's tweak the styling with some custom CSS.

**1** If necessary, open **tours.html** in Live view.

Make sure the document window is at least 1200 pixels wide.

2 Select the heading on one of the images in the carousel.

The Element Display appears focused on the <h5> element. Since all the headings are <h5> elements, you can select any of them to style all of them. As always, the first step in modifying CSS styling is to check to see if there are any existing rules styling this element.

3 In CSS Designer, click the Current button.
Inspect the rules displayed in the Selectors pane.
Identify the rule or rules responsible for the styling of these headings.

There are three rules targeting <h5> elements. But these do not supply the specific styling seen in the carousel. That can be found in the rule `.carousel-caption`.

4 In CSS Designer, select the All button.

5 Choose **favorite-styles.css** in the Sources pane.
Click the Add Selector icon ✚.

A new selector appears in the Selectors pane targeting the carousel caption element, but the selector is too specific.

6 Edit the selector name to `.carousel-caption`.
Press Enter/Return to complete the selector.

▶ **Tip:** Unless you know what the other classes do, it's a good practice not to use them in a selector. Leaving them in the name could reformat other elements unintentionally.

7 Create the following properties in `.carousel-caption`:
```
font-size: 130%
font-weight: 700
text-shadow: 0px 2px 5px rgba(0, 0, 0, 0.8)
```

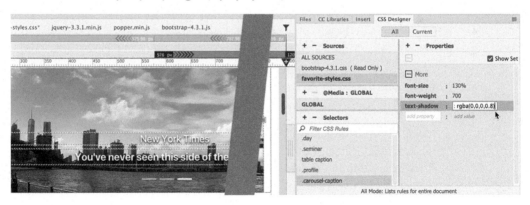

The increased font size and text shadow make the text easier to read. But the <h5> element did not get any bigger. That means another rule is blocking the new styling. A separate rule targeting the <h5> should do the trick.

8 Create the following rule: `.carousel-caption h5`

9  In the rule `.carousel-caption h5`, add the following properties:
   `font-size: 130%`
   `font-weight: 700`

The heading resizes and appears bolder. The text is much more readable now.

10 Choose File > Save All Related Files.

You have learned several ways to insert and work with images in this lesson. It's time to put those skills to the test.

## Self-paced exercise: Inserting images in child pages

You've replaced image placeholders and inserted images in Live view, Design view, and Code view. In this self-paced exercise, you will finish the pages **tours.html** and **cruises.html** by replacing the placeholder images remaining in the file.

1  If necessary, open **tours.html** in Live view.
   Make sure the document window is at least 1200 pixels wide.

   Nine tour descriptions on the page contain image placeholders.

2  Using any of the techniques you have learned in this lesson, replace the placeholders as indicated:
   London Tea: **london-tour.jpg**
   French Bread: **paris-tour.jpg**
   When in Rome: **rome-tour.jpg**
   Chicago Blues: **chicago-tour.jpg**
   Dreams of Florence: **florence-tour.jpg**
   Back Canal Venice: **venice-tour.jpg**

New York Times: **nyc-tour.jpg**
San Francisco Days: **sf-tour.jpg**
Normandy Landings: **normandy-tour.jpg**

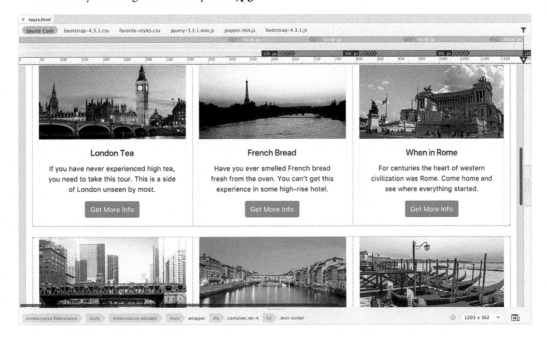

The placeholders have all been replaced.

3 Choose Save All. Close the file.

4 If necessary, open **cruises.html** in Live view.
Make sure the document window is at least 1200 pixels wide.

This page features an image carousel and three cruise descriptions.

5 Use the following content in the carousel for Item 1:
Item 1 placeholder: `sf-cruise-carousel.jpg`
Item 1 Heading: `Coastal California`
Item 1 Description: `Monterey to San Francisco, nuff said!`

6 Use the following content in the carousel for Item 2:
Item 2 placeholder: `ny-cruise-carousel.jpg`
Item 2 Heading: `Beans to Big Apples`
Item 2 Description: `Come see a new perspective of Boston and New York`

7 Use the following content in the carousel for Item 3:
Item 3 placeholder: `miami-cruise-carousel.jpg`
Item 3 Heading: `Southern Charm`
Item 3 Description: `Breathtaking views and amazing seafood`

8  Using any of the techniques you have learned in this lesson, replace the cruise placeholders as indicated:

Coastal California: **sf-cruise.jpg**

Beans and Big Apples: **nyc-cruise.jpg**

Southern Charm: **jacksonville-cruise.jpg**

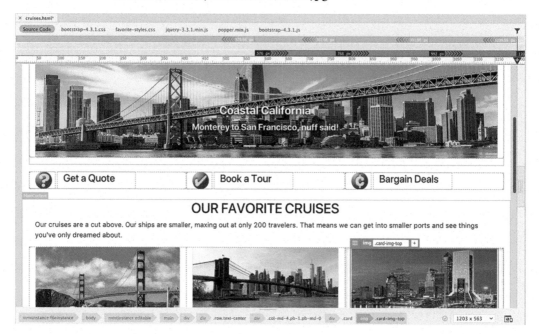

The placeholders have all been replaced.

9  Choose Save All. Close the file.

Congratulations! You've learned how to work with web-compatible images in a variety of ways in Dreamweaver, including inserting images into a layout, replacing image placeholders, making them responsive to various screen sizes, and resizing them.

## Review questions

1 What are the three factors that determine raster image quality?

2 What file formats are specifically designed for use on the web?

3 Describe at least two methods for inserting an image into a webpage using Dreamweaver.

4 True or false: You cannot insert Photoshop files directly in Dreamweaver.

5 How can you resize an image that has already been inserted into Dreamweaver.

## Review answers

1 Raster image quality is determined by resolution, image dimensions, and color depth.

2 The image formats that are compatible for the web are GIF, JPEG, PNG, and SVG.

3 One method to insert an image into a webpage using Dreamweaver is to use the Insert panel. Another method is to use the Insert command in the Assets panel. Images can also be copied and pasted from Photoshop.

4 True. Dreamweaver no longer supports the direct insertion of Photoshop files, but you can use the Extract panel to create web-compatible images from Photoshop documents.

5 You can resize an image that is already in Dreamweaver by right-clicking the image and selecting Edit With > Adobe Photoshop 2021. This will open the image in Photoshop, where you can resize the image. When you save the changes, the inserted image will be updated automatically.

# 10 WORKING WITH NAVIGATION

## Lesson overview

In this lesson, you'll learn how to do the following:

- Create a text link to a page within the same site.

- Create a link to a page on another website.

- Create an email link.

- Create an image-based link.

- Create a link to a location within a page.

 This lesson will take about 2 hours to complete. To get the lesson files used in this lesson, download them from the webpage for this book at www.adobepress.com/DreamweaverCIB2021. For more information, see "Accessing the lesson files and Web Edition" in the "Getting Started" section at the beginning of this book.

Dreamweaver can create and edit many types of links—from text-based links to image-based links—and does so with ease and flexibility.

# Hyperlink basics

The World Wide Web, and the internet in general, would be a far different place without the hyperlink. Without hyperlinks, HTML (HyperText Markup Language) would simply be ML (Markup Language). The *hypertext* in the name refers to the functionality of the hyperlink. So what is a hyperlink?

A hyperlink, or *link*, is an HTML-based reference to a resource available on the internet or within the computer hosting a web document. The resource can be anything that can be stored and displayed by a computer, such as a webpage, an image, a movie, a sound file, a PDF—in fact, almost any type of computer file. A hyperlink creates an interactive behavior specified by HTML and CSS, or by the programming language you're using, and is enabled by a browser or other application.

An HTML hyperlink consists of the anchor <a> element and one or more attributes.

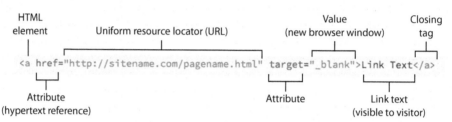

## Internal and external hyperlinks

The simplest hyperlink—an *internal* hyperlink—takes the user to another part of the same document or to another document stored in the same folder or hard drive on the web server that hosts the site. An *external* hyperlink is designed to take the user to a document or resource outside your hard drive, website, or web host.

Internal and external hyperlinks may work differently, but they have one thing in common: they are enabled in HTML by the <a> *anchor element.* This element designates the address of the destination of the hyperlink and can then specify how it functions using several attributes. You'll learn how to create and modify the <a> element in the exercises that follow.

## Relative vs. absolute hyperlinks

A hyperlink address can be written in two ways. When you refer to a target according to where it is stored in relation to the current document, it is known as a *relative* link. This is like telling a friend that you live next door to the blue house. If she were driving down your street and saw the blue house, she would know where you live. But those directions don't really tell her how to get to your house or even to your neighborhood. A relative link frequently will consist of the resource name and perhaps the folder it is stored within, such as `tours.html` or `content/tours.html`.

Sometimes you need to spell out precisely where a resource is located. In those instances, you need an *absolute* hyperlink. This is like telling someone you live at 123 Main Street in Meredien. This is typically how you refer to resources outside your website. An absolute link includes the entire uniform resource locator, or URL, of the target and may even include a filename—such as **https://www.adobe.com/products/dreamweaver.html**—or just a folder within the site.

Both types of links have advantages and disadvantages. Relative hyperlinks are faster and easier to write, but they may not work if the document containing them is moved to a different folder or location within the website. Absolute links always work no matter where the containing document is saved, but they can fail if the targets are moved or renamed. A simple rule that most web designers follow is to use relative links for resources within a site and absolute links for resources outside the site. Of course, whether you follow this rule or not, it's important to test all links before deploying the page or site. And then monitor your links from time to time to make sure they are still working.

# Previewing the completed files

To see the final version of the files you will work on in this lesson, let's preview the completed page in the browser.

1 Launch Adobe Dreamweaver CC (2021 release) or later.

2 If necessary, press F8 to open the Files panel.
Select lesson10 from the site list.

3 In the Files panel, expand the lesson10 folder.

4 In the Files panel, navigate to the lesson10/finished folder and right-click **aboutus-finished.html**. Choose Open In Browser from the context menu, and select your favorite browser.

● **Note:** Before beginning this exercise, download the project files and define a new site based on the lesson10 folder using the instructions in the "Getting Started" section at the beginning of the book.

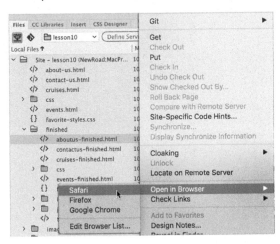

The **aboutus-finished.html** file appears in the browser you selected. This page features only internal links in the horizontal menu.

5 Position the cursor over the horizontal navigation menu.
Hover over each button and examine the behavior of the menu.

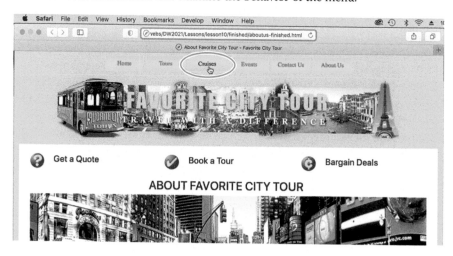

The menu is the same one created and formatted in Lesson 6, "Creating a Page Layout," with a few changes.

6 Click the *Tours* link.

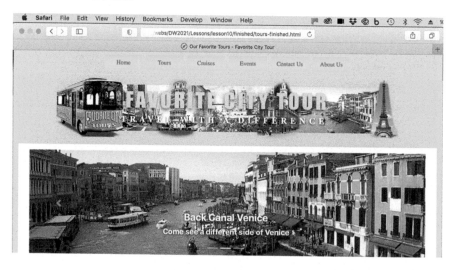

**Tip:** Most browsers display the destination of a hyperlink in the status bar at the bottom of the browser window. In some browsers, this status bar may be turned off by default.

The browser loads the finished *Tours* page.

7 Position the cursor over the *Contact Us* link.
Observe the browser to see whether it's displaying the link's destination anywhere on the screen.

Typically, the browser shows the link destination in the status bar.

**8** Click the *Contact Us* link.

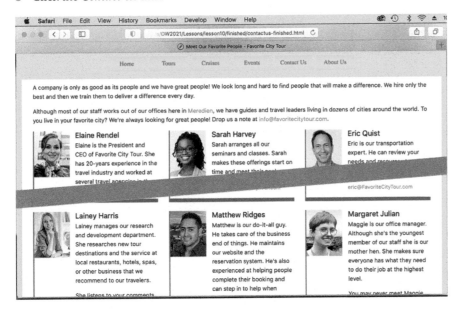

The browser loads the finished *Contact Us* page, replacing the *Tours* page. The new page includes internal, external, and email links.

**9** Position the cursor over the *Meredien* link in the second paragraph of the main content area. Observe the status bar.

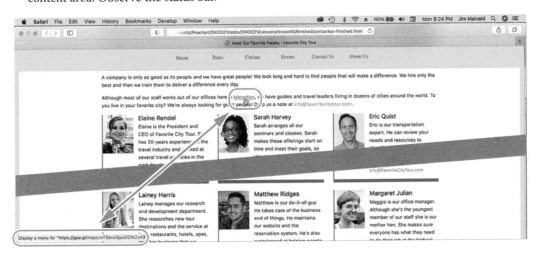

The status bar displays a Google Maps link.

⬤ **Note:** The display in Google Maps may differ from the one pictured.

10  Click the *Meredien* link.

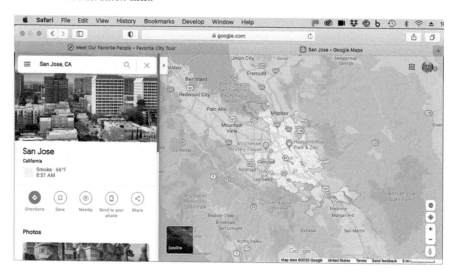

A new browser window appears and loads Google Maps. The link is intended to show the visitor where the Meredien Favorite City Tour Association offices are located. If desired, you can even include address details or the company name in this link so that Google can load the exact map and directions.

Note that the browser opens a separate window or document tab when you click the link. This is a good behavior to use when directing visitors to resources outside your site. Since the link opens in a separate window, your own site is still open and ready to use. This practice is especially helpful if your visitors are unfamiliar with your site and may not know how to get back to it once they click away.

11  Close the Google Maps window.

The *Contact Us* page is still open in the browser. Note that each employee has a link applied to their email address.

12  Click an email link for one of the employees.

● **Note:** Many web visitors don't use email programs installed on their computers. They use web-based services such as AOL, Gmail, Hotmail, and so on. For these visitors, email links like the one you tested won't work. The best option is to create a web-hosted form on your site that sends the email to you via your own server.

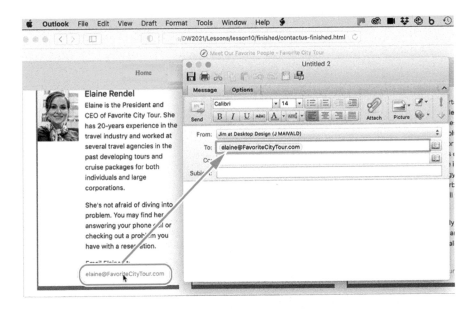

The default mail application launches on your computer. If you have not set up this application to send and receive mail, the program will usually start a wizard to help you set up this functionality. If the email program is set up, a new message window appears with the email address of the employee automatically entered in the To field.

13 Close the new message window, if necessary, and exit the email program.

14 Scroll down to the page footer.

Note that the menu sticks to the top of the page as you scroll down.

15 Click the *Events* link.

The browser loads the *Festivals and Seminars* page. The browser focuses on the table containing the list of upcoming events near the top of the page. Notice that the horizontal menu is still visible at the top of the browser.

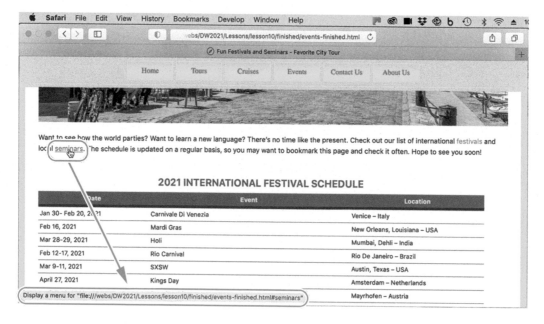

**16** Click the *Seminars* link in the first paragraph.

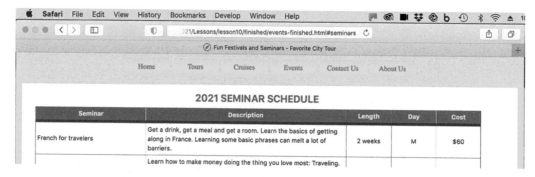

The browser jumps down to the list of upcoming seminars at the bottom of the page.

**17** Click the *Return to top* link that appears above the class schedule.

You may need to scroll up or down the page to see it. The browser jumps back to the top of the page.

**18** Close the browser and switch to Dreamweaver, if necessary.

You have tested a variety of different types of hyperlinks: internal, external, relative, and absolute. In the following exercises, you will learn how to build each type.

# Creating internal hyperlinks

Creating hyperlinks of all types is easy with Dreamweaver. In this exercise, you'll create relative text-based links to pages in the same site, using a variety of methods. You can create links in Design view, Live view, and Code view.

## Creating relative links

Dreamweaver provides several methods for creating and editing links. Links can be created in all three program views.

1 Open **about-us.html** from the site root folder in Live view. Make sure the document window is at least 1200 pixels wide.

2 In the horizontal menu, position the cursor over any of the menu items. Observe the type of cursor that appears.

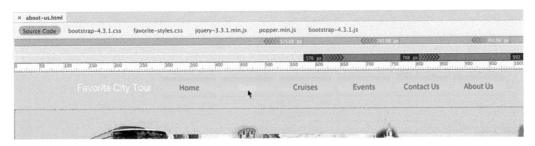

The pointer icon 🖑 indicates that the menu item is structured as a hyperlink. The links in the horizontal menu are not editable in the normal way, but this is something you can actually see only in Design view.

3 Switch to Design view.
Position the cursor over any item in the horizontal menu again.

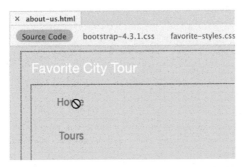

● **Note:** The Template category is not visible in Live view. You will see it only in Design view and Code view or when no document is open.

The "no" symbol ⊘ appears, indicating that this section of the page is uneditable. The horizontal menu was not added to any of the editable regions you created in Lesson 7, "Working with Templates." That means it is considered part of the template and is locked within Dreamweaver. To add hyperlinks to this menu, you'll have to open the template.

4  Choose Window > Assets. Click the Templates icon in the Assets panel. Right-click **favorite-temp** and choose Edit from the context menu.

5  In the horizontal menu, insert the cursor into the *Tours* link.

The horizontal menu is editable in the template.

6  If necessary, choose Window > Properties.
Examine the contents of the Link field in the Property inspector.

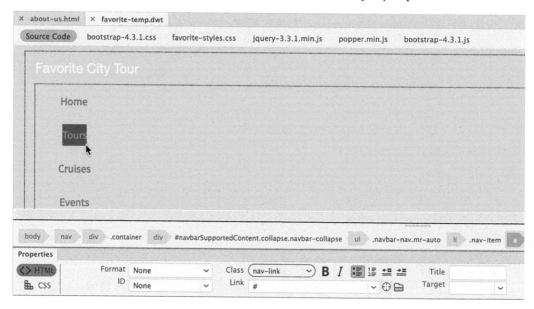

> ▶ **Tip:** When editing or removing an existing hyperlink, you don't need to select the entire link; you can just insert the cursor anywhere in the link text. Dreamweaver assumes you want to change the entire link by default.

To create links, the HTML tab must be selected in the Property inspector. The Link field shows a hyperlink placeholder (#).

7  In the Link field, click the Browse For File icon 📁.

A file selection dialog appears.

8   Navigate to the site root folder, if necessary.
    Select **tours.html** from the site root folder.

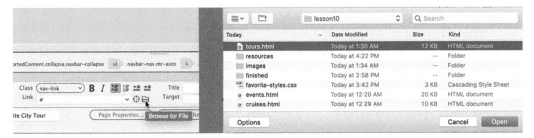

9   Click OK/Open.

**Note:** The link won't have the typical hyperlink appearance—a blue underscore—because of the special formatting you applied to this menu in Lesson 5, "Web Design Basics."

The link `../tours.html` appears in the Link field in the Property inspector. You've created your first text-based hyperlink.

Since the template is saved in a subfolder, Dreamweaver adds the path element notation (`../`) to the filename. This notation tells the browser or operating system to look in the parent directory of the current folder.

This is necessary if the child page is saved in a subfolder, but it is unnecessary if the page is saved in the root of the site. Luckily, when you create a page from the template, Dreamweaver rewrites the link, adding or removing path information as needed.

If desired, Dreamweaver enables you to type links in the field manually.

10  Insert the cursor in the *Home* link.

The home page does not exist yet. But that doesn't stop you from entering the link text by hand.

11  In the Property inspector Link field, select the hash (#) symbol, type `../index.html` to replace the hash symbol placeholder, and press Enter/Return.

At any time, you may insert a link by typing it manually just this way. But entering links by hand can introduce a variety of errors that can break the very link you are trying to create. If you want to link to a file that already exists, Dreamweaver offers other interactive ways to create links.

**12** Insert the cursor in the *Cruises* link.

**13** Click the Files tab to bring the panel to the top, or choose Window > Files.

You need to make sure you can see the Property inspector and the target file in the Files panel.

**14** In the Property inspector, drag the Point To File icon ⊕—next to the Link field—to **cruises.html** in the site root folder displayed in the Files panel.

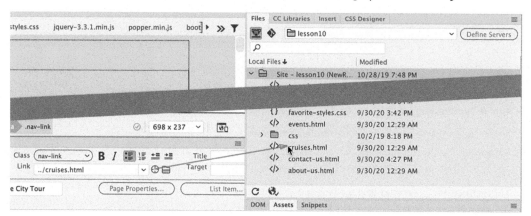

**▶ Tip:** If a folder in the Files panel contains a page you want to link to but the folder is not open, drag the Point To File icon over the folder and hold it in place to expand that folder so that you can point to the desired file.

Dreamweaver enters the filename and any necessary path information into the Link field.

**15** Create the rest of the links as shown here using any of the methods you've learned:

Events: **../events.html**

Contact Us: **../contact-us.html**

About Us: **../about-us.html**

For files that have not been created, you will always have to enter the link manually. Remember that all the links added to the template pointing to files in the site root folder must include the **. . /** notation so that the link resolves properly. Remember also that Dreamweaver will modify the link as needed once the template is applied to the child page.

## Creating a home link

Most websites display a logo or company name, and this site is no different. The Favorite City Tour logo appears in the header element—a product of a background graphic and some text. Frequently, such logos are used to create a link back to the site home page. In fact, this practice has become a virtual standard on the web. Since the template is still open, it's easy to add such a link to the Favorite City Tour logo.

1   Insert the cursor in the *Favorite City Tour* text in the `<header>` element.

Dreamweaver keeps track of links you create in each editing session until you close the program. You can access these previously created links from the Property inspector.

2   Click the h2 tag selector. In the Property inspector Link field, choose `../index.html` from the dropdown menu.

**Note:** You can select any range of text to create a link—from one character to an entire paragraph or more; Dreamweaver will add the necessary markup to the selection.

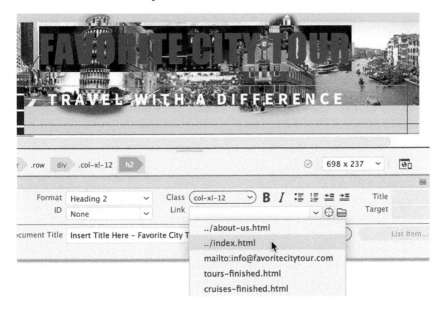

This selection will create a link to the home page that you will build later. The `<a>` tag now appears in the tag selector interface.

You probably noticed that the logo has changed color to blue. If you have used the internet for a while, you have probably seen lots of links formatted in this color. In fact, it's part of the default styling of hyperlinks.

In Lesson 3, "CSS Basics," you learned that some HTML tags are styled by default. The `<a>` tag is one of those, and it comes with a full set of specifications and behaviors. To get a better understanding of what's involved, check out the sidebar "Hyperlink pseudo-classes."

Although some people may want normal hyperlinks to be styled this way, the logo is not supposed to be blue. It's a simple fix with CSS.

**Tip:** You may need to select the All button first to see **favorite-styles.css.**

3   In the CSS Designer, select **favorite-styles.css.**
In the Selectors pane, select the rule `header h2`.
Create the following selector:
`header h2 a:link, header h2 a:visited`

This selector will target the "default" and "visited" states of the link within the logo.

**Tip:** If you select an existing rule first, the new rule will be added directly after the selection. This is a good way to organize the rules in your style sheets.

# Hyperlink pseudo-classes

Default styling of HTML elements can sometimes get pretty elaborate. For example, the <a> element (hyperlink) provides five states, or distinct behaviors, that can be modified individually by CSS using what are known as *pseudo-classes*. A pseudo-class is a CSS feature that can add styling, special effects, and functionality to certain selectors. Here are the pseudo-classes for the <a> tag.

- a:link creates the default display and behavior of the hyperlink and in many cases is interchangeable with the a selector in CSS rules. But a:link is *more* specific and will override specifications assigned to a less specific selector if both are used in the style sheet.

- a:visited formats the link after it has been visited by the browser. This state can be reset to the default styling by deleting the browser cache, or history.

- a:hover formats the link when the cursor passes over it.

- a:active formats the link when the mouse clicks it.

- a:focus formats the link when accessed via keyboard as opposed to mouse interaction.

When used, the pseudo-classes must be declared in the order listed here to be effective. Remember that, whether declared in the style sheet or not, each state has a set of default formats and behaviors.

4 Add the following properties to the rule:

```
color: inherit
text-decoration: none
```

5    Switch to Live view.

These properties will cancel the hyperlink styling and return the text to its original appearance. By using `inherit` for the color value, the color applied by the `header h2` rule will be passed automatically to the text. That way, if the color in the `header h2` rule changes, the hyperlink will be styled in turn without any additional work or redundant code.

● **Note:** The company name will display in blue in Design view, but it will appear correctly in Live view and in a browser.

There's one more link to create and style before we save the template. In the horizontal menu, the company name appears on the left side of the buttons. The text was part of the original Bootstrap starter layout that you customized with the company name.

If you review the mockup design from Lesson 5, the header element and its contents are hidden on tablets and smartphones. The company name appearing next to the horizontal menu is supposed to replace the company logo on those smaller screens. Visitors using tablets and smartphones should be able to tap this text to take them to the home page when the header element is hidden. Let's add the home page link to this text.

6    Switch to Design view.

7    Select the text *Favorite City Tour* at the top of the menu.

     The link placeholder (#) should appear in the Link field of the Property inspector.

8    In the Property inspector Link field, choose `../index.html` from the dropdown menu.

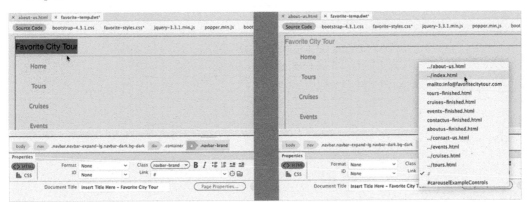

The link is complete, but you're not finished with it yet. Although the text is intended for tablets and smartphones, there's no need for it to be visible on desktop computers. Let's create some styling that will hide the text on desktop computers.

9 If necessary, select the a.navbar-brand tag selector.

10 In the CSS Designer, select **favorite-styles.css**.
Click the Add Selector icon ✚.
Press the up arrow to create the following selector:
.container .navbar-brand

11 Add the following property to the new rule:
display: none

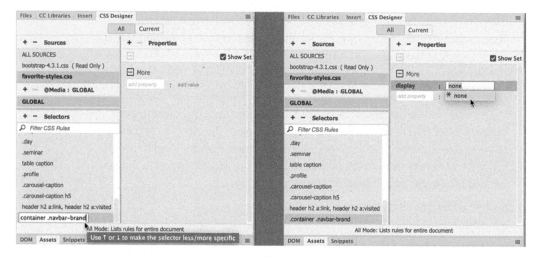

12 Switch to Live view.

The company name is no longer visible beside the horizontal menu. But now the menu has moved over to the left side of the layout. It would look better centered on the page. The menu is created using the element ul.navbar-nav.mr-autolist.

13 In the CSS Designer, select **favorite-styles.css**.
In the Selectors pane, select the rule .bg-dark.
Create the following selector:
ul.navbar-nav

**14** Add the following property to the new rule:

```
margin: 0 auto
```

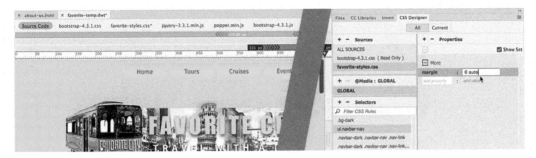

The horizontal menu aligns to the center of the layout.

So far, all the links you've created and the changes you've made are only on the template. The whole purpose of using the template is to make it easy to update pages in your site.

## Updating links in child pages

To apply the links you've created to all the existing pages based on this template, all you have to do is save it.

**1** Choose File > Save.

The Update Template Files dialog appears. You can choose to update pages now or wait until later. You can even update the template files manually, if desired.

**2** Click Update.

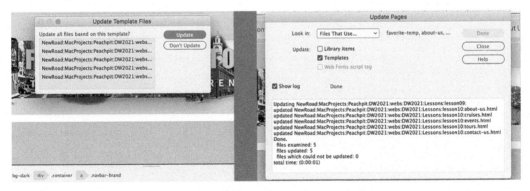

Dreamweaver updates all pages created by this template. The Update Pages dialog appears and displays a report listing the updated pages. If you don't see the list of updated pages, click the Show Log option in the dialog.

**Note:** When you close templates or webpages, Dreamweaver may ask you to save changes to **favorite-styles.css**. Whenever you see these warnings, always save the changes; otherwise, you could lose all your newly created CSS rules and properties.

3 Close the Update Pages dialog.
Close **favorite-temp.dwt**.

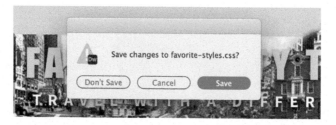

Dreamweaver prompts you to save **favorite-styles.css**.

4 Click Save.

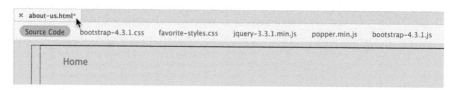

The file **about-us.html** is still open. Note the asterisk in the document tab; this indicates that the page has been changed but not saved.

5 Save **about-us.html**.

Although Live view provides an excellent method to preview your HTML content and styling, the best way to preview links by far is in a web browser. Dreamweaver provides an easy way to preview webpages in your favorite browser.

6 Right-click the document tab for **about-us.html**.
Select Open In Browser. Choose your preferred browser from the context menu.

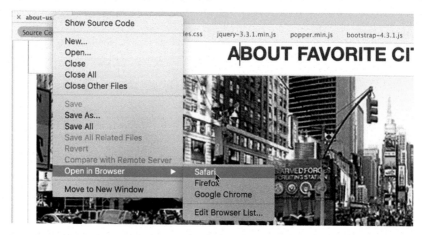

7 Position the cursor over the *Home* and *Tours* links.

If you display the status bar in your browser, you can see the links applied to each item. When the template was saved, it updated the locked regions of the page, adding the hyperlinks to the horizontal menu. Child pages that are closed at the time of updating are automatically saved. Open pages must be saved manually or you will lose changes applied by the template.

8 Click the *Contact Us* link.

The *Contact Us* page loads to replace the *About Us* page in the browser.

● **Note:** The display of the target URL in your browser may require you to activate a feature in your browser first.

▶ **Tip:** Thoroughly test all links you create on every page.

9 Click the *About Us* link.

The *About Us* page loads to replace the *Contact Us* page. The links were added even to pages that weren't open at the time.

● **Note:** When you make and save changes to a document already open in the browser, remember that you have to reload the page before the changes will be visible.

10 Close the browser.

You learned three methods for creating hyperlinks with the Property inspector: typing the link manually, using the Browse For File function, and using the Point To File tool.

# Creating an external link

The pages you linked to in the previous exercise were all stored within the current site. You can also link to any page—or other resource—stored on the web if you know the URL.

## Creating an absolute external link in Live view

In the previous exercise, you used Design view to build all your links. As you build pages and format content, you'll use Live view frequently to preview the styling and appearance of your elements. Although some aspects of content creation and editing are limited in Live view, you can still create and edit hyperlinks. In this exercise, you'll apply an external link to some text using Live view.

1 Open **contact-us.html** from the site root folder in Live view. Make sure the document window is at least 1200 pixels wide.

  The first thing we need to do is add some text to the file.

2 In the Files panel, open **contact-link.txt** from the lesson10/resources folder.

3 Select all the text and copy it.

4 Switch to **contact-us.html** in Dreamweaver. Insert the cursor into the paragraph starting with *A company is only as good as its people...*

5 Select the p tag selector.

6 Choose Insert > HTML > Paragraph.

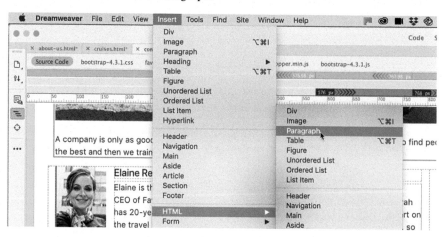

The Position Assist dialog appears.

**7** Click After.

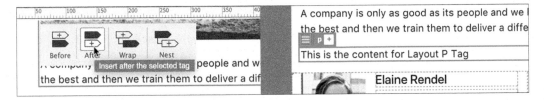

A new paragraph element appears with placeholder text.

**8** Select the placeholder text and paste the text copied in step 3.

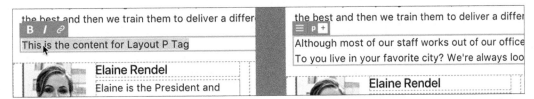

The text is in place for two of our sample links.

**9** In the new <p> element, note the word *Meredien*.

You'll link this text to the Google Maps site.

**10** Launch your favorite browser.
In the URL field, type **google.com/maps** and press Enter/Return.

▶ **Tip:** For this exercise, you can use any search engine or web-based mapping application.

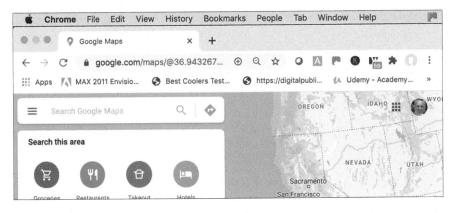

Google Maps appears in the browser window.

● **Note:** In some browsers, you can type the search phrase directly in the URL field.

● **Note:** We're using the Adobe headquarters in place of the fictional city of Meredien. Feel free to use your own location or another search term in its place.

11 Type **San Jose, CA** into the search field and press Enter/Return.

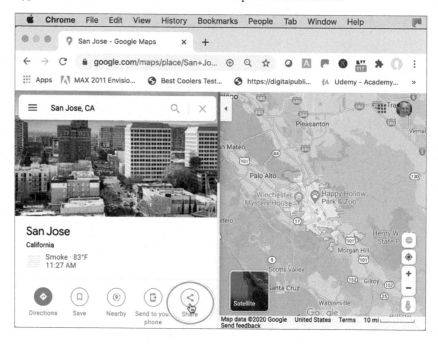

San Jose appears on a map in the browser. In Google Maps, somewhere on the screen you should see a settings or share icon.

● **Note:** The technique for sharing map links is implemented differently in various browsers and search engines and may change over time.

12 Open the sharing or settings interface as appropriate for your chosen mapping application.

Search engines and browsers may display their link-sharing and embedding interface slightly differently than does the one pictured. Google Maps, Map-Quest, and Bing usually offer at least two separate code snippets: one for use within a hyperlink and the other to generate an actual map that you can embed in your site.

Note that the link contains the entire URL of the map, making it an *absolute* link. The advantage of using absolute links is that you can copy and paste them anywhere in the site without worrying about whether the link will resolve properly.

13 Copy the link.

14 Switch to Live view in Dreamweaver.
Select the word *Meredien*.

In Live view, you can select an entire element or insert the cursor within the element to edit or add text or apply hyperlinks, as desired. When an element or section of text is selected, Text Display will appear. The Text Display interface allows you to apply `<strong>` or `<em>` tags to the selection or (as in this case) to apply hyperlinks.

15 Click the Hyperlink icon ![icon] in the Text Display. Press Ctrl+V/Cmd+V to paste the link in the Link field. Press Enter/Return to complete the link.

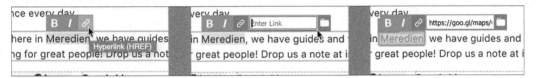

The selected text displays the default formatting for a hyperlink.

▶ **Tip:** Double-click to select text in Live view.

16 Save the file and preview it in the default browser.
Test the link.

When you click the link, the browser takes you to the opening page of Google Maps, assuming you have a connection to the internet. But there is a problem: clicking the link replaced the *Contact Us* page in the browser; it didn't open a new window, as it did when you previewed the page at the beginning of the lesson. To make the browser open a new window, you need to add a simple HTML attribute to the link.

17 Switch to Dreamweaver.
Click the *Meredien* link in Live view.

The Element Display appears focused on the `<a>` element. The Property inspector displays the value of the existing link.

**18** Choose _blank from the Target menu in the Property inspector.

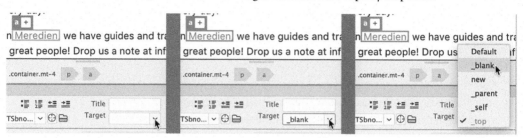

▶ **Tip:** Note the other options in the dropdown menu. You can access the Target attribute in the Property inspector.

Note the other options in the dropdown menu.

**19** Save the file and preview the page in the default browser again. Test the link.

This time when you click the link, the browser opens a new window or document tab.

**20** Close the browser windows and switch back to Dreamweaver.

As you can see, Dreamweaver makes it easy to create links to both internal and external resources.

## Where are you going?

The Target menu has six options. The *target* attribute specifies where to open the designated page or resource.

Default does not create a target attribute in the markup. The default behavior of hyperlinks is to load the page or resource in the same window or tab.

_blank loads the page or resource in a new window or tab.

new is an HTML5 value that loads the page or resource in a new window or tab.

_parent loads the linked document in the parent frame or parent window of the frame that contains the link. If the frame containing the link is not nested, then the linked document loads in the full browser window.

_self loads the linked document in the same frame or window as the link. This target is the default, so you usually don't have to specify it.

_top loads the linked document in the full browser window, thereby removing all frames.

Many of the target options were designed decades ago for sites using framesets, which are now outdated. As a result, the only option you need to consider today is whether the new page or resource replaces the existing window content or loads in a new window.

# Setting up email links

Another type of link takes the visitor not to another page but to the visitor's email program. Email links can create automatic, pre-addressed email messages from your visitors for customer feedback, product orders, or other important communications. The code for an email link is slightly different from the normal hyperlink, and—as you probably guessed already—Dreamweaver can create the proper code for you automatically.

1   If necessary, open **contact-us.html** in Design view.

2   Select the email address (info@favoritecitytour.com) in the second paragraph underneath the heading CONTACT FAVORITE CITY TOUR.

3   Choose Insert > HTML > Email Link.

▶ **Tip:** The Email Link menu can be accessed in Live view, but it doesn't work properly. You can use the menu in Design view or Code view, or you can just create the links by hand in any view.

The Email Link dialog appears. The text selected in the document window in step 2 is automatically entered into the Text and Email fields.

4   Click OK.
    Examine the Link field in the Property inspector.

▶ **Tip:** If you select the text before you access the dialog, Dreamweaver enters the text in the field for you automatically.

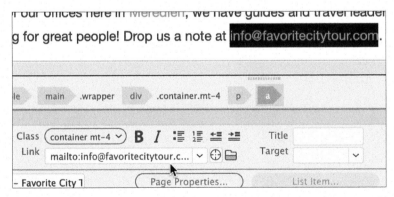

Dreamweaver inserts the email address into the Link field and also enters an additional notation, `mailto:`, that tells the browser to automatically launch the visitor's default email program.

5 Save the file and open it in the default browser.
Test the email link.

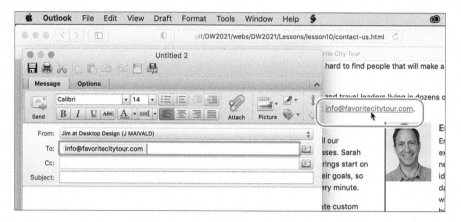

If your computer has a default email program installed, it will launch and create a new email message using the email address provided in the link. If there is no default email program, your computer's operating system may ask you to identify or install one.

6 Close any open email program, related dialogs, or wizards. Switch to Dreamweaver.

You can also create email links manually.

7 Select and copy the email address for Elaine that appears at the end of her description.

8 Type `mailto:` in the Property inspector Link field. Paste Elaine's email address directly after the colon. Press Enter/Return to complete the link.

● **Note:** Be sure that there are no spaces between the colon and the link text.

The text `mailto:elaine@favoritecitytour.com` appears in the Text Display link field in Live view.

9 Save the file.

You have learned a few techniques to add links to text content. You can add links to images too.

# Creating an image-based link

Image-based links work like any other hyperlink and can direct users to internal or external resources. You can use the Insert menu in Design view or Code view or apply links and other attributes using the Element Display interface in Live view.

## Creating image-based links using the Element Display

In this exercise, you will create and format an image-based link using the email addresses of each Favorite City Tour employee via the Element Display.

1 If necessary, open **contact-us.html** in Live view from the site root folder. Make sure the document window is at least 1200 pixels wide.

2 Select the image of Elaine in the card-based content section.

The Element Display appears focused on the img element. The hyperlink options are hiding in the Quick Property inspector.

3 In the Element Display, click the Edit HTML Attributes icon ▤.

The Quick Property inspector opens and displays options for the image attributes src, alt, link, width, and height.

4 Click in the Link field. If the email address is still in memory from the previous exercise, simply enter mailto: and paste the address in the Link field. Otherwise, enter mailto:elaine@favoritecitytour.com in the Link field after the colon and press Enter/Return to complete the link. Press the Esc key to close the Quick Property inspector.

The hyperlink that is applied to the image will launch the default email program in the same fashion as it did with the text-based link earlier.

5 Select and copy the email address for Sarah.
Repeat steps 2 through 4 to create an email link for Sarah's image.

6 Create image links for the remaining employees using the appropriate email address for each.

7 Load the page in a browser and test each link.

● **Note:** In the past, images that featured a hyperlink were automatically styled with a blue border. That styling was deprecated in HTML5.

All the image-based links on the page are complete. You can create text-based links using the Text Display too.

## Creating text links using the Text Display

In this exercise, you will create text-based email links as needed for the remaining employees.

1   If necessary, open **contact-us.html** in Live view. Make sure the document window is at least 1200 pixels wide.

2   Select and copy the email address for Sarah.

3   Double-click to edit the paragraph containing Sarah's email address. Select her email address.

    The Text Display appears around the selected text.

4   Click the Link icon.

    A Link field appears. A folder icon displays on the right side of the Link field. If you were linking to a file on the website, you could click the folder to target the file. In this case, we're creating an email link.

5   Insert the cursor in the Link field, if necessary.
    Enter `mailto:` and paste Sarah's email address.
    Press Enter/Return.

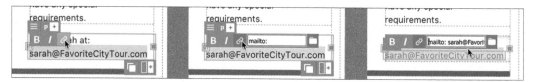

6   Using the Text Display, create email links for the remaining email addresses displayed on the page.

When you are finished, you may notice that Matthew's email address is extending beyond the edges of the second column.

Normally, when text gets close to the end of a column, it will wrap to the next line, but Matthew's email address is treated as one long word and cannot wrap. There is also no hyphenation and no practical way to break the address either. The best way to deal with this issue is to apply a special CSS style for the email address.

7  Insert the cursor in Matthew's email address.
Select the a tag selector.

The Element Display appears on the `<a>` element containing Matthew's email address.

8  If necessary, click the All button in CSS Designer.

9  Select **favorite-styles.css** in the Sources pane.
Click the Add Selector icon ✚.

A new selector, `.media-body p a`, appears in the Selector pane. This selector will target only the links within the list-based content section. Since there are no other text-based links in these profiles, the selector should be fine as is.

10 Press Enter/Return to create the new selector.
Add the following property to the rule `.media-body p a`:
`font-size: 90%`

All the email addresses resize. Matthew's email address now fits entirely within the column. This styling should take care of the spacing problem for the moment.

11 Save and close all files.

## Attack of the killer robots

Although on the surface it sounds like a good idea to add email links to make it easier for your customers and visitors to communicate with you and your staff, email links are a double-edged sword. The internet is awash in bad actors and unethical companies that use intelligent programs, or robots, to constantly search for live email addresses (and other personal information) that they can flood with unsolicited email and spam. Putting a plain email address on your site as shown in these exercises is like putting a sign on your back that says "kick me."

In place of active email links, many sites use a variety of methods for limiting the amount of spam they receive. One technique uses images to display the email addresses, since robots can't read data stored in pixels (yet). Another leaves off the hyperlink attribute and types the address with extra spaces, like this:

```
elaine @ favoritecitytour .com
```

However, both of these techniques have drawbacks; if visitors try to use copy and paste, it forces them to go out of their way to remove the extra spaces or try to type your email address from memory. Either way, the chances of you receiving any communication decrease with each step the user has to accomplish without additional help.

At this time, there is no foolproof way to prevent someone from using an email address for nefarious purposes. Coupled with the fact that fewer users actually have a mail program installed on their computers anymore, the best method for enabling communication for your visitors is to provide a means built into the site itself. Many sites create web-hosted forms that collect the visitor's information and message and then pass them along using server-based email functionality.

## Targeting page elements

As you add more content, the pages get longer and navigating to that content gets more difficult. Typically, when you click a link to a page, the browser window loads the page and displays it starting at the top. But it can be helpful to provide convenient methods for users to link to a specific point on a page, especially when the content they are looking for may be a fair distance from the top.

HTML 4.01 provided two methods to target specific content or page structures: a *named anchor* and an *id* attribute. In HTML5, the named anchor method has been deprecated in favor of ids. If you or your website have used named anchors in the past, don't worry—they won't suddenly cease to function. But from this point on, you should start using ids exclusively.

# Creating internal targeted links

In this exercise, you'll work with id attributes to create the target of an internal link. You can add ids in Live, Design, or Code view.

1   Open **events.html** in Live view. Make sure the document window is at least 1200 pixels wide.

2   Scroll down to the table containing the seminar schedule.

When users move down this far on the page, the navigation menus are out of sight and unusable. The farther down the page they read, the farther they are from the primary navigation. Before users can navigate to another page, they have to use the browser scroll bars or the mouse scroll wheel to get back to the top of the page.

Older websites dealt with this situation by adding a link to take visitors back to the top, vastly improving their experience on the site. Let's call this type of link an *internal targeted* link. Modern websites simply freeze the navigation menu at the top of the screen. That way, the menu is always visible and accessible to the user. You will learn how to do both techniques. First, let's create an internal targeted link.

Internal targeted links have two parts: the link itself and the target, or destination. Which one you create first doesn't matter.

3   Click in the 2021 *Seminar Schedule* table.
    Select the table's parent `section` tag selector.

The Element Display appears focused on the `section` element.

4   Open the Insert panel.
    Select the HTML category.
    Click the Paragraph item.

    The Position Assist dialog appears.

5  Click Before.

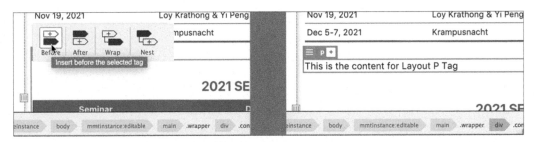

A new paragraph element appears in the layout, with the placeholder text *This is the content for Layout P Tag.*

6  Select the placeholder text.
   Type **Return to top** to replace it.

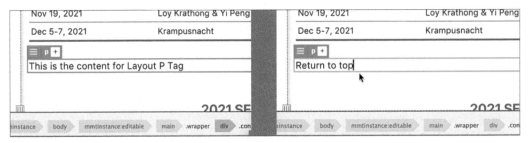

The text is inserted between the two tables, formatted as a `<p>` element. The text would look better centered. Bootstrap has a rule already defined for centering text that has been applied to all the content section headings.

7  Click the Add Class/ID icon ⊞ for the new `<p>` element.

8  Type `.text-center` in the text field and press Enter/Return, or choose `.text-center` from the hinting menu.

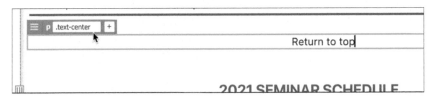

The *Return to top* text is aligned to the center. The tag selector now displays `p.text-center`.

9  Select the element *Return to top*. Click the Edit HTML Attributes ▤ icon and type `#top` in the Link field.

Press Enter/Return to complete the link.

By using `#top`, you have created a link to the top of the current page. This target is now a default function in HTML5. If you use the plain hash (#) symbol or `#top` as the link target, the browser automatically assumes you want to jump to the top of the page. No additional code is needed.

10  Save all files.

11  Open **events.html** in a browser.

12  Scroll down to the *Seminar* table.
Click the *Return to top* link.

The browser jumps back to the top of the page.

You can copy the *Return to top* link and paste it anywhere in the site you want to add this functionality.

13  Switch to Dreamweaver.
Click the text *Return to top*. If necessary, select the p tag selector for the link and press Ctrl+C/Cmd+C to copy the <p> element and its link.

14  Insert the cursor in the *Seminar* table.
Select the `section` tag selector.
Press Ctrl+V/Cmd+V to paste.

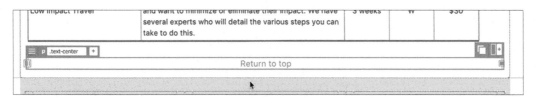

A new p element and link appear at the bottom of the page.

15  Save the file and preview it in the browser.
Test both *Return to top* links.

Both links can be used to jump back to the top of the document. In the next exercise, you'll learn how to create link targets using element attributes.

# Creating a destination link in the Element Display

In the past, destinations were often created by inserting a standalone element known as a *named anchor* within the code. Today, id attributes have replaced the named anchor in HTML5. In most cases, there's no need to add any extra elements to create hyperlink destinations, since you can simply add an id attribute to a handy element nearby.

In this exercise, you will use the Element Display to add id attributes to the tables for navigation purposes.

1   Open **events.html** in Live view. Make sure the document window is at least 1200 pixels wide.

▶ **Tip:** Since the hyperlink behavior focuses the browser on any element featuring the id, it is better to apply it to the section instead of to the table element.

2   Click the *2021 International Festivals Schedule* table. Select the `section` tag selector.

The Element Display and the Property inspector display the attributes currently applied to the `section` element containing the Events table. You can add an id using either tool.

3   Click the Add Class/ID icon. Type #

If any ids were defined in the style sheet but unused on the page, a hinting list would appear. Since nothing appears, it means that there are no unused ids. Creating a new one is easy.

4   Type `festivals` and press Enter/Return.

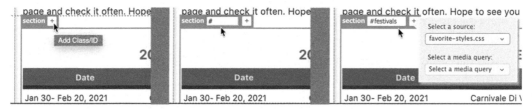

● **Note:** When creating ids, remember that they need to have names that are used only once per page. They are case sensitive, so look out for typos.

The CSS Source dialog appears. You do not need to add the id to any style sheet.

5   Press Esc to close the dialog.

The tag selector now displays `#festivals` and no entry was made in the style sheet. Since ids are unique identifiers, they are perfect for targeting specific content on a page for hyperlinks.

> ● **Note:** There is no need for a CSS selector for this id. If one is accidentally created, feel free to delete the selector in CSS Designer.

You also need to create an id for the *Seminars* table.

6   Repeat steps 2 through 5 to create the id #seminars on the section element containing the *Seminars* table.

The tag selector now displays #seminars.

7   Save all files.

You'll learn how to link to these ids in the next exercise.

● **Note:** If you add the id to the wrong element, simply delete it and start over.

## Targeting id-based link destinations

By adding unique ids to both tables, you have provided ideal targets with which internal hyperlinks can navigate to a specific section of your webpage. In this exercise, you will create a link to each table.

1   If necessary, open **contact-us.html** in Live view. Make sure the document window is at least 1200 pixels wide.

2   Scroll down to the profile of Sarah Harvey.

3   Select the word *festivals* in the second paragraph of the profile.

4   Using the Text Display, type events.html to create a link to the file.

This link will open the file, but you're not finished. You now have to direct the browser to navigate down to the *Festivals* table.

5   Type #festivals at the end of the filename to complete the link, and press Enter/Return.

▶ **Tip:** You can select single words by double-clicking them.

● **Note:** Hyperlinks cannot contain spaces; make sure the id reference follows the filename immediately.

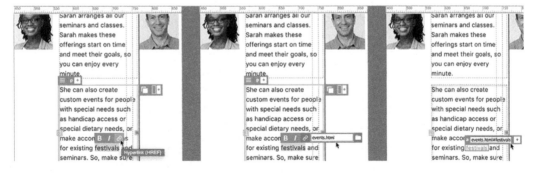

The word *festivals* is now a link targeting the *Festivals* table in the events.html file.

6 Select the word *seminars*.

Create a link to the events.html file.

Type #seminars to complete the link and press Enter/Return.

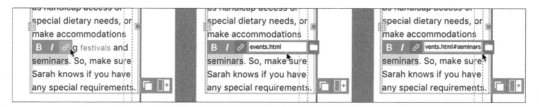

7 Save the file and preview the page in a browser.

Test the links to the *Festivals* and *Seminars* tables.

The links open the *Events* page and jump to the appropriate tables. You've learned how to create a variety of internal and external links. There are only a few more chores remaining.

## Locking an element on the screen

Most elements you encounter on a webpage will move with the page as you scroll down through the content. This is the default behavior in HTML. For specific purposes you may want to freeze an element so that it stays on the screen. This has become very popular, especially with navigation menus. Keeping the menu visible at all times provides handy navigation options whenever desired.

The navigation menu is not editable directly in the child pages created from the template. The change you need to make has to be done in the template.

1 Open **favorite-temp.dwt** in Live view. Make sure the document window is at least 1200 pixels wide.

The navigation menu appears at the top of the page but scrolls with the rest of the content.

A bug in Dreamweaver makes it difficult to work with elements in the noneditable regions of the page in Live view. In most cases, you won't be able to directly select many elements in the document window. But you can use the DOM panel.

2 Choose Window > DOM to open the DOM panel, if necessary. Locate the nav element in the DOM panel.

Note that there are several Bootstrap classes assigned to this element already; you'll assign one more.

3 Double-click to edit the classes assigned to the nav element.

4   Insert the cursor at the end of the array of classes.
    Press the spacebar to insert a space.
    Type `.fixed-`

    The hinting menu displays a list of defined classes and filters them as you type.
    The class `.fixed-bottom` would position the horizontal menu at the bottom of
    the browser window. The class `.fixed-top` positions it at the top.

5   Select the class `.fixed-top` and press Enter/Return to complete the change.

As soon as you add the class, the `header` element shifts under the horizontal
menu. If you scroll down the page, you will see that in Live view the menu stays
at the top of the window. It should work the same way in a browser.

The effect is close to what we wanted but not complete. Although the menu
is fixed to the top of the screen, it obscures part of the header. Applying this
Bootstrap class has basically taken the menu out of the normal flow of the document. It now exists in a separate world, floating above the other elements.

To make the rest of the content reorient properly to the original page design,
you'll have to add spacing above the `header` element to move everything back
into place. To move it down below the menu, you need to add some space to the
rule formatting it.

6   Add the following property to the `header` rule:
    `margin-top: 2.6em`

    ▶ **Tip:** Using em measurements for menus and other controls ensures that the structure will
    adapt better if visitors use larger font sizes, since ems are based on the font size.

The `header` element shifts back down to its original position.

**7** Save and update all files.

The menu is almost complete. You may have noticed that some of the formatting of the horizontal menu is a bit off. Let's adjust the colors to better match the site color scheme.

## Styling a navigation menu

A close inspection of the horizontal menu will identify inconsistent styling, especially when you interact with the menu items.

**1** If necessary, open **favorite-temp.dwt** in Live view. Make sure the document window is at least 1200 pixels wide.

**2** Position the cursor over any menu item and observe the behavior of its styling. Move the cursor to another item and note any changes.

As the cursor passes over a menu item, the text color changes from blue to white. This change is enabled by the pseudo-class :hover. Since you did not create any styling for the :hover behavior, you can assume it is part of the Bootstrap framework.

In Lesson 6, you defined several rules to override the default styling of the horizontal menu. Two in particular style the individual menu items, or buttons. To modify the styling fully, you will have to create two new rules. The easiest method is by duplicating the two existing rules.

**3** In CSS Designer, select the All button, if necessary.
Select **favorite-styles.css** in the Sources pane.

**4** Select the rule .navbar-dark .navbar-nav .nav-link.
Examine the properties of the rule.

This rule formats the color of the text. The current :hover styling changes the text to white, which makes it hard to read. Let's change it to black instead.

**5** Right-click the rule .navbar-dark .navbar-nav .nav-link.

**6** Select Duplicate from the context menu.

An exact copy of the rule is created. Note that the selector is editable.

**7** Click at the end of the class `.nav-link`.

Type `:hover` and press Enter/Return.

● **Note:** The pseudo-class must be added directly to the end of the class `.nav-link` with no spaces.

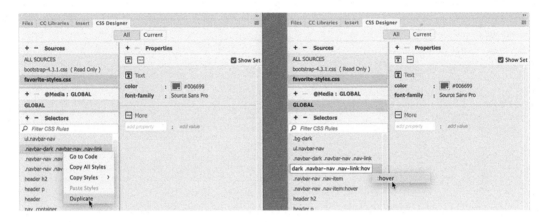

The new rule targets the `:hover` state of the link text.

**8** Change the following property `color:#000`

Click the Remove CSS Property 🗑 icon in CSS Designer to delete the property `font-family source sans pro`

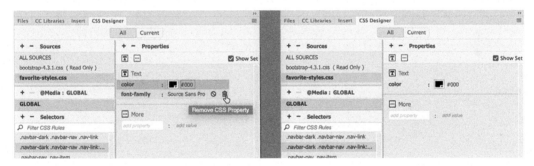

When you create a pseudo-class, you need to declare only the properties that change from one state to the next. Therefore, there's no need to keep the `font-family` property.

**9** Position the cursor over any of the menu items.

Move the cursor to another item.

The link text changes from blue to black. That looks much better, but the change could be a bit more dramatic. A change in the background property would enhance the `:hover` effect.

**10** Right-click the rule `.navbar-nav .nav-item`.

Select Duplicate from the context menu.

Edit the selector as highlighted:

```
.navbar-nav .nav-item:hover
```

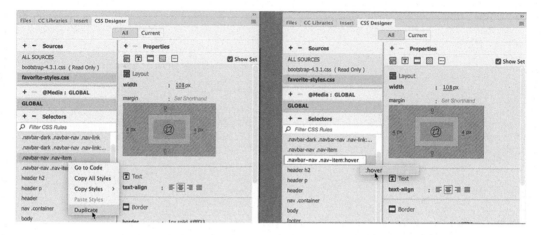

The original rule styles the button. One of the properties sets a gradient background. Reversing the direction of the gradient would create a dramatic effect. First, you need to delete all the properties that are unneeded.

11 Delete the following properties in the new rule: ~~width~~, ~~margin~~, ~~text-align~~, and ~~border~~.

The only property remaining is background-image.

12 Click the Gradient Color Picker in the Properties pane.

13 Change the angle to 0.
Press Enter/Return to complete the change.

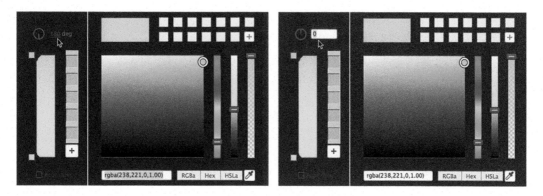

**14** Position the cursor over any of the menu items.

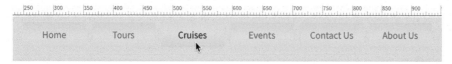

The gradient background reverses direction and the text displays in black. The effect provides a nice interactive behavior to the menu items.

Before you save the template and update all the pages, there's a new kind of link you should add to the site: a telephone link.

# Adding a telephone link

Clicking to dial a phone number on a website was not a "thing" before the debut of the smartphone. Today, millions of people surf the internet using smartphones every day. A telephone link is an essential component of any page if you want to get customers to call your business.

In this exercise, you will learn how to create a clickable telephone link.

**1** Scroll down to the bottom of the template.

The address block in the `<footer>` element features the company phone number.

Some phones are smart enough to automatically recognize phone numbers. Adding a link to the number will ensure that all phones will be able to click to dial it. Since this is a template, you probably won't be able to select the phone number and add a link to it in Live view.

2  Switch to Design view.
   Select the phone number.

   When creating a phone link, leave off any formatting characters and enter it exactly how it should be dialed. Don't use hyphens or parentheses, and add the country code.

3  In the Property inspector, enter `tel:14085551212` in the Link field.

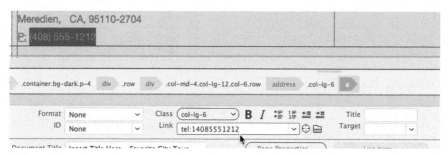

4  Press Enter/Return.

   When you press Enter/Return, you should see an <a> element added to the tag selectors. The telephone link is complete. Now there's only one item left to address. Below the phone number there is an email link.

5  Select and copy the email address info@favoritecitytour.com.

6  Using any of the methods you learned in this lesson, create the link **mailto:info@favoritecity.com** on the text.

7  Save the template and update all pages.
   Close the Update Pages dialog.

8  Close the Template.
   Save changes to **favorite-styles.css**.

You have learned how to create links in a variety of ways and even learned how to format an interactive behavior on the horizontal menu as well as freeze it to the top of the screen. Creating the hyperlinks is just the first part of the job; you next need to learn how to test them.

## Checking your page

Dreamweaver can check your page, as well as the entire site, for valid HTML, accessibility, and broken links. In this exercise, you'll learn how to check your links sitewide.

1  If necessary, open **contact-us.html** in Live view.

2  Choose Site > Site Options > Check Links Sitewide.

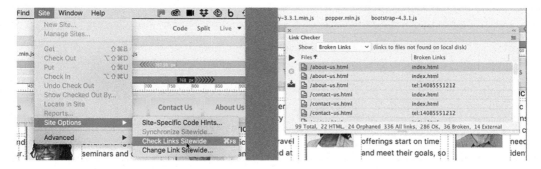

The Link Checker panel appears. The panel reports broken links, orphaned links, and external links, among other things. Use this panel before publishing your site to identify problems with your hyperlinks. One item you should notice is that the panel reports a broken link to the file **index.html**. This is a link to a currently nonexistent page. Don't worry, you'll create this page in an upcoming lesson, so you can ignore this error for now.

The panel also reports that the link #top is broken. Although the link works, there's no actual target defined in any of the pages, so the panel reports it anyway. If you expect to get visitors who use older browsers, you might want to add the id #top to the nav element in the template.

The report also identifies a link to an SVG graphic defined in the Bootstrap style sheet. As you can see, the Link Checker will also find broken links to external sites and resources. Although the total number of errors seems large, none of them should affect the operation of the site, and the links to the home page will be fixed once you create that page in Lesson 11, "Publishing to the Web."

● **Note:** The total number and types of missing and broken links may vary from those pictured.

3  Close the Link Checker panel, or, if it's docked, right-click the Link Checker tab and choose Close Tab Group from the context menu.

You've made big changes to your pages in this lesson by creating links in the main navigation menu, within text blocks, to specific destinations on pages, to email, and to a phone number. You also applied links to images and learned how to check your site for broken links.

## Self-paced exercise: Adding additional links

First, using the skills you have just learned, open **events.html** and create destination links for the words *festivals* and *seminars* in the intro paragraph above the tables.

Remember that each word should link to the appropriate table on that page. Can you figure out how to construct these links properly? If you have any trouble, check out the **events-finished.html** file in the lesson10/finished folder for the answer.

● **Note:** Be sure to add target _blank to these links.

At the bottom of each of the pages there are three link placeholders with the text *Link Anchor*. You'll have to open the site template to edit these links. Point them to the following external targets:

- Link Text: **US State Dept**
- Link URL: `https://travel.state.gov`
- Link Text: **US Customs**
- Link URL: `https://cbp.gov/travel`
- Link Text: **Overseas Shipping**
- Link URL: `https://usps.com/international`

When you finish, don't forget to save the template and update pages.

# Review questions

1 Describe two ways to insert a link into a page within the site.

2 What information is required to create a link to an external webpage?

3 What's the difference between standard page links and email links?

4 What attribute is used to create destination links to specific elements on a page?

5 What limits the usefulness of email links?

6 Can links be applied to images?

7 How can you check to see whether your links will work properly?

# Review answers

1 Select text or a graphic, and then, in the Property inspector, click the Browse For File icon next to the Link field and navigate to the desired page. A second method is to drag the Point To File icon to a file within the Files panel.

2 To link to an external page, you must type or copy and paste the full web address (a fully formed URL, including http:// or other protocol) in the Link field of the Property inspector or the Text Display.

3 A standard page link opens a new page or moves the view to a position somewhere on the page. An email link opens a blank email message window if the visitor has an email application installed on their system.

4 You apply unique id attributes to any element to create a link destination, which can appear only once in each page.

5 Email links may not be very useful because many users do not use built-in email programs, and the links will not automatically connect with internet-based email services.

6 Yes, links can be applied to images and used in the same way text-based links are.

7 Run the Link Checker report to test links on each page individually or sitewide. You should also test every link in a browser.

# 11 PUBLISHING TO THE WEB

## Lesson overview

In this lesson, you'll publish your website to the internet and do the following:

- Define a remote site.
- Define a testing server.
- Put files on the web.
- Cloak files and folders.
- Update out-of-date links sitewide.

 This lesson will take about 1 hour to complete. To get the lesson files used in this lesson, download them from the webpage for this book at www.adobepress.com/DreamweaverCIB2021. For more information, see "Accessing the lesson files and Web Edition" in the "Getting Started" section at the beginning of this book.

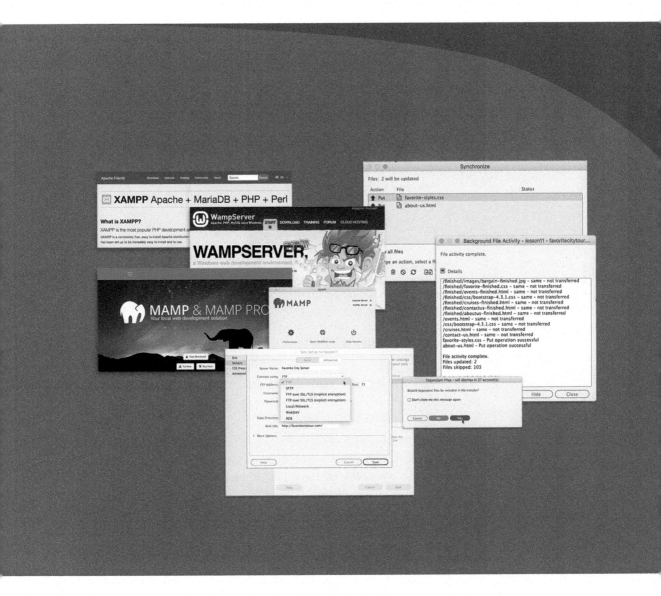

The goal of all the preceding lessons is to design, develop, and build pages for a remote website. But Dreamweaver doesn't abandon you there. It also provides powerful tools with which to upload and maintain a website of any size over time.

# Defining a remote site

● **Note:** If you have not already downloaded the project files for this lesson to your computer from your Account page and defined a site based on this folder, make sure to do so now. See "Getting Started" at the beginning of the book.

Dreamweaver's workflow is based on a two-site system. One site is in a folder on your computer's hard drive and is known as the *local site*. All work in the previous lessons has been performed on your local site. The second site, known as the *remote site*, is established in a folder on a web server, typically running on another computer, and is connected to the internet and publicly available. In large companies, the remote site is often available only to employees via a network-based intranet. Such sites provide information and applications to support corporate programs and products.

Dreamweaver supports several methods for connecting to a remote site.

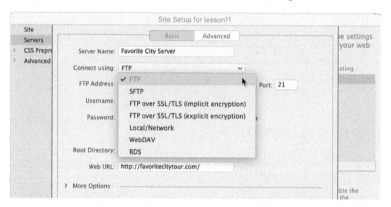

- **FTP** (File Transfer Protocol): The standard method for connecting to hosted websites.

- **SFTP** (Secure File Transfer Protocol): A protocol that provides a method to connect to hosted websites in a more secure manner to preclude unauthorized access or interception of online content.

- **FTP over SSL/TLS** (implicit encryption): A secure FTP (FTPS) method that requires all clients of the FTPS server be aware that SSL is to be used on the session. It is incompatible with non-FTPS-aware clients.

- **FTP over SSL/TLS** (explicit encryption): A legacy-compatible secure FTP method on which FTPS-aware clients can invoke security with an FTPS-aware server without breaking overall FTP functionality with non-FTPS-aware clients.

- **Local/network:** A local or network connection is most frequently used with an intermediate web server, known as a *staging server*. Staging servers are typically used to test sites before they go live. Files from the staging server are eventually published to an internet-connected web server.

- **WebDav** (Web Distributed Authoring and Versioning): A web-based system also known to Windows users as Web Folders and to Mac users who use AirDrop or Air Sharing with their devices.

- **RDS** (Remote Development Services): Developed by Adobe for ColdFusion and primarily used when working with ColdFusion-based sites.

Dreamweaver can now upload larger files faster and more efficiently and as a background activity, allowing you to return to work more quickly. In the following exercises, you'll set up a remote site using the two most common methods: FTP and local/network.

## Setting up a remote FTP site (optional)

The vast majority of web developers rely on FTP to publish and maintain their sites. FTP is a well-established protocol, and many variations of the protocol are used on the web—most of which are supported by Dreamweaver.

1 Launch Adobe Dreamweaver CC (2021 release) or later.

2 Choose Site > Manage Sites, or choose Manage Sites from the site list dropdown menu in the Files panel.

In the Manage Sites dialog is a list of all the sites you may have defined.

3 Make sure that the current site, lesson11, is selected. Click the Edit icon ✏.

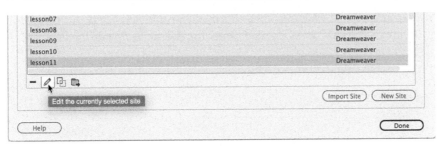

4 In the Site Setup dialog for lesson11, click the Servers category.

The Site Setup dialog allows you to set up multiple servers so that you can test several types of installations, if desired.

◆ **Warning:** To complete the following exercise, you must have a remote server already established. Remote servers can be hosted by your own company or contracted from a third-party web-hosting service.

5  Click the Add New Server icon ＋.

Enter **Favorite City Server** in the Server Name field.

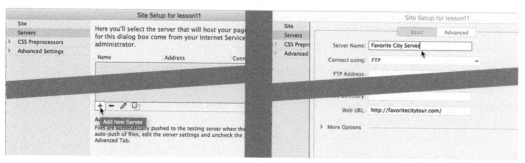

6  From the Connect Using pop-up menu, choose FTP.

● **Note:** If neces-
sary, select a different
protocol to match your
available server.

▶ **Tip:** If you are in
the process of moving
an existing site to a
new internet service
provider (ISP), you may
not be able to use the
domain name to upload
files to the new server.
In that case, the IP
address can be used to
upload files initially.

7  In the FTP Address field, type the URL or IP (Internet Protocol) address of your
FTP server.

If you contract a third-party service as a web host, you will be assigned an
FTP address. This address may come in the form of an IP address, such as
192.168.1.100. Enter this number into the field exactly as it was sent to you.
Frequently, the FTP address will be the domain name of your site, such as
**ftp.favoritecitytour.com**. But don't enter the characters *ftp* into the field.

● **Note:** The username
and password will be
provided by your host-
ing company.

8  In the Username field, enter your FTP username.
In the Password field, enter your FTP password.

Usernames may be case sensitive, but password fields almost always are; be sure you enter them correctly. Often, the easiest way to enter them is to copy them from the confirmation email from your hosting company and paste them into the appropriate fields.

9  In the Root Directory field, type the name of the folder that contains documents publicly accessible to the web, if any.

**Tip:** Check with your web-hosting service or IS/IT manager to obtain the root directory name, if any.

Some web hosts provide FTP access to a root-level folder that might contain nonpublic folders—such as cgi-bin, which is used to store common gateway interface (CGI) or binary scripts—as well as a public folder. In these cases, type the public folder name—such as httpdocs, public, public_html, www, or wwwroot—in the Root Directory field. In many web-host configurations, the FTP address is the same as the public folder, and the Root Directory field should be left blank.

10 If necessary, select the Save checkbox if you don't want to re-enter your username and password every time Dreamweaver connects to your site.

11 Click Test to verify that your FTP connection works properly.

**Tip:** If Dreamweaver does not connect to your host, first check the username and password, as well as the FTP address and root directory, for any errors.

Dreamweaver displays an alert to notify you that the connection was successful or unsuccessful.

12 Click OK to dismiss the alert.

If Dreamweaver connects properly to the webhost, skip to step 14. If you received an error message, your web server may require additional configuration options.

13 Click the More Options triangle to reveal additional server options.

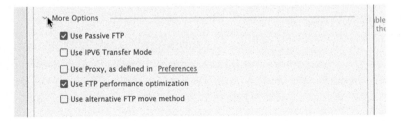

The default options selected in Dreamweaver should work, but if they don't, consult your hosting company to select the appropriate options for your specific FTP server:

- **Use Passive FTP:** Allows your computer to connect to the host computer and bypass a firewall restraint. Many web hosts require this setting.

- **Use IPV6 Transfer Mode:** Enables connection to IPV6-based servers, which use the most recent version of the internet transfer protocol.

- **Use Proxy:** Identifies a secondary proxy host connection, as defined in your Dreamweaver preferences.

- **Use FTP Performance Optimization:** Optimizes the FTP connection. Deselect this option if Dreamweaver can't connect to your server.

- **Use Alternative FTP Move Method:** Provides an additional method to resolve FTP conflicts, especially when rollbacks are enabled or when moving files.

Once you establish a working connection, you may need to configure some advanced options.

## Troubleshooting your FTP connection

Connecting to your remote site can be frustrating the first time you attempt it. You can experience numerous pitfalls, many of which are out of your control. Here are a few steps to take if you have issues connecting:

- If you can't connect to your FTP server, double-check your username and password and re-enter them carefully. Remember that usernames may be case sensitive on some servers, while passwords frequently are. (This is the most common error.)

- Select Use Passive FTP and test the connection again.

- If you still can't connect to your FTP server, deselect the Use FTP Performance Optimization option and click Test again.

- If none of these steps enables you to connect to your remote site, check with your IS/IT manager or your remote site administrator or web-hosting service.

14 Click the Advanced tab.

Select from the following options for working with your remote site:

- **Maintain Synchronization Information:** Automatically notes the files that have been changed on the local and remote sites so that they can be easily synchronized. This feature helps you keep track of your changes and can be helpful if you change multiple pages before you upload. You may want to use cloaking with this feature. You'll learn about cloaking in an upcoming exercise. This feature is usually selected by default.

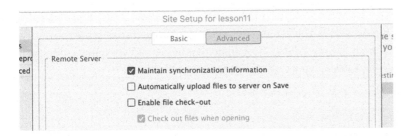

- **Automatically Upload Files To Server On Save:** Transfers files from the local to the remote site when they are saved. This option can become annoying if you save often and aren't yet ready for a page to go public.

- **Enable File Check-Out:** Starts the check-in/check-out system for collaborative website building in a workgroup environment. If you choose this option, you'll need to enter a check-out name and, optionally, an email address. If you're working by yourself, you do not need to select this option.

It is acceptable to leave any or all these options unselected, but for the purposes of this lesson, select the Maintain Synchronization Information option, if necessary.

15 Click Save to finalize the settings in the open dialogs.

The server setup dialog closes, revealing the Servers category in the Site Setup dialog. Your newly defined server is displayed in the window.

16 The Remote option should be selected by default once the server is defined. If you have more than one server defined, click the Remote option for Favorite City Server.

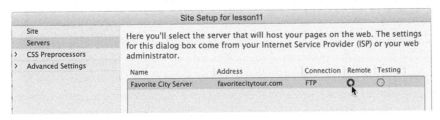

17 Click Save to finish setting up your new server.

A dialog may appear, informing you that the cache will be re-created because you changed the site settings.

18 If necessary, click OK to build the cache.
When Dreamweaver finishes updating the cache, click Done to close the Manage Sites dialog.

You have established a connection to your remote server. If you don't currently have a remote server, you can instead substitute a local testing server as your remote server. See the sidebar "Installing a testing server" for information on installing and setting up a testing server in Dreamweaver.

## Installing a testing server

When you produce sites with dynamic content, you need to test the functionality before the pages go live on the internet. A testing server can fit that need nicely. Depending on the applications you need to test, the testing server can simply be a subfolder on your actual web server, or you can use a local web server such as Apache or Internet Information Services (IIS) from Microsoft.

For detailed information about installing and configuring a local web server, check out the following links:

- Apache/ColdFusion: https://tinyurl.com/settingup-coldfusion
- Apache/PHP: http://tinyurl.com/setup-apachephp
- IIS/ASP: https://tinyurl.com/settingup-asp
- WAMP server https://www.wampserver.com/en/

Once you set up the local web server, you can use it to upload the completed files and test your remote site. In most cases, your local web server will not be accessible from the internet or be able to host the actual website for the public.

## Cloaking folders and files

▶ **Tip:** If disk space is not a concern, you might consider uploading the template files to the server as a means of creating a backup.

Not all the files in your site root folder may need to be transferred to the remote server. For example, there's no point in filling the remote site with files that won't be accessed or that will remain inaccessible to website users. Minimizing files stored on the remote server may also pay financial dividends, since many hosting services base part of their fee on how much disk space your site occupies. If you selected Maintain Synchronization Information for a remote site using FTP or a network server, you may want to cloak some of your local materials to prevent them from being uploaded. *Cloaking* is a Dreamweaver feature that allows you to designate certain folders and files that will not be uploaded to or synchronized with the remote site.

Folders you don't want to upload include the *Templates* and *resource* folders. Some other non-web-compatible file types used to create your site, such as Photoshop (.psd), Flash (.fla), or Microsoft Word (.doc or .docx), also don't need to be on the remote server. Although cloaked files will not upload or synchronize automatically, you may still upload them manually, if desired. Some people like to upload these items to keep a backup copy of them online.

The cloaking process begins in the Site Setup dialog.

1 Choose Site > Manage Sites.

2 Select lesson11 in the site list, and click the Edit icon.

3 Expand the Advanced Settings category and select the Cloaking category.

4 Select the Enable Cloaking and Cloak Files Ending With options, if necessary.

The field below the checkboxes is already populated with a variety of extensions. The actual extensions you see may differ from those pictured.

5 Insert the cursor after the last extension, and insert a space, if necessary. Type **.docx .csv .xslx** in the field.

**Note:** Add any extension you may be using as your own source files.

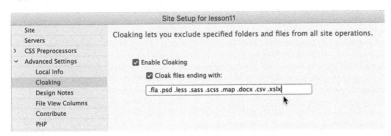

Be sure to insert a space between each extension. By specifying the extensions of file types that don't contain desired web content, you prevent Dreamweaver from automatically uploading and synchronizing these file types no matter where they appear in the site.

6 Click Save. If Dreamweaver prompts you to update the cache, click OK. Then, click Done to close the Manage Sites dialog.

Although you have cloaked several file types automatically, you can also cloak specific files or folders manually from the Files panel.

7 Open the Files panel.

**Note:** Any resource uploaded to the server can be accessed by search engines and accessed by the public. Sensitive material or content should not be uploaded if you are concerned that it may be seen by the public.

In the site list, you will see a list of the files and folders that make up the site. Some of the folders are used to store the raw materials for building content. There's no need to upload these items to the web. The Templates folder is not needed on the remote site, because your webpages do not reference these assets in any way. If you work in a team environment, it may be handy to upload and synchronize these folders so that each team member has up-to-date versions of each on their own computers. For this exercise, let's assume you work alone.

8  Right-click the Templates folder.
From the context menu, choose Cloaking > Cloak.

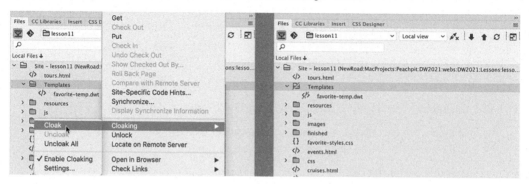

A warning dialog appears, saying that cloaking affects only Put and Get commands and not batch operations.

9  In the warning dialog, click OK.

The selected folder shows a red slash, indicating that it is now cloaked.

Using the Site Setup dialog and the Cloaking context menu, you cloaked file types, folders, and files. The synchronization process will ignore cloaked items and will not automatically upload or download them.

## Wrapping things up

Over the last 10 lessons, you have learned how to use Dreamweaver and built an entire website, beginning with a starter layout and then adding text, images, and navigational content, but a few loose strings remain for you to tie up. Before you publish your site, you'll need to create one important webpage and make some crucial updates to your site navigation.

The file you need to create is one that is essential to every site: a home page. The home page is usually the first page most users see on your site. It is the page that loads automatically when a user enters your site's domain name into the browser window. That means when a visitor enters favoritecitytour.com into the browser's URL field and presses Enter/Return, the home page will appear even if you don't know its actual name. Since the page loads automatically, there are a few restrictions on the name and extension you can use.

Basically, the name and extension depend on the hosting server and the type of applications running on the home page, if any. Today, the majority of home pages will simply be named *index*. But *default*, *start*, and *iisstart* are also used.

Extensions identify the specific types of programming languages used within a page. A normal HTML home page will use an extension of .htm or .html.

Extensions like .asp, .cfm, and .php, among others, are required if the home page contains any dynamic applications specific to that server model. However, you may still use one of these extensions—if they are compatible with your server model—even if the page contains no dynamic applications or content. But be careful—in some instances, using the wrong extension may prevent the page from loading altogether. Check with your server administrator or IT manager for the proper extension.

The specific home page name or names honored by the server are normally configured by the server administrator and can be changed, if desired. Most servers are configured to honor several names and a variety of extensions. If the primary name doesn't exist, the server will load the next one on the list. Check with your IS/IT manager or web-server support team to ascertain the recommended name and extension for your home page. In the upcoming exercise, you will use *index* for the name of the home page.

## Creating a home page

In this exercise, you'll create a new home page and populate the content placeholders.

1 Create a new page from the site template.
Save the file as **index.html** or use a filename and extension compatible with your server model.

2 Open **home.html** from the lesson11 site root folder in Design view.

The file contains content for the text-based content section that appears below the image carousel. Since the file has no CSS styling, the display will look different than that of the Bootstrap layout, but it has the identical HTML structure.

3 Insert the cursor in the heading *WELCOME TO FAVORITE CITY TOUR*
Select the `div.container.mt-4` tag selector and cut the content.

**Note:** Moving content from one file to another is easier in Design view or Code view. Remember that you must use the same view in both the source and target documents.

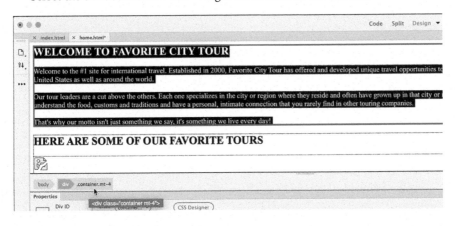

4 Switch to **index.html**, and select Design view.

Select the heading *ADD HEADLINE HERE* in the text-based content placeholder just below the image carousel.

5 Select the `div.container.mt-4` tag selector.

The selected placeholder structure matches the content you cut in step 3.

6 Paste to replace the selection.

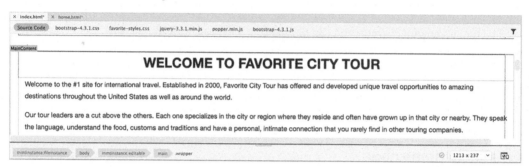

**Note:** Pasting to replace an element with another works only in Design view and Code view.

The text-based content section placeholder in the new layout is replaced.

7 Switch to **home.html**.

8 Insert the cursor in the heading *HERE ARE SOME OF OUR FAVORITE TOURS*. Select the `div.container.mt-4` tag selector.

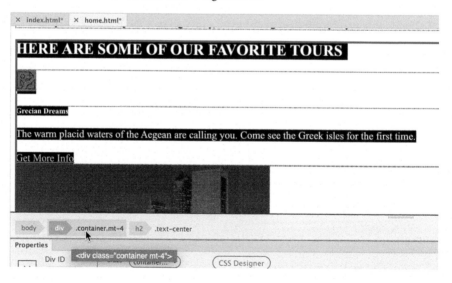

9 Cut the content.

The file **home.html** should be empty.

10 Close **home.html**. Do not save the changes.

The **index.html** file appears alone in the document window.

**11** In **index.html**, select the heading *ADD HEADLINE HERE* in the card-based content section.

**12** Select the `div.container.mt-4` tag selector.
Paste to replace the selection.

The text-based and card-based content section placeholders have been replaced. You don't need the list-based section placeholders. Let's delete them.

**13** Scroll down to the list-based section placeholders.

**14** Select the heading *ADD HEADLINE HERE* in the list-based content section.

**15** Select the `div.container.mt-4` tag selector and press Delete.

The list-based content section is deleted. The new home page is nearly finished. Let's add some content to the image carousel.

## Completing the home page

In this exercise, you will finish the home page by adding images and text to the Bootstrap image carousel. In most cases, you'll find working with the image carousel easier in Code view.

**1** Switch to Split view.

The document window is divided into two parts. One shows Design view, the other Code view. The advantage of using Split view is that it makes it easier to find components within the code.

2　In Design view, scroll up to the image carousel and click one of the image placeholders.

## 1920 x 500

```
51 ▼    <div class="carousel-inner">
52 ▼      <div class="carousel-item active"> <img class="d-block w-100" src="images/1920x500.gif" alt="First slide">
53 ▼        <div class="carousel-caption d-none d-md-block">
54            <h5>Item 1 Heading</h5>
55            <p>Item 1 Description</p>
56          </div>
57        </div>
58 ▼      <div class="carousel-item"> <img class="d-block w-100" src="images/1920x500.gif" alt="Second slide">
```

mmtinstance:fileinstance ⟩ body ⟩ mmtinstance:editable ⟩ div ⟩ div ⟩ div ⟩ div ⟩ div ⟩ div ⟩ .carousel-item.active ⟩ img ⟩ .d-block.w-100 　　⊘　HTML ⌄　1213 x 275 ⌄　INS　52:48 　🔲

When you select an element in Design view, the code structure of that element is highlighted automatically in Code view.

The highlighted code belongs to one of the image placeholders, but it may not be the first one. Examine the highlighted code and locate the first image placeholder in the carousel structure. The first placeholder can be found around line 52.

3　Select the code `1920x500.gif` and type `fl`

As you type, Dreamweaver provides hinting to complete the name of the image source.

4　Select `florence-tour-carousel.jpg` from the hinting menu.

If you position the cursor over the filename in Code view, a preview image pops up.

● **Note:** If this were a real website, you would also add alt and title attributes to each image.

5　Below the image source reference, select the text `Item 1 Heading` and type `Dreams of Florence` to replace it.

6　Select the text `Item 1 Description` and type `This tour is no fantasy. Come live the dream.`

7　Use the following content in the carousel for Item 2:
Item 2 placeholder: `greek-cruise-carousel.jpg`
Item 2 Heading: `Cruise the Isles`
Item 2 Description: `Warm waters. Endless Summer. What else do you want?`

8 Use the following content in the carousel for Item 3:

Item 3 placeholder: `rome-tour-carousel.jpg`

Item 3 Heading: `Roman Holiday`

Item 3 Description: `All roads lead to Rome. Time to find out why.`

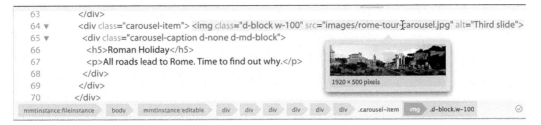

```
63          </div>
64 ▼        <div class="carousel-item"> <img class="d-block w-100" src="images/rome-tour-carousel.jpg" alt="Third slide">
65 ▼          <div class="carousel-caption d-none d-md-block">
66            <h5>Roman Holiday</h5>
67            <p>All roads lead to Rome. Time to find out why.</p>
68          </div>
69        </div>
70      </div>
```

mmtinstance:fileinstance  body  mmtinstance:editable  div  div  div  div  div  div  .carousel-item  img  .d-block.w-100

9 Switch to Live view.

The home page is nearly complete. The `title` and `meta` description place-holders still need to be updated.

10 In the Property inspector, select the placeholder text `Insert Title Here` and type `Welcome to travel with a difference`

11 Switch to Code view, select the text `add description here` (around line 15), and type `Welcome to the home of travel with a difference`

12 Save and close all files.

These changes should be good enough for now. Let's assume you want to upload the site at its current state of completion. This happens in the course of any site development. Pages are added, updated, and deleted over time; missing pages will be completed and then uploaded at a later date. Before you can upload the site to a live server, you should always check for and update any out-of-date links and remove dead ones.

# Putting your site online (optional)

**Note:** This exercise is optional, since it requires that you set up a remote server beforehand.

For the most part, the local site and the remote site are mirror images, containing the same HTML files, images, and assets in identical folder structures. When you transfer a webpage from your local site to your remote site, you are publishing, or *putting*, that page. If you *put* a file stored in a folder on your local site, Dreamweaver transfers the file to the equivalent folder on the remote site. It will even automatically create the remote folder or folders if they do not already exist. The same is true when you download files.

Using Dreamweaver, you can publish anything—from one file to a complete site—in a single operation. When you publish a webpage, by default Dreamweaver asks if you would also like to put the dependent files too. Dependent files are the images, CSS, HTML5 movies, JavaScript files, server-side includes (SSI), and other files necessary to complete the page.

You can upload one file at a time or the entire site at once. In this exercise, you will upload one webpage and its dependent files.

1   Open the Files panel and click the Expand icon ⊡, if necessary.

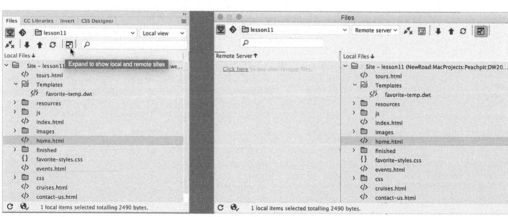

The files panel expands to take up the entire interface in Windows. In macOS, the files panel pops up as a floating window. The window is divided in half, showing the local site on the right. The left side will show the remote site once you connect to the hosting server.

● **Note:** The Expand icon will appear only when a remote server is defined in the site.

2   Click the Connect To Remote Server icon 🚀 to connect to the remote site.

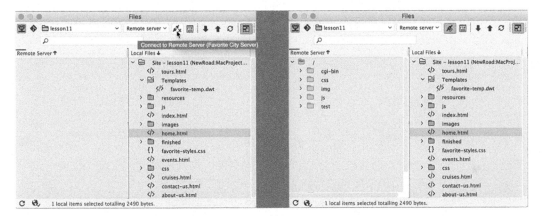

If your remote site is properly configured, the Files panel will connect to the site and display its contents on the left half of the panel. When you first upload files, the remote site may be empty or mostly empty. If you are connecting to your internet host, specific files and folders created by the hosting company may appear. Do not delete these items unless you check to see whether they are essential to the operation of the server or your own applications.

● **Note:** Dependent files include but are not limited to images, style sheets, and JavaScript used within a specific page and are essential to the proper display and function of the page.

3   In the local file list, select **index.html**.

4   In the Files panel toolbar, click the Put icon ↑ .

◆ **Warning:** Dreamweaver does a good job trying to identify all the dependent files in a particular workflow. But in some cases, it may miss files that are crucial to a dynamic or extended process. It is imperative that you do your homework to identify these files and make sure they are uploaded.

5   By default, Dreamweaver will prompt you to upload dependent files. If a dependent file already exists on the server and your changes did not affect it, you can click No. Otherwise, for new files or files that have had any changes, click Yes. There is an option within Preferences where you can disable this prompt, if desired.

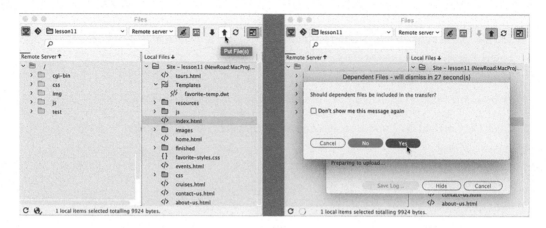

6 Click Yes.

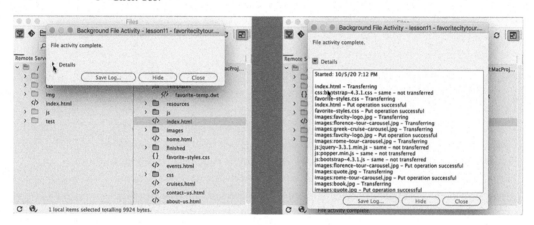

▶ **Tip:** When the File Background Activity dialog appears, you may need to click to see the details to review all files uploaded.

Dreamweaver uploads **index.html** and all images, CSS, JavaScript, and other dependent files needed to properly render the selected HTML file. A Background File Activity dialog appears, listing all the files uploaded to the server. Although you chose only one file to put, you can see that 27 files and three folders were uploaded.

The Files panel enables you to upload multiple files as well as the entire site at once.

7 Close the Background File Activity dialog, if necessary.
Select the site root folder for the local site, and then click the Put icon in the Files panel.

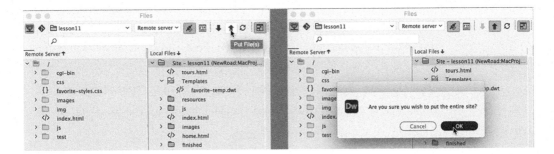

An unnamed dialog appears, asking you to confirm that you want to upload the entire site.

8   Click Yes or OK as appropriate.

> **Tip:** If you are using a third-party web-hosting service, be aware that they often create placeholder pages on your domain. If your home page does not automatically appear when you access your site, you may need to delete the placeholder page.

● **Note:** A file that is uploaded or down-loaded will auto-matically overwrite any version of the file at the destination.

Dreamweaver begins to upload the site. It will re-create your local site structure on the remote server. Dreamweaver uploads pages in the background so that you can continue to work in the meantime. Often the Background File Activity dialog disappears before you can see the report. The Files panel has an option that allows you to display the full report at any time.

9   Click the File Activity icon 🔥 in the lower-left corner of the Files panel.

> **Tip:** You may need to click the Details option to see the entire report.

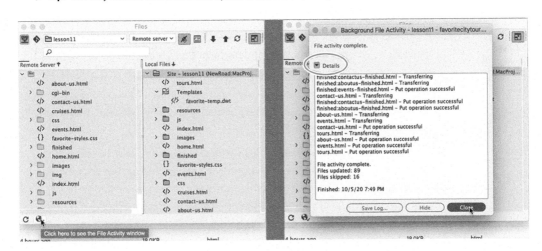

When you click the File Activity icon, the Background File Activity dialog appears, displaying a list featuring the filenames and the status of the selected operation. You can even save the report to a text file, if desired, by clicking the Save Log button.

Note that neither the cloaked Templates folder nor the file stored within it was uploaded. Dreamweaver will automatically ignore all cloaked items when putting individual folders or an entire site. If desired, you can manually select and upload individually cloaked items.

10 Right-click the Templates folder and choose Put from the context menu.

Dreamweaver prompts you to upload dependent files for the Templates folder.

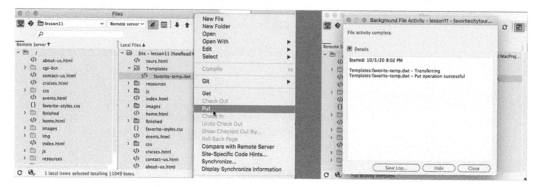

11 Click Yes to upload dependent files.

The Templates folder is uploaded to the remote server. The log report may show some dependent files uploaded, if any changes were made to them.

● **Note:** When accessing Put and Get, it doesn't matter whether you use the Local or Remote pane of the Files panel. Put always uploads to Remote; Get always downloads to Local.

If you look in the Remote Server pane, you can see the Templates folder listed. Note that the remote Templates folder displays a red slash, indicating that it, too, is cloaked. At times, you will want to cloak local and remote files and folders to prevent these items from being replaced or accidentally overwritten. A cloaked file will not be uploaded or downloaded automatically. But you can manually select any specific files and perform the same action.

The opposite of the Put command is Get, which downloads any selected file or folder to the local site. You can get any file from the remote site by selecting it in the Remote pane and clicking the Get icon. Alternatively, you can drag the file from the Remote pane to the Local pane.

12 If you were able to successfully upload your site, use a browser to connect to the remote site on your network server or the internet. Type the appropriate address in the URL field—depending on whether you are connecting to the local web server or to the actual internet site—such as:
http://localhost/*domain-name* or http://www.*domain-name*.com.

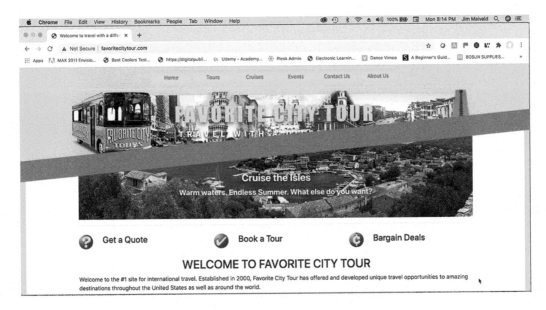

The Favorite City Tour site appears in the browser.

13 Click to test the hyperlinks in the horizontal menu to view each of the completed pages for the site.

Once the site is uploaded, keeping it up to date is an easy task. As files change, you can upload them one at a time or synchronize the whole site with the remote server.

Synchronization is especially important in workgroup environments where files are changed and uploaded by several individuals. You can easily download or upload files that are older, overwriting files that are newer in the process. Synchronization can ensure that you are working with only the latest versions of each file.

## Synchronizing local and remote sites

Synchronization in Dreamweaver keeps the files on your server and your local computer up to date. It's an essential tool when you work from multiple locations or with one or more co-workers. Used properly, it can prevent you from accidentally uploading or working on out-of-date files.

At the moment, your local and remote sites should be very similar if not identical. Remember that there may be some placeholder files in the server created by your hosting service. To better illustrate the capabilities of synchronization, let's make a change to one of the site pages.

When the Files panel is expanded, the Expand icon becomes the Collapse icon.

1 Collapse the Files panel by clicking the Collapse icon 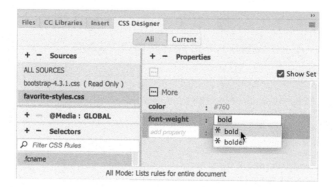, if necessary.

Clicking the Collapse icon re-docks the panel on the right side of the program, if necessary.

2 Open **about-us.html** in Live view.

3 In the CSS Designer, click the All button.
Select **favorite-styles.css**.
Create a new selector: `.fcname`

4 Add the following properties to the new rule:
`color: #760`
`font-weight: bold`

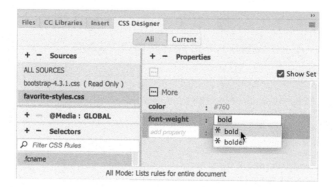

5 In the first paragraph of the text content, select the first occurrence of the text *Favorite City Tour*.

6 Select `.fcname` from the Class dropdown menu in the Property inspector.

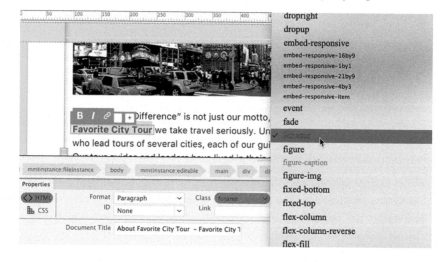

7 Apply the `fcname` class to each occurrence of the name *Favorite City Tour* anywhere on the page where it appears in the text content.

8 Save all files and close the page.

9 Open and expand the Files panel.
In the Document toolbar, click the Synchronize icon ⟳.

The Synchronize With Remote Server dialog appears.

**Note:** The Synchronize icon looks similar to the Refresh icon but is located on the upper-right side of the Files panel.

10 From the Synchronize pop-up menu, choose the option Entire 'lesson11' Site. From the Direction dropdown menu, choose Get And Put Newer Files.

● **Note:** Synchronize does not compare cloaked files or folders.

11 Click Preview.

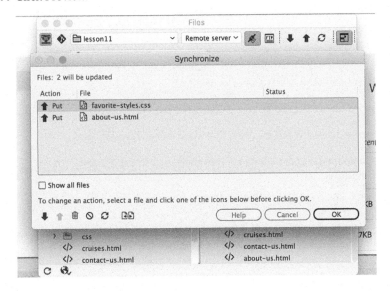

The Synchronize dialog appears, reporting what files have changed or do not exist on the remote or local site, and whether you need to get or put them.

Since you just uploaded the entire site, the files you modified—**about-us.html** and **favorite-styles.css**—should appear in this list, which indicates that Dreamweaver wants to put them to the remote site.

The dialog also may list a number of files that already exist on the remote server, placed there by your web-hosting company or service, that do not appear in the local site folder. These files, in most cases, will be needed only by the placeholder content itself. The content you created within Dreamweaver is completely self-sufficient and should not require these files and resources. Of course, I cannot guarantee that this is always the case.

If the Synchronize dialog has marked any of the preexisting files on the remote server with the action Get, these files will be downloaded to your local site. Any files already on your server are not required to support your site and there would be no reason to download them. You have two choices in that case: you can ignore the files or delete them altogether.

12 Mark any file on the remote site to be ignored ⊘ or for deletion 🗑 if you do not need them.

## Synchronization options

During synchronization, you can choose to accept the suggested action or override it by selecting one of the other options in the dialog. Options can be applied to one or more files at a time.

⬇ **Get** downloads the selected file(s) from the remote site.

⬆ **Put** uploads the selected file(s) to the remote site.

🗑 **Delete** marks the selected file(s) for deletion.

⊘ **Ignore** ignores the selected file(s) during synchronization.

↻ **Synchronized** identifies the selected file(s) as already synchronized.

▤▤ **Compare** uses a third-party utility to compare the local and remote versions of a selected file.

**13** Click OK to upload the two files and perform any other actions you selected.

The Background File Activity dialog appears and reports the progress of synchronizing the content of the local and remote sites.

● **Note:** The files shown in the screen shots are typical of the webhosting service I used. The files on your service may be totally different.

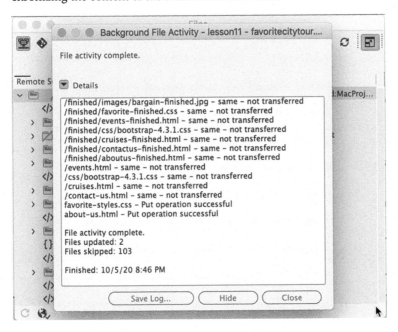

**14** If necessary, click to close the Background File Activity dialog. In the Files panel, click the Collapse icon ⬚ to dock the panel again.

If other people can access and update files on your site, remember to run synchronization *before* you work on any files to be certain you are working on the most current versions of each file in your site. Another technique is to set up the check-out/check-in functionality in the advanced options of the server's setup dialog.

In this lesson, you set up your site to connect to a remote server and uploaded files to that remote site. You also cloaked files and folders and then synchronized the local and remote sites.

Congratulations! You've designed, developed, and built an entire website and uploaded it to your remote server. By completing the exercises in this book to this point, you have gained experience in most aspects of the design and development of a standard website compatible with desktop computers. In the remaining lessons, you will learn to adapt your content to the dynamic Bootstrap site framework so that it will work not only on desktop computers but also with cellphones, tablets, and other mobile devices.

## Review questions

1 What is a remote site?

2 Name two types of file transfer protocols supported in Dreamweaver.

3 How can you configure Dreamweaver so that it does not synchronize certain files in your local site with the remote site?

4 True or false: You have to manually publish every file and associated image, JavaScript file, and server-side include that is linked to pages in your site.

5 What service does synchronization perform?

# Review answers

1 A remote site is typically the live version of the local site stored on a web server connected to the internet.

2 FTP (File Transfer Protocol) and local/network are the two most commonly used file transfer methods. Other file transfer methods supported in Dreamweaver include Secure FTP, WebDAV, and RDS.

3 Cloaking the files or folders prevents them from synchronizing.

4 False. Dreamweaver can automatically transfer dependent files, if desired, including embedded or referenced images, CSS style sheets, and other linked content, although some files may be missed.

5 Synchronization automatically scans local and remote sites, comparing files on both to identify the most current version of each. It creates a report window to suggest which files to get or put to bring both sites up to date, and then it will perform the update.

# APPENDIX

## Tiny URLs

At several points in the book, I reference external information available on the internet. The uniform resource locators (URLs) for this information are often long and unwieldy, so we have provided custom TinyURLs in many places for your convenience. Unfortunately, the TinyURLs sometimes expire over time and no longer function. If you find that a TinyURL doesn't work, look up the actual URL in the following table.

| PAGE | TINY URL | FULL URL |
|---|---|---|
| **Lesson 3** | | |
| 80 | https://tinyurl.com/css-inheritance | www.w3.org/TR/CSS2/propidx.html |
| 81 | https://tinyurl.com/special-selectors | https://w3schools.com/cssref/css_selectors.asp |
| 94 | tinyurl.com/shorten-CSS | https://developer.mozilla.org/en-US/docs/Web/CSS/Shorthand_properties |
| **Lesson 5** | | |
| 151 | https://tinyurl.com/generate-photoshop | https://helpx.adobe.com/photoshop/using/generate-assets-layers.html |
| 151 | https://tinyurl.com/asset-generator | https://helpx.adobe.com/photoshop/using/generate-assets-layers.html |
| **Lesson 9** | | |
| 320 | https://tinyurl.com/broadband-coverage | www.fcc.gov/reports-research/reports/broadband-progress-reports/eighth-broadband-progress-report |
| **Lesson 11** | | |
| 414 | https://tinyurl.com/settingup-coldfusion | www.adobe.com/devnet/coldfusion/articles/setup_dev.html |
| 414 | http://tinyurl.com/setup-apachephp | www.adobe.com/devnet/archive/dreamweaver/articles/setup_php.html?PID=4166869 |
| 414 | https://tinyurl.com/settingup-asp | www.webassist.com/tutorials/Set-up-a-test-server-on-Windows |
| **Lesson 12** | | |
| online | https://tinyurl.com/CSS-media-rules | www.w3schools.com/cssref/css3_pr_mediaquery.asp |

# INDEX

## NUMBERS

## A

## B

# C

Cache
  defining Dreamweaver site, 14
  remote FTP site setup, 413
Captions, table, 303–305
Card-based content, 28
Card-based section
  adding boilerplate/placeholders, 225–226
  as content model for template in this book, 209
  creating and styling text, 263–268
  creating lists, 273–274, 276
  deleting unused sections from child page, 252–253
  editable regions, 232
  removing components, 209–212
Cascade theory, CSS styles, 78, 82
Cascading style sheets. See CSS (cascading style sheets)
Case sensitivity, usernames/passwords, 411
Cells, styling table, 292–293
Character entities, HTML, 62–63
Check page, navigation, 402–403
Check Spelling dialog, webpages, 305–306
Child pages
  adding content, 244–245
  adding CSS classes to template, 349–351
  adding metadata, 246–247
  adding unique content. See Editable regions, templates
  creating from template, 208, 242
  creating new, 242–243
  inserting images, 356–358
  removing optional region from, 251–252
  removing unused sections from, 252–253
  updating links, 377–379
Class attribute
  conventions for element references, 3
  creating, 94–95
  writing code automatically, 108
Classes
  adding CSS, to template, 348–351
  controlling table display, 296–298
Cloaked folders and files
  publishing to web and, 414–416
  synchronization and, 429
  will not be uploaded, 426
Code
  accessing Split Code view, 134–135
  collapsing, 133–134
  commenting, 112–113

creating HTML, 102–103
CSS preprocessors and. See CSS preprocessors
expanding, 134
lesson overview, 100–101
linting support, 128–129
multicursor support, 110–111
previewing assets in Code view, 136–137
review Q&A, 138–139
selecting, 129–133
validating HTML, 230–231
writing automatically, 106–110
writing manually, 103–105
Code font, 2
Code hinting
  adding images to Bootstrap carousel, 353
  inserting images in Split view, 346
  locking element onscreen, 397
  writing code manually, 104
Code Navigator, 82–87
Code Theme window, 24–25
Code view
  adding images to Bootstrap carousel in, 352–354
  customizing workspace in, 25
  Find And Replace text in, 307–309
  inserting images in, 345
  interface preference settings in, 23
  previewing assets in, 136–137
  Split view and, 27
  swapping with Live view, 70
  templates work properly in, 244
  writing code automatically in, 106–110
  writing code manually in, 102–105
Coding toolbar. See Common toolbar
Collapsing code, 133–134, 427–428
Color
  nesting CSS selectors, 124–126
  raster graphics and, 318–319
  theme, 9, 24
Columns
  Bootstrap layout modification, 216–221
  content structures based on lists, 275–278
  CSS Designer displaying, 44, 88–89
  CSS multicolumn layouts, 157
  HTML formatting and, 70
  inserting tables from other sources, 299
  new Bootstrap structures, 193–194
  new list-based items, 279–280
  removing unneeded, 213
  responsive web design for, 145
  table display, 296–298

IP (Internet Protocol) address, remote FTP
   sites, 410
IPV6 Transfer Mode, default FTP server, 412

## J

JPEG (Joint Photographic Experts Group), raster
   images, 320

## K

Keyboard shortcuts
   customizing, 38–40
   Windows vs. macOS, 3–4

## L

Laptops, web design questions, 143–144
Launch, getting started, 8
Layers pane, 333
Layout
   Developer workspace, 30
   page. *See* Page layout
   Standard workspace, 29–30
LESS, CSS preprocessor
   choosing Sass vs., 115
   creating CSS source file, 116–119
   defined, 113
   enabling, 113–116
Lesson files for this book, accessing online
   content, 6–7
Lesson order, recommended in this book, 7–8
<li> element (list item), 61, 106–107
Line numbers, selecting code, 129–130
Link Checker panel, 403
Linked, applying CSS formatting as, 77
Links. *See* Hyperlinks; Navigation
Linting support, live code error checking, 128–129
List-based content section
   adding boilerplate/placeholders, 226
   as content model for template in this book, 209
   creating new list-based items, 279–282
   in editable regions, 232
   modifying Bootstrap layout, 216
   removing unneeded components, 212–216
   removing unused sections from child page,
      252–253
Lists, creating
   content structures based on, 275–278
   deleting unused Bootstrap components, 267–268
   Find And Replace text, 307–312
   lesson overview, 256–257
   new list-based items, 279–282

ordered, 270–271
overview of, 268–270
pasting multiple elements in Live view, 278–279
previewing completed file, 258–260
review Q&A, 313
spell-checking webpages, 305–306
unordered, 271–274
Live code error checking, 128–129
Live Code mode, customizing workspace, 28
Live view
   absolute external links in, 380–384
   activating Live Code mode, 28
   customizing workspace, 26–27
   Dreamweaver usually defaults to, 71
   inserting images in, 347
   pasting elements in, 278–279
   Split view pairs Code view with, 27
   styling heading and text in Bootstrap carousel,
      354–356
   styling tables in, 290–292
   swapping with Code view window, 70
   updating template in, 248–249
   web images for mobile design, 335
Local/network, connecting to remote site, 408
Local sites, 408, 427–431
Locking element, screens, 396–398
Logo. *See* Company logo
Lorem generator, 109

## M

macOS, vs. Windows instructions, 3–4
<main> element, writing code automatically, 109
Maintain Synchronization Information, 412–414
Manage Sites, remote FTP site setup, 409
Marcotte, Ethan, 145
Margin spacing, web images for mobile design, 340
Master page, template as type of, 208
Math, vector graphics and, 316
@Media pane, CSS Designer
   modifying Bootstrap layout, 217
   overview of, 46
   styling layout elements with Extract, 166
   troubleshooting in, 88–89
Menu items
   creating with copy/paste, 181–182
   inserting new, 176–179
Meta description element
   basing content structures on lists, 275–276
   creating lists, 268–269
   importing text, 261–264
   inserting editable optional region, 241

# Production Notes

*Adobe Dreamweaver CC Classroom in a Book (2021 release)* was created electronically using Adobe InDesign. Art was produced using Adobe InDesign, Adobe Illustrator, and Adobe Photoshop. References to company names in the lessons are for demonstration purposes only and are not intended to refer to any actual organization or person.

## Images

Photographic images and illustrations are intended for use with the tutorials. Photographic images used to create the webpages in the *Adobe Dreamweaver Classroom in a Book (2021 release)* lessons are copyright Shutterstock, shutterstock.com:

- London composite images © s4svisuals/shutterstock.com
- Brooklyn Bridge and lower Manhattan across East River, NYC, composite images @ ARK NEYMAN/shutterstock.com

## Screenshot credits

Screenshots on pages 152, 361, 366, 381, 382 © 2020 Google LLC. Screenshot on page 386 © Microsoft 2020. Screenshots on page 407 © 2020, Apache Friends, © 2018 Alter Way, and © MAMP GmbH 2020.

## Contributors

Jim Maivald began his career as the editor of an architectural and engineering magazine. Since then he has edited two other magazines and written over 10 books and dozens of articles on electronic design and production. He founded his own graphic design practice in 1991 and has worked with companies big and small crafting corporate identities, brochures, and custom illustrations. He started learning HTML in late '90s and was an early adopter of Dreamweaver. Jim now specializes in web-based content management systems and document automation.

## Special thanks

I would like to thank my wife and kids for suffering through the days and long weekends as I worked hard to write this new edition and make the critical deadlines.

# The fastest, easiest, most comprehensive way to learn
# Adobe Creative Cloud

**Classroom in a Book®**, the best-selling series of hands-on software training books, helps you learn the features of Adobe software quickly and easily.

The **Classroom in a Book** series offers what no other book or training program does—an official training series from Adobe Systems, developed with the support of Adobe product experts.

**To see a complete list of our Classroom in a Book titles covering the 2021 release of Adobe Creative Cloud go to:**
www.adobepress.com/CC2021

**Adobe Photoshop Classroom in a Book (2021 release)**
ISBN: 9780136904731

**Adobe Illustrator Classroom in a Book (2021 release)**
ISBN: 9780136805533

**Adobe InDesign Classroom in a Book (2021 release)**
ISBN: 9780136870289

**Adobe Dreamweaver Classroom in a Book (2021 release)**
ISBN: 9780136875239

**Adobe Premiere Pro Classroom in a Book (2021 release)**
ISBN: 9780137280926

**Adobe Dimension Classroom in a Book (2021 release)**
ISBN: 9780136870104

**Adobe After Effects Classroom in a Book (2021 release)**
ISBN: 9780136815648

**Adobe Animate Classroom in a Book (2021 release)**
ISBN: 9780136887423

**Adobe Photoshop Lightroom Classic Classroom in a Book (2021 release)**
ISBN: 9780136885382

 Adobe Press